# THE CRITICS ARE STARKLY R*
## (AND MADLY PASSIONATE
## ABOUT THIS BOOK AND ITS AUTHOR:

**RAY BRADBURY, America's Leading Fantasy Writer:**
*"Everybody should read this book! EVERYBODY!"*

**ELVIRA, Mistress of the Dark:**
*"John Stanley has definitely shaped a well-rounded study of American horror hosts, but
I seriously doubt he will ever be able to keep abreast of me."*

**ROGER CORMAN, Master of Low Budget Sci-Fi and Horror Films**
*"This insightful, enjoyable book reveals a diverse array of first-class (if idiosyncratic) talents
from the golden age of science-fiction and horror whose work tapped into the audience's
unconscious fears and desires."*

**TOM HANKS, Who Grew Up in the Bay Area Watching "Creature Features":**
*"I would never have been scared by 'Night of the Living Dead' and countless Hammer
horror masterpieces were it not for gentle Bob Wilkins, cracking jokes in his rocking
chair. Thanks, John Stanley, for putting it down in print."*

**SARA KARLOFF, Daughter of the Frankenstein Monster**
*"What fun it is to know John Stanley!  Even more fun to read his book!"*

**JOE BOB BRIGGS, Drive-In Movie Host and Film Historian**
*"John Stanley is probably the most knowledgeable of all horror hosts. He knows more
about horror movies than any person alive."* – From the Documentary "American Scary"

# CULT OF THE HORROR HOST RELIVED

MEET JOHN STANLEY, WHO HOSTED THE POPULAR "CREATURE FEATURES" SERIES
IN THE SAN FRANCISCO-BAY AREA . . . DISCOVER A HISTORY OF THE TERROR
ENTERTAINMENT WORLD AS HE DISCOVERED IT DURING HIS SIX YEARS AS A
HORROR HOST, AND DURING HIS 33 YEARS AS AN INTERVIEWER FOR THE SAN
FRANCISCO CHRONICLE, COVERING FIRST-RUN MOVIES AND NETWORK TV . . .

## STARTLING REVELATIONS ABOUT GENRE ICONS:

✳ **BOB WILKINS:** *The Strangest Story of All TV Horror Hosts –* **He Wore No Costume!**
✳ **GENE RODDENBERRY:** *Career Betrayal Behind the Scenes of* **STAR TREK**
✳ **WILLIAM SHATNER:** *Your Modest and Humble Captain . . . of the Universe!*
✳ **VINCENT PRICE:** *He Tried to Deny His True Heritage as a Horror Movie Star*
✳ **THE REAL "STAR WARS" HEROES:** *The True Faces of the Faceless Ones*
✳ **WILLIAM CASTLE:** *He Was Pure Hype But Turned Out to Be the* **REAL TINGLER**
✳ **CHRISTOPHER LEE:** *He Almost Walked Off the Set and Left Stanley Bloodless*
✳ **RAY HARRYHAUSEN:** *This Assistant to the Man Who Moved King Kong Became a
Master of Stop-Motion Special Effects for Monsters With Personality and Class*
✳ **ANTHONY PERKINS:** *He Hesitated to Pick Up a Butcher Knife – Bad for One's Image?*

# PLUS 559 PHOTOGRAPHS
*NUMEROUS ONES IN PRINT FOR THE VERY FIRST TIME!*

# *DEDICATION PAGE*

## To the People in My Life and Career Who Made
## Many Great Things Possible – Especially This Book

To my beautiful wife **Erica,** without whom I would have never succeeded at Anything. This provocative woman has consistently displayed her special intellectual prowess and philosophical viewpoints with charm, sophistication and devotion to duty. Thanks to her my son Russ, daughter Trista and I all turned out to be law-biding citizens. Could the fact she had a six-shooter strapped to her hip during those years have something to do with it?

My deepfelt thanks to **Dr. Thomas Mullooly,** our family dentist, a devoted professional always probing for the root of all problems and going at his work tooth and nail. He recently informed me rather intensely, *"I've Looked into the Mouth of Horror and I'm Still Alive to Tell About It."* Thanks also goes to his wife Kitty, a charming sophisticate who once again, by popular demand, is the Mayor of Hillsborough, CA.

To my collaborator **Kenn Davis**, with whom I co-made the horror film "Nightmare in Blood," and wrote the novel "Bogart '48." And with whom I helped to create the San Francisco private eye Carver Bascombe in "The Dark Side." Kenn is now retired and lives in Roseville, CA., where he creates oil paintings.

And finally a grand thanks to the industrious, hard-working Tom Wyrsch, the Most Dedicated Creature Features Fan of All. He alone inspired me (nay, forced me over two years) to write this book. Thanks also goes to Tom's wife Lisa and their wonderful kids, Nikki and Jeff.

# I WAS A TV HORROR HOST

OR

MEMOIRS
OF A
CREATURE
FEATURES
MAN

## BY JOHN STANLEY

# I WAS A TV HORROR HOST
## AKA MEMOIRS OF A CREATURE FEATURES MAN

First Edition in a Trade Paperback Format
@ 2007 by John Stanley

**Creatures at Large Press**
**1082 Grand Teton Drive**
**Pacifica, CA 94044**

FOR DESIGNING the cover of this book, my thanks to Scott Moon, editor of Planet X Magazine. Scott is a professional printing designer and major contributor to the Bob Wilkins website. Thanks, Scott, for your continued support over many years. Check out the **Moon website at** www.scottmoon.net.

## TO BUY COPIES
## OF THIS BOOK:
Send Check or Money Order for $23
(That Includes Postage/Handling) to
**John Stanley**
**1082 Grand Teton Drive**
**Pacifica, CA 94044**
You Can Also Make Contact at
creature@netwiz.net
Or Go to Our Website at
www.stanleybooks.net
## When You Order the Book
## Be Sure to Tell Us to Whom It
## Should Be Autographed and
## John Stanley Will Sign It
## As You Request

International Standard Book Numbering Agency
Information: **ISBN: 978 - 0 - 940064 - 11 - 9**

# AN INTRODUCTION TO THE IMPACTS OF LIFE

## GHOST WRITTEN BY JOHN STANLEY

D on't whip me again! Hate cat-o-nine tails. Hate barbed comments. And keep those damned bloodhounds back! The snarling ones . . with the glowing eyes, the slobbery tongues! And . . . *gag* . . . don't let those shambling corpses come any closer. *What corpses?* Those flesh-crumbling things over on the other side of the dungeon! The ones near the crocodile pit! With all those . . . *gulp* . . . maggots crawling freely! You know, the slithery things shambling their way past the Iron Maiden! *What Iron Maiden?* The one with the rivers of blood! Gushing through the holes! Loosen my bonds and I'll talk. I'll confess. I'll blab. I'll spill my intestinal fortitude.

Yeah, sure, I'll tell you what you want to know. The whole . . . *gasp* . . . ungodly thing:

*I was a TV horror host.*

Yeah, me. The ordinary guy without a monster suit. I was one of those who introduced monster flicks on Saturday night. Horror classics and non-classics sixty minutes before the arrival of the Witching Hour.

Yeah, let the truth be heard throughout the dungeon, throughout the castle of madmen:

I was a "Creature Features" man.

If you think some people will do anything to make a buck, let me square with you:

Some unredeeming people will.

*And I was loving it.*

In America, being a TV horror host means something special. Something bigger than life. Death even. Something greater than the Universe itself. You almost become eternal, at least in the eyes of your fans. Never forgotten, even after you should be forgotten.

Dare I say it: One becomes a legend! Well, in one's own mind, anyway. But not quite. Well, yeah, it's kind of complicated, so here goes:

See, a monster-flick host or a "Creature Features" guru inescapably becomes a symbol for the enormous love and appreciation millions of devoted fans have for science-fiction, fantasy and horror flickers. These impressionable wide-eyed beings spearhead a special gang of tomorrow that loves and longs for the magical, wondrous things in life. They are fascinated by cinematic imagery, sci-fi books, TV "Star Trek" spinoffs, Tolkien theories and the roots of the Ent tree people, hulking entities, costumes worn by Conan, Hercules and Xena and

My first ever publicity photo, designed to please . . . the popcorn trade?

When I was a boy watching TV in the 1950s, my favorite weekly series was "You Axed for It."

just about anything else imaginatively dealing with the fantastique.

They are filled with what Ray Bradbury calls "Our Sense of Wonder," a concept I will be telling you more about later when I describe the author of "The Martian Chronicles," one of the most fascinating people I have ever met. (In fact, I'm going to describe a slew of fascinating people because being a horror host allows you to meet these inspirational creators first-hand and become their chronicler.)

A horror host, in the minds of these devotees, becomes an icon. Okay, maybe I am overdoing it a little. If not someone as notorious as Jennifer Lopez or as dashing as Tom Cruise or as shapely as Britney Spears or as sexually intellectual as Madonna, a horror host becomes a focal point, a conduit, for all the adulation and devotion. If you dig the movies, you gotta dig the guy/gal bringing them to you in all their bloodthirsty glory. A horror host talks the talk and walks the walk of the horror crowd, and usually tries to tickle the fans' funnybones because people like us need to spoof ourselves, to let others know that while we mean horror-ible business, we can also laugh at our images and put each other on once in a while. Tongue-in-cheek goes with being a TV horror host and the fans know and appreciate this whimsical, lampoonish touch.

Here's more confession: I was a TV horror-movie host for less than six years–January 1979 through August 1984–but my life continues to seem like one long horror story. Because those years–which are so long ago in my past and should seem less important now–keep coming back to haunt me. Those years, strangely enough, remain vitally fresh. *And important.* They remain at the forefront of my memories and my everyday activities. In a way, they now seem more important than when they were happening. (Could this irony be called nostalgia? The passage of years does give one fresh perspective.)

Believe me, there is no escape. Once a horror host, eternally a horror host.

My six years at KTVU (Channel 2) in Oakland, CA., next door to Jack London Village and just a bone's throw from Jack London Square, have never gone away. They revisit me nightly, as if they were those restless corpses in George Romero's "Night of the Living Dead" clawing at the windows of my house, trying to get inside and tear me into bloody shreds of quivering human flesh. That ringing in my ears . . . the screams . . . it's

Old PR shots off an aging contact sheet, proving the job did on occasion tend to bring out the devil in me.

horror-hosting of my past, as alive in-the-rotting-flesh today as then.

Get a lode of this golden whackiness: I still make appearances at the annual conventions, such as San Francisco's Wondercon and assorted "Star Trek" shows. I'm still selling my "Creature Features Movie Guide" series (six editions in all), DVDs of old "Creature Features" programs I produced so long ago, and CDs of music and sounds from my horror-host past.

There's even "The John Stanley Scrapbook" (a pictorial history of my experiences at KTVU-TV) littering the shelves of a few thousand fans (poor souls) and even, I am told, a few Bay Area libraries. Is there no accounting for taste?

The author, Tom Wyrsch, was himself a devoted "Creature Features" fan during my time and he has made a cottage (cheesy?) industry out of keeping the old memory of the show freshly alive for the old generations that lived through the experience and the new generations that are just discovering its magic. Wyrsch symbolizes the kind of people who

Tom Wyrsch, a living fan who resurrected a dead TV show ("Creature Features") in the '90s with horror-ific scrapbooks.

love and revere horror hosts. He is among the resurrectors of the dead and undead and he will be important to these eccentric and arcane memoirs. Despite everything else I have done in my life that I'm happy to confess to, especially my 33 years as an entertainment writer for a major American big-town newspaper, my horror past remains the one thing that comes screaming down on my head. Take my word for it: The phrase "TV horror host" will definitely be in the lead paragraph of my eagerly-awaited obituary.

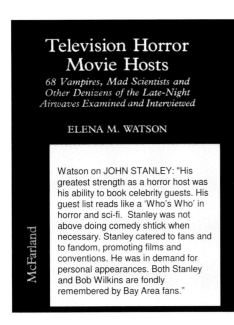

Television Horror Movie Hosts
*68 Vampires, Mad Scientists and Other Denizens of the Late-Night Airwaves Examined and Interviewed*

ELENA M. WATSON

Watson on JOHN STANLEY: "His greatest strength as a horror host was his ability to book celebrity guests. His guest list reads like a 'Who's Who' in horror and sci-fi. Stanley was not above doing comedy shtick when necessary. Stanley catered to fans and to fandom, promoting films and conventions. He was in demand for personal appearances. Both Stanley and Bob Wilkins are fondly remembered by Bay Area fans."

McFarland

A dire sweet lady, the late Elena M. Watson, even wrote a book about us: "Television Horror Movie Hosts: 68 Vampires, Mad Scientists and Other Denizens of the Late-Night Airwaves Examined and Interviewed" (McFarland, 1991). And yes, if you ask the inevitable question, there is a chapter about this humble one.

So there I had been for almost six years, every Saturday night just before the Witching Hour, introducing a movie. But there was more to it than talking about the plot or the actors. I also had to produce about 30 minutes of original material each week.

I was always interviewing colorful guests – from local oddball gurus who believed in UFOs and time travel to leading fantasy and mystery writers (Harry Harrison, Joe Gores, Poul Anderson, Chelsey Quinn Yarbro, etc.) to top-of-the-movie-industry film-makers (Roger Corman, to name but one) to wannabee film-makers. (I once did a program about amateur films and their creators called "The Star Wars Gang of Tomorrow" followed by the sequel "Eat Your Heart Out, George Lucas").

And there were special effects artists (Dennis Murin, Phil Tippet, etc.) as well as wanna be special-effects artists. The fascinating thing about the wanna-bes: Some of them went on to be what they wanted to be. Talk about being inspired – many a horror host has given many a wanna-be the inspiration to go do the real thing. Another reason TV horror hosts don't get completely forgotten, no matter how gray their hair turns or how gnarly their teeth form curvatures or how snarly they become as old age sets in.

Along the way I talked to every member of the "Star Trek" franchise at least once, I was there to put on record the thoughts of all the principals involved with the making of "The Empire Strikes Back," did amazing-to-me interviews with Ray Bradbury, and helped to perpetuate the legend of Robert Bloch, author of "Psycho" and hundreds of other classic horror stories, by not only exposing him on "Creature Features" but by publishing an anthology of comedy short stories under the title "Lost in Time and Space with Lefty Feep."

I also chatted with old stars (Buster Crabbe, Christopher Lee) and new ones (Arnold Schwarzenegger, making his debut in "Conan the Barbarian," and let me tell you – he governed the interview from beginning to end.). There was also a newcomer to movies named Chuck Norris who showed up for a night of marital-arts comedy action with his brother Aaron.

And of course there is a fella named Bob Wilkins who started the Creature Features phenomena in the San Francisco Bay Area. Bob preceded me for eight years at KTVU Channel 2. Single-handedly he created "Creature Features" and made it a legend

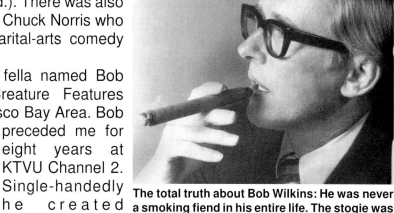

The total truth about Bob Wilkins: He was never a smoking fiend in his entire life. The stogie was intended only as a prop to help disguise the fact he was one nervous TV host.

in his own right (if not in his own mind). And he's still a legend today, signing twice the autographs I am asked to sign. (I'm lying–he signs five to my one.) He dominated a market in prime time TV while I was a late-night guy, when all the decent folks had gone to bed to dream happy nightmares.

In the beginning I was just one of his fans, contacting Bob by mail or phone to share my enthusiasm. But then he became my mentor when it was time for me to take over his Saturday night slot, and he initially guided me and helped me to find my own way into the world of TV horror-hosting. So it was that from this still-beloved, perennial king of TV horror hosts that I came to learn what it was going to take to be a successor, and I'm going to tell you readers the full, uncensored behind-the-scenes Wilkins story–even incriminating stuff he doesn't want printed.

This PR photo was captioned: Getting a Head in Life.

About those fans I mentioned earlier? I'm still surrounded by them through the world of fandom – a rarified place where the fan, or the amateur, meets the professional: the comic book artist and writer, the film producer, writer and director, the painter and illustrator, and of course the TV horror-movie host.

Even I, at a recent Wondercon Convention in San Francisco, discovered Elvira sitting just behind me. That beautiful one-time "curvaceous, cuddly creature" in a black outfit plunging down to here and up to there, with slits that slithered toward erotica, would rather I identify her as serious-minded actress Cassandra Peterson, although the world will always remember her as the Vampira-like brunette of doom, whose cleavage sent shock quakes through the horror-host world back in the 1980s. (What she has that I don't have is something I will try to explain later, after I have talked to an anatomist who lives down my street.)

Fandom, in case you don't read Fangoria or Scary Monsters Magazine, is composed of conventions and specialty shows, from the annual comic book extravaganza held at the San Diego Convention Center to the Wondercon at the San Francisco Moscone Center, or the annual World Fantasy Con. In between are hundreds of other similar events, big and small, sponsored by magazines, studios and horror icons the likes of Forrest J. Ackerman.

And thus is the world of an aging, long-retired TV horror-host like myself. But there's more I want to share.

Queen B Productions
**Elvira, Mistress of the Dark**

In these pages I want to tell you about a golden time for science-fiction and fantasy, a time that now seems long ago and far away. A time when "Alien" set new trends in horror/sci-fi, when "Star Trek" became a fascinating franchise, when the initial "Star Wars" trilogy exploded in all its onscreen brilliance. When movie special effects were given new birth and achieved new heights of cinematic thrills. The B movie of yesterday had become the A movie of today, but now with newfound respect and class.

That reminds me of Sid Ganis, who during my hosting days was the Director of Marketing for a fella named George Lucas. I had worked on many promotions for Lucas films and Sid and I had become well acquainted. When the excitement for Sid of working for George slowed after the producer's divorce in 1984, Sid left the Bay Area for Los Angeles to become president of world-wide marketing and distribution for Columbia. (Today he is president of the Academy of Motion Pictures Arts & Sciences.) I hadn't seen him for a few years when suddenly he showed up in San Francisco in 1990 promoting "Amos and Andrew," a Nicolas Cage vehicle.

We began reminiscing about the "good old days" and I remarked,

**Sid Ganis then and now**

"You know, Sid, there was something really wonderful and special happening back in the early '80s when you were working for Lucas . . . but it's something I don't feel anymore."

Sid sighed and looked melancholy: "John, those were great days. And you're right. It doesn't feel the same anymore."

It's that great time and place that I hope to take you back to. I also hope to take you into other dark corners of Hollywood, to a world of celebrityhood and stardom that no longer exists. This was the world of TV and movies I explored while serving as an entertainment writer for the San Francisco Chronicle for three decades.

Due to my special areas of interest, I was to explore many science-fiction and horror themes of the 1960s and '70s, years before becoming a TV horror host. By intermeshing my personal stories about Hollywood with those of horror hosting, I think you will discover a unique glimpse of show business. Yes, I met Leonard Nimoy and William Shatner as a horror host, but I also met them as a newspaperman, and hence can now bring two viewpoints to the fore.

Hang it all - I was always being roped by Larry Ett into behaving like a noose-paperman on my "Creature Features" set – knot!

In addition to my own experiences, I'm also going to take you into my time machine and whiz you through the years, to chronicle historically the "hosts" of early feature films in the horror vein starting with the original "Frankenstein." And then I'll take you into the Golden Age of Radio, to a time when I was there, a kid glued to an old radio set, the kind found today only in museums and hock shops.

I will focus heavily on the horror storytellers of that Golden Age, when "Inner Sanctum Mysteries" and "Lights Out," "Quiet Please" and "The Witch's Tale" dominated the airways and a generation of listeners was challenged by what has been described as "The Theater of the Mind." It was a rich time for listening, when the radio fan could conjure up his or her own images of horror and imaginations could run rampant. You didn't need a TV set or computer to show you what it's like to see someone turned outside in. Or inside out. The imagination is the best special-effects device ever created. I'll also trace the coming of Vampira (and Ed Wood Jr. too) in the early 1950s and how her creation of the very-first-TV-horror-host-of-all was to inspire and set into motion a trend of ghoulish and comedic hosts that inundated mankind after the 1958 release of Universal's "Shock!" package of horror and sci-fi films. A new trend was created.

The PR Photo for my amateur-films special "The Star Wars Gang of Tomorrow" and its equally well-viewed sequel, "Eat Your Heart Out, George Lucas."

After that I will take you to the Magic Castle in Hollywood to meet a number of popular horror hosts. Then we're off into time and space to the universe of "Star Trek," a robot killer who turned into a killer politician, the faceless ones of "Star Wars," and a magical mixture of personalities who once dominated the world of film making and literature.

And now allow me, after reviewing literally thousands of movies in order to produce six editions of "The Creature Features Movie Guide," a spinoff of my TV show in which I attempted to critique or review every science-fiction, fantasy and horror movie made since the invention of the movie camera by Thomas Alva Edison, to tell you what it's like to be exposed to such material.

It's mind-numbing. It's soul-crushing. It's devastating.

And I had a helluva time.

So, fans, here we go:

*Once upon a time I became trapped in a dungeon of horror, captive to eviscerated evils unimaginable, a prisoner of putrescent pandemonium. Buried up to my armpits in a gorepool created by a thousand vampiric bites, fanged werewolf attacks, baying hellhound teeth gnashes and man-made monsters gurgling their insanity in and out of laboratories.*

*A gorepool in which float hundreds of chainsawed arms and legs, filled with buckets of blood from a thousand gaping wounds made by axes, butcher knives, swords, skewers,*

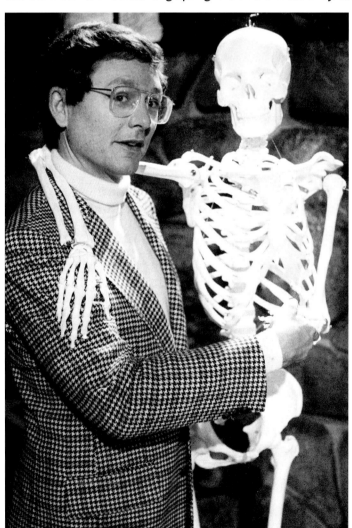

*pikes and picks. I was awash in an abyss of blood, wallowing in its gory atmosphere of horrific violence.*

But relax. It was only a cinematic gorepool in which I was up to my armpits.

It was in the dungeon-like darkness of movie theaters wherein I cringed, stricken by the sound of a thousand soul-piercing screams and where I have observed 2,000 maniacs performing their ungodly hackwork. Yes, while mangling butter-soaked popcorn pieces to bits and gurgling Cokes to death, I have been to the edge of the pit of Hell and back more than once.

And of course, being the pure-of-heart TV horror-host that I am, I was loving it. Every moment, every scene. So brace yourself and prepare for an excursion into a rarified and special world of the fantastic, as I have seen it, lived it and enjoyed it.

Now that I have you in the mood, prepare to have your brain turned inside out.

**– John Stanley, Pacifica, CA
2007 A.D. (After Dracula)**

# HORROR HOSTING B.T.
## (BEFORE TELEVISION)

A N ANTHROPOLOGICAL THEORY persists that the first true "horror-storyteller" was a flamboyant caveman, sporting a leopard-skin wraparound, who sat cross-legged with several enraptured peers around a blazing campfire, spinning tall primeval yarns about life in the horrible old days of man vs. nature. Of course, we could add that the symbols scratched into the walls of caves were the first actual stories recounting horrific events or heroic encounters of those primordial periods.

Our motion pictures have tended to distort this potential truth by having those campfire patrons listening to terror tales about flesh-hungry tyrannosaurus rexes, pterodactyls attacking from the sky and other reptilian denizens of a million years ago. Since man and dinosaur never existed together in the same historical time zone, that's hogwash reserved for those ridiculous movies that have depicted this major historical inaccuracy, all in the name of vicarious entertainment. I refer to "One Million Years B.C." (a 1966 film with a human creature named Raquel Welch) and "One Million B.C." (a 1940 release with Lon Chaney Jr. as virile caveman Akhoba, in hot pursuit of yet another curvaceous creature, Carole Landis). Check out "Jurassic Park" and sequels for a modern variation.

From behind the curtain steps Edward Van Sloan in 1931 to introduce Universal's horror classic "Frankenstein."

Prehistoric literacy aside, we must turn to the age of modern popular culture to find our first contemporary "horror host," the man who introduces us to *things* to come. That gentleman would be Edward Van Sloan, who prefaced the 1931 film "Frankenstein" by stepping out from behind a theatrical-style curtain to welcome viewers into Mary Shelley's world of gothic horror. In this brief introduction, his face overly lit to give him an element of menace, Van Sloan became our first official horror host of the 20th Century with this gleeful greeting:

*"How do you do. Mr. Carl Laemmle* [founder of Universal Studios and the film's "presenter"] *feels it would be a little unkind to present this picture without just a word of friendly warning. We are about to unfold the story of Frankenstein, a man of science who sought to create a man after his own image without reckoning upon God. It is one of the strangest tales ever told. It deals with the two great mysteries of creation: Life and Death. I think it will thrill you. It may shock you. It might even . . . horrify you. So if any of you feel you do not care to subject your nerves to such a strain, now is your chance to uh . . . well . . . we warned you."*

Not only was Van Sloan the film's "horror host," but he also appeared in the film as Dr. Waldman. Significantly, Van Sloan contributed more than his share to the Universal horror cycle by also playing Professor Abraham Van Helsing in "Dracula" (1933) and "Dracula's Daughter" (1936), Dr. Muller in "The Mummy" (1932) and Professor Carlyle in the disaster spectacle "Deluge" (1933)." (Van Sloan lived a full 82 years of life.)

How The Shadow was depicted on the cover of a 1938 pulp magazine.

Almost simultaneous with the release of "Frankenstein" in 1931, radio made its initial foray into the field of horror with what would be the first personality host/story-teller. A strange flesh-and-blood entity with a name and a distinct identity designed to tap into our fears and vulnerabilities and intrigue us with the promise of a terrifying experience. That sinister story-telling force was an entity hosting "The Shadow." The idea was for the host (James La Curto, replaced after a few weeks by Frank Readnick) to tell the week's mystery, adapted from the then-popular Detective Story Magazine. It was good promotion for newsstands, something being tried for the first time in this new listening medium grabbing the nation's imagination.

According to Anthony Tollin in his "The Shadow: The Making of a Legend," the program "started with a laugh . . . a disembodied, haunting laugh that seemed to come from nowhere and everywhere. The mocking voice that accompanied it was strange and venomous; a voice that sent chills down the spines of early radio listeners." The voice was meant to mock the listener: *"I . . . am The Shadow. Conscience is a taskmaster no crook can escape. It is a jeering shadow even in the blackest lives. The Shadow knows . . . and you too shall know if you listen as Street and Smith's 'Detective Story Magazine' relates for you the story of . . . "*

"Who Knows What Evil Lurks in the Hearts of Men . . ."

A publicity photo designed to promote "The Shadow" radio series in the late 1930s.

The claim of those early audiences that chills traveled along their spines cannot be verified today because not a single episode of "The Shadow" radio show from the early 1930s has survived. But because listeners began asking for "that magazine with 'The Shadow' in it," Street and Smith decided to publish such a magazine devoted to The Shadow. A magician-turned writer named Walter Gibson came up with a new concept. Writing under the pen name of Maxwell Grant, Gibson created a character who combined elements of stage magic, Tibetan mysticism and crime-fighting and who would seemingly fit the persona of the unseen radio personality. The first issue of The Shadow Magazine sold out and listeners could now imagine a cloaked figure in black clothing, his face hidden in the shadows created by his oversized slouch hat and high collar, hovering over the microphone with that sneer on his lips as he unfolded the latest mystery adventure.

Despite the magazine's leap in circulation, the radio version continued with The Shadow (played by both Readnick and James La Curto at various times) as only the storytelling host, not a story character. So it went throughout the Depression years, when such escapist pulp magazines as The Shadow, Weird Tales and Argosy fascinated the reading public. Finally in 1937 radio history would be made and "The Shadow" would become synonymous with old-time radio's great love for the mystery program. The radio character no longer

"Crime Does Not Pay"

Orson Welles in his radio role as The Shadow, aka Lamont Cranston, 1937.

merely introduced the stories but now became the central figure in a series that would run for the next 15 years. For radio was a burgeoning medium that allowed one to exercise the full depth of the imagination – a "theater of the mind" where one could conjure up monsters far worse-looking than anything designed by a special-effects artist for a visual medium.

It began with the coming of Orson Welles on September 26, 1937, in the episode "Death House Rescue." "The Shadow" now focused on a man-about-town named Lamont Cranston, who would cloak himself in invisibility to track down criminals. The thrilling new opening would become known to several generations of Americans: after a brief rendition from "Omphale's Spinning Wheel" . . .

. . . The Shadow laughed diabolically, not unlike a fiend, and proclaimed: *"Who knows what evil lurks in the hearts of men. The Shadow knows. Heh heh heh heh."* Then announcer Ken Roberts told us: *"The Shadow, Lamont Cranston, a man of wealth, a student of science, and a master of other people's minds, devotes his life to righting wrongs, protecting the innocent, and punishing the guilty. Using advanced methods that may ultimately become available to all law enforcement agencies, Cranston is known to the Underworld as The Shadow. Never seen, only heard, as haunting to superstitious minds as a ghost, as inevitable as a guilty conscience.*

*"Cranston has learned the hypnotic power to cloud men's minds so they cannot see him. Cranston's friend and companion, the lovely Margo Lane, is the only person who knows to whom the voice of the invisible Shadow belongs. Today's story . . . "*

"The Shadow," with plots that ranged from routine underworld-crime stories to ghoulish tales about mad scientists, crazed witch doctors and killer gorillas, was played by Welles (with Agnes Moorehead as his Margo Lane) through two seasons, then he would pass the cloak of invisibility to Billy Johnstone, a versatile radio actor who held the job until 1943. Movie actor John Archer took over for two years, then in 1945 Bret Morrison would grab onto the role and maintain it for the duration of the run. The episodes during those 15 years always concluded with: *"The Weed of Crime bears bitter fruit. Crimes does not pay. The Shadow knows. Heh heh heh heh."*

John Archer, a Hollywood film actor, would play The Shadow for two seasons.

Agnes Moorehead, the first Margo Lane opposite Orson Welles' Shadow, 1937.

Bret Morrison also left behind a voice legacy in another way. After the heyday of radio, he began his own movie-dubbing business in New York City, hiring other great voices from the Golden Age of Radio to provide English-speaking soundtracks for countless foreign-made motion pictures. I've jumped out of my chair more than once while watching these old chestnuts. Suddenly it was like listening to an old episode of "The Shadow" as Morrison's voice boomed forth from my TV set.

"The Shadow" was but the beginning of an explosion in radio. At the forefront of establishing a brand-new characterization to serve as horror host for the new medium was an imaginative writer named Alonzo Deen Cole. He decided to submerge himself totally into the world of the supernatural with the creation of "The Witch's Tale," a chilling collection of original ghost and horror tales featuring restless spirits, ancient curses, slithering monstrosities, evil genii, walking corpses and all the other imagery of classic horror stories. At the heart of each twisted tale was a driven character who

Bret Morrison would play Lamont Cranston aka The Shadow for 15 years, proving crime did pay – for radio actors with versatile voices.

would ultimately lose his soul if not his/her life. The series, which ran on radio WOR in New York from 1931-38, introduced Nancy the Old Witch of Salem and Satan, "her wise black cat." Nancy would become the prototype that inspired E.C. comic book publisher William Gaines to create "The Haunt of Fear," featuring the Old Witch as yarn-spinner, as well as

"Cackle Cackle"

"Eeek!"

Alonzo Deen Cole in a "Witch's Tale" publicity pose with leading lady Adelaide Fitz-Allen in the background.

"Tales From the Crypt" (with the Crypt-Keeper) and "Vault of Horror" (with the Vault-Keeper) during the 1950s.

Portraying the cackling hag was stage actress Adelaide Fitz-Allen, who was 75 when she took to the microphone for the first time. Despite Dean's weird tales now sounding a bit dated and simplistic, and despite the sometimes Shakespearean-like hysterical qualities Cole brought to his bravura writing, "The Witch's Tale" still stands as a landmark radio horror show.

Each episode opened wth a bell tolling against an eerie wind, then a burst from Leginski's "Orgie and the Spirits," and a grim narrator's voice (WOR personality Roger Bower) intoning *"The Witch's Tale . . . a fascination of the eerie . . . weird, blood-chilling tales told by Old Nancy, the Witch of Salem, and Satan, her wise black cat. They are waiting, waiting for you . . . Now!"* This was always followed by a cackling "heh heh heh heh" as Fitz-Allen brilliantly conjured up the image of the old witch. (Later her audio interpretation would be visually enjoined on the movie screen by Margaret Hamilton when she portrayed the quintessential hag, the Wicked Witch of the West, in 1939's MGM classic "The Wizard of Oz" opposite Judy Garland's wonderful portrayal of Judy.)

You could see Old Nancy in your mind's eye, huddled in a wretched hut hidden away in a dark forest of gnarly trees, perhaps a cauldron of slimy ooze nearby, perhaps her broomstick leaning against the corner. Always the cat Satan sat beside her, eyes glowing an evil red. And next to them the fireplace and the burning embers – embers ablaze like Satan's piercing eyes.

Inserted into Old Nancy's introductions was the mewing of Satan, who purred menacingly (voice provided by Cole himself) at the appropriate moment as Nancy cackled on: *"A hundred and three year old I be today. Yes sir, a hundred and three year old. Heh heh heh. Well, Satan, me and you'd better plan to see folks are treated to a pretty little yarn tonight. Heh heh heh."* . . . *"Meow . . . meoowww . . ."* . . . *"Douse all them lights. That's it. Make it nice and dark and cheerful when you hear them bedtime stories. Now draw up to the fire and gaze into the embers, gaze into 'em deep and soon you'll see . . . "* At this point Nancy would describe the setting for the first piece of action, with Satan still making felinely purrful asides.

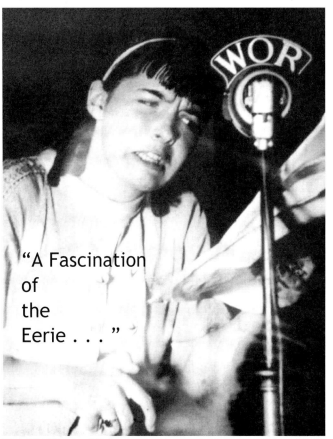

"A Fascination of the Eerie . . . "

The Old Witch of Salem wasn't so old after all – Miriam Wolff was only 13 when she took over the role of Nancy after the death of Adelaide Fitz-Allen.

It has been speculated that Cole was able to sell this then-unusual idea to WOR because most of what night-time radio was presenting in the early 1930s was non-dramatic: long musical interludes, or occasional comedy shows featuring the up-and-coming talents of Ed Wynn, Jack Benny and Eddie Cantor. Because "The Witch's Tale" offered something far from the ordinary, the series was an instant hit and would set the stage for similar radio horror hosts to follow.

Fitz-Allen, who had a reputation for never missing a performance, suddenly fell ill and died in the third year of the show's run. She was replaced by Miriam Wolff, who had previously played a witch on "Let's Pretend," a CBS Saturday morning series. What's amazing is that Wolff was all of 13 years old, and yet managed to convey all the old-woman qualities that Fitz-Allen had so ably established. (Wolff still holds the record for being the youngest of horror hosts.)

The show was heard eight years throughout the land and is still much coveted by radio-show collectors. In 1998 David S. Siegel, who claims to own one of the largest collections of old-time radio shows in America, edited a script collection as "The Witch's Tale: Stories of Gothic Horror from the Golden Age of Radio" (Dunwich Press/Book Hunter Press), with the surviving Ms Wolff providing opening and closing comments.

"The Witch's Tale" proved to be a worthy stepping stone for Cole, who went on to work in numerous radio series, including "Gangbusters," "The Kate Smith Hour" and a few episodes of "The Shadow." He finally discovered a new niche for himself with the creation of "Casey, Crime Photographer," a relative routine crime-solving series that ran from 1943-55. He attempted a TV version of "The Witch's Tale" in 1955. A pilot episode was shot, but upon seeing that the finished results were poor, Cole abandoned the project.

After the success of radio's "The Witch's Tale," listeners began to hear the sounds of horror all over the radios of America, often showcased by a grisly storyteller. First to blatantly copy the Alonzo Deen Cole style was "The Hermit's Cave" which went through two incantations.

The first was from 1935-40 at Radio WJR in Detroit, Mi, with John Kent portraying the storyteller: a cackling old geezer, obviously demented in mind and body, living in a cave surrounded by howling wolves. *"Ghost Stories . . . Weird Stories . . . And murders too! The Hermit knows of them all. Turn out your lights. Turn them out. Ahhhhh . . . Have you heard tonight's story? Then listen while the Hermit tells you the story. Heh heh heh heh heh heh . . . "* And thus would begin such yarns as "House of Purple Shadows," "Spirit Vengeance," "Buried Alive," "From Another World" and "Plantation Mystery."

A troupe of Detroit radio actors known as "The Mummers" contributed the character parts, and listeners would recognize some of the voices from "The Lone Ranger," also done in Detroit. The second incantation for "The Hermit's Cave" ran at Radio KMPC in Beverly Hills, Ca., from 1940-43.

This version also specialized in flat-out ghost and ghoul stories with ample eerie sound effects. Almost every episode featured some horrendous death (or multiple deaths) caused by crazed killers, slobbering ghouls, attacking vampires or cackling dastards.

This second version opened with the same howling wolves but now with the voice of radio actor Mel Johnson as the campy yet unforgettable desert rat.

One could almost see his blazing eyes, wretched clothing and beard-covered face as he hunched forward in the dankness of his cave, surrounded by the crying beasts of the night. In addition to keeping alive radio's horror cycle, "The Hermit's Cave" also introduced newcomers William Conrad and John Dehner, who would both make major contributions to the radio version of "Gunsmoke" in the 1950s.

Another newcomer who was first heard on "The Hermit's Cave," Bill Forman, would soon make history as the weird host of what is now considered radio's finest, and most mature, long-lasting mystery show. While "The Whistler" (which ran from 1942 to 1955) never dealt directly with the supernatural

Bill Conrad provided plenty of weird characters for the Golden Age of Radio but his most memorable role was the original version of Marshal Matt Dillon on "Gunsmoke" when it first premiered on radio in 1952.

world Nancy specialized in, and never delved into realms of fantasy, it nevertheless had some of the best spine-tinglers ever heard on radio. Call it the horror of the human mind—or psychological ghastliness.

This ghoulish-like leading character was a sinister figure who walked the dark streets of American towns and cities, and who talked like a calculating specialist in the arts of murder, deceit and deception. Each program opened with a whistling theme (by Wilbur Hatch, who also supplied the incidental and oft-impactful music) followed by Forman's hard-edge reading: *"I am The Whistler and I know many things for I walk by night. I know many strange tales hidden in the hearts of men and women who have stepped into the shadows. Yes, I know the nameless terrors of which they dare not speak."*

Bill Forman, as The Whistler, symbolized the worst traits of the diabolical, psychotic and murderous mind. And he was such a sweet-looking man.

Unlike Old Nancy and the Old Hermit, who were horror-story cliches played with a tongue-in-cheek style, Forman brought a cold harshness and heartlessness to the character. Although The Whistler himself was only the storyteller, and never a character within the stories, he was an omnipresent observer of the dark deeds of men and women obsessed by greed and betrayal.

From the outset, the listener followed the perpetrator step by step as he/she carried out an intricate plan. The Whistler would interject gloating comments about how clever these schemes were, and how the dastardliness was going to turn out so well. Call The Whistler the Voice of one's conscience.

Also, "The Whistler" was different because it was always written in the second-person, present tense. *"Yes, you intend to kill your wife, don't you, Frank. But you know it's dangerous and so you'll have to proceed with care. You have to be clever in how you carry out your plan. Step by step, you go over it in your mind. Knowing that one slip and it will be over for you, won't it, Frank? But you know you can do it because you love Cynthia too much to let her go . . . Yes, beautiful Cynthia. The woman who takes your breathe away, the woman you'll stop at nothing to have as your own, to hold tightly in your arms."* You could almost see the omniscient Whistler hunkering just out of sight, following every step of the nefarious plans being carried out by the characters, and then darting forward to whisper evil designs into the ears of his doomed characters.

In the final moments of "The Whistler" the evil doer would make one fatal mistake or fate would intervene to thwart the scheme and bring about ironic justice. In one of the more memorable episodes a disc jockey cuts a record to play while he sneaks out of the radio studio to rush home and murder his wife.

As he's standing over her dead body, gloating and listening to himself on the radio, he suddenly hears the record stick—and realizes his alibi has just been shattered. So it went—23 excellent years of first-rate stories in an adult vein, with conniving, sexy ladies and adulterous affairs often driving the plots.

Forman, as excellent as he was playing the title role, never enjoyed much fame from it – his identity as the real star of "The Whistler" was kept secret for nine years, not being revealed to the public until 1951. Radio listeners had thought of him only as the light-hearted, jovial announcer of "The Alice Faye-Phil Harris Show" which ran 1946-54.

Because radio's "The Whistler" was film-noirish in tone, and because radio shows often inspired movie versions, Columbia produced a series of low-budget films beginning with "The Whistler" in 1944. Unfortunately, the writers played down the second-person, present-tense voiceover and The Whistler remained nothing but a shadow on a wall or sidewalk and never took on a life of his/its own. What had made the radio shows unique and singular was largely lost on the screen in what became nothing more than a quintessential B-movie series often featuring one-time leading man Richard Dix.

However, the director of the first film, William Castle, was beginning to distinguish himself at the studio and would direct most of the other films in the series in his newfound noirish style. "The Whistler" series would prove to be the first of several building blocks that would eventually turn Castle into a variation on a horror host. In the late 1950s and into the '60s he would produce and introduce on screen a series of horror films (see my chapter "He Tried to Scare the Pants Off America!" for an accounting of my meetings and unusual interviews with Castle – on page 187.)

Other films in this marginal series followed, and I list them strictly for the record: "The Mark of the Whistler" (1944), "Voice of the Whistler" (1945), "Mysterious Intruder" (1946), "The Secret of the Whistler" (1947), "The Thirteenth Hour" (1947) and "Return of the Whistler" (1948). There was also a 1954-55 TV version which wisely recast Bill Forman as the voiceover narrator but it still wasn't as dynamic or well-received as the radio series.

While radio's "The Whistler" was to be taken seriously, "Inner Sanctum Mysteries" was another matter entirely, mixing tongue-in-cheek black comedy with over-the-top haunted house thrills. "The Whistler" always dealt with seemingly real people in identifiable situations, while "Inner Sanctum" was purely made up of graveyard humor with devilish twists. A listener never knew if the supernatural or horrific elements of a story were real, or events had been concocted by a character to mislead others. Sometimes it really was the ghost that returned for revenge, other times it was a set-up to trick someone into confessing or revealing the hiding place of the treasure map or the family jewelry.

A protagonist would often become an antagonist at episode's end, or vice versa. (i.e., innocent young thing is really a hatchet murderess with ten bodies to her credit; crazed woman locked in a mental asylum discovers she really isn't a fiendish killer after all and is reunited with her lover.) There was always a surprise switch awaiting the listener. Almost always told with wind blowing in the background, or thunderbolts cracking outside the windows of the narrative. It was an early hokey version of what attendees would experience years later at the Disneyland Haunted Mansion.

It was created by the brilliant writer-producer-director Himan Brown (see pages 16-17).

Vera Allen (center) is the horrified heroine of a 1949 "Inner Sanctum Mysteries" radio-series episode, assisted by Frank Mellow and Arlene Blackburn.

# THE INNER SANCTUM OF . . .

THE FIRST TIME I met Himan Brown he described himself as "a man reborn." He proved it by filling the air around us with verbal fire and fury. "I'd watched my greatest love, radio, die at the end of the 1950s, and I spent the next 15 years working my head off to bring it back to life." What he wanted to resurrect was dramatic radio, that which had held the nation captive listeners throughout the 1930s and '40s.

Brown had spearheaded the era as a wunderkind by producing and directing an estimated 40,000 programs. At 18 he had produced "The Goldbergs," a long-running soap opera about a Jewish family in the Bronx, but he soon found himself better suited to mystery material

**Horror/mystery specialist Himan Brown directs actress Joan Hackett during the recording of a "CBS Radio Mystery Theater" episode entitled "Mother Love" which first aired on January 30, 1974.**

and daily turned out 15 minutes of "Dick Tracy." "The Adventures of the Thin Man" and "Bulldog Drummond" became Himan Brown's other successes. But his greatest hit was "Inner Sanctum Mysteries" (1941-52), earmarked by the sound of a creaking door slowly opening. It became the most familiar sound effect of his age, the Golden Age of Radio.

The year of our meeting was 1978. Brown, then 68, was passing through San Francisco to promote his then-popular "CBS Radio Mystery Theater," at the time the only dramatic program of its kind playing nightly on 236 syndicated stations. Opening with the creaking door right out of "Inner Sanctum Mysteries," the series was a well-written and -acted package of mysteries, science-fiction adventures and outright horror tales (some were based on classic stories, most were originals) but there was a totally different kind of host: E. G. Marshall was no fiend or ghoul but a learned introducer who commented philosophically and intellectually on the program themes.

As I sat across a table from Brown in a San Francisco restaurant whose name I have forgotten, I could sense his rejuvenation of spirit. He had found the

Fountain of Youth and Elixir of Life through his radio series. "We have become a nation of starers," he told me with all the passion that is Himan Brown. "We lost the joy of listening. Hell, we don't even listen to each other anymore. You see, radio is beautiful because it forces your brain to create images and faces. Through 'Mystery Theater' I can reach out and touch and talk to you. I can get into your emotions. And that's making a form of contact that TV can never accomplish." His 365-episodes-a-year series was just reaching its zenith when we met. And it would continue with a mixture of original shows and reruns through 1982.

Brown has always been noted for his unique use of sound. He told me they needed the sound of a human skull being crushed by a crowbar. He achieved this, after much trial and error, by dropping a cantelope on a solid surface. The blaring of foghorns and the bong of Big Ben became the motif for "Bulldog Drummond" and there was the characteristic laugh of the obese, armchair-bound Nero Wolfe.

"Today," said Brown, "sound is much more sophisticated, but unfortunately, because of the natural sounds of television, creating sound effects has almost become a lost art. We're always creating some new sound for our science fiction stories, and I like to think we're keeping that part of it alive.

"Dialogue has changed over the years," he said. "Idiom has changed. What we try to capture on the show is the sound of today, of now. We're not redoing the old days. We never play down to our listeners. E.G. Marshall, for instance, doesn't crack macabre jokes on Raymond's level, that would never work with today's audiences. Instead he's on a higher literary level."

My second conversation with Himan Brown was in the spring of 2004 via telephone at his Central Park West digs. And I heard a different voice, a voice that lacked all the positive energy of 1978. At 93, he was totally unhappy about the state of radio and leveled a diatribe against a modern world that denied him opportunities to find new listening markets (his plans for exposure on National Public Radio had repeatedly failed, even though he had been reborn again with a 1999 Peabody Award).

"There's no radio anymore. Just 14,000 stations with commercials, interrupted once in a great while by a non-commercial." He was also angry about those selling his '40s radio shows without sharing the profits.

It was difficult to get Brown to talk about the origins of "Inner Sanctum Mysteries," but bits and pieces of information filtered through. For example, I learned that the creaking door of "Inner Sanctum Mysteries" was the first sound effect to be given a trademark notice by the Library of Congress.

He also told me about the opening format of "Grand Central Station," which still ranks as one of the most dramatic signatures of the radio years . . .

# ... Horror Master Himan Brown

**Himan Brown directing "Inner Sanctum Mysteries" during his career heyday.**

I was knocked out by that opening: *"As a bullet seeks its target, shining rails in every part of our great country are aimed at Grand Central Station, heart of the nation's greatest city. Drawn by the magnetic force of the fantastic metropolis, day and night great trains rush toward the Hudson River, sweep down its eastern bank for 140 miles, flash briefly by the long red row of tenement houses south of 125th Street, dive with a roar into the two-and-one-half-mile tunnel which burrows beneath the glitter and swank of Park Avenue and then . . . (train hissing to a stop) . . . Grand Central Station! Crossroads of a million private lives. Gigantic stage on which are played a thousand dramas daily!")*

I finally got Brown onto the subject of Raymond Edward Johnson, the first "Inner Sanctum" host. There was nothing much good he had to say: "Johnson was a shit. Not a nice man. After the show became popular, Johnson came to me and demanded that he be given credit as the host. And I told him no, that would spoil the grand illusion of 'Inner Sanctum.' I'll admit, Johnson had a good voice but it was still the imagination of the individual listener that brought the witches and goblins to life. Not him. He stormed off to AFTRA [the radio actors guild] and filed a grievance against me. I couldn't fire him so I compromised. I told him he could identify himself as Raymond. Just that."

Once the war was over, Brown replaced Johnson with Paul McGrath, who is pleasantly remembered by Brown as "a much nicer man, he was wonderful."

I had to end my 2004 conversation with Brown on that note. But research has uncovered a couple of other truths (or legends?). The story goes that there was a cellar door in one of the radio studios where Himan Brown worked.

He repeatedly heard it squeaking shut, and he decided one day to use that sound as part of the opening signature for a new idea for a horror-mystery show. He thought "The Creaking Door" was an excellent title. However, the story goes, an executive decided

**Himan Brown, circa 1980**

instead to call the show "Inner Sanctum Mysteries." At that time Simon & Schuster was publishing a line of mystery books under that title, and it would be a way of cross-promoting the two product lines. Ironically, the title "The Creaking Door" would be used in the 1960s to identify a South African radio horror series that was a direct steal of "Inner Sanctum Mysteries." You can almost hear Himan Brown screaming the top of his head off.

One of the pleasures of producing-directing dramatic radio in the 1970s is that Brown is his own boss. "I used to have to put up with incredible pressures from the sponsors back in the 1940s. They'd demand rewrite after rewrite and rehearsal after rehearsal until the program was a washed-out dishrag.

"But now, radio is very much creative and alive again -- and I feel very much alive. I'm doing something that I took for granted all my life. I'll never take it for granted again. Radio is too special to too many people." ❑

**Himan Brown in 1994 at the age of 84.**

Raymond Edward Johnson, the first host of Himan Brown's "Inner Sanctum Mysteries."

Paul McGrath, the second host of "Inner Sanctum Mysteries," and the one Himan Brown preferred.

"Inner Sanctum Mysteries" was set in a crypt of the mind managed by a cheekier version of Old Nancy or the Hermit. His name was Raymond, a vault/crypt/tomb-keeper who relished in the wordplay of horror. Before he spoke there was the sound of a heavy door opening, its hinges desperately in need of oil. Then a burst of grimmer-than-grim organ music, as if a funeral for Satan himself was in progress.

*"Good evening, friends of the Inner Sanctum,"* Raymond would croak. *"This is your host inviting you through the creaking door into the Inner Sanctum for another story to help settle your nerves."* But then Raymond would start to get cute: *"Slither in, won't you? Hmmmm? Sorry the place is such a mess. I'll sweep it up later. Those are just chips off the old block. Been doing my bone work. Heh heh heh. Didn't I tell you? I'm going back to skull this term. All cozy now, ready to swing with us for a while? Hah hah. After all, this is a noose-paper story. And we have a story to jell you . . . Death of a Doll."* Yes, Raymond was good at "scaring the yell" out of you. Each show ended with the door groaning shut again, with Raymond saying: *"And now it's time to close the creaking door. Good night. Pleasant . . . dreams . . . ?"*

"Raymond" was named after the first actor to bring him to ghoulish life: Raymond Edward Johnson, who had once taught, ironically, voice and diction control at the University of Indiana. He maintained the role from 1941-45, and then went on to work in most of the major radio shows of the 1940s.

He hosted Mutual Radio's "Crime Club" (1946-47) and portrayed a character called The Hungarian Giant on a spy thriller, "Cloak and Dagger," in 1950. he might have had a good film career but muscular sclerosis plagued him for years until his death in 2001 at the age of 90. Johnson must be credited with at least establishing the audio qualities of the ghoulish/comedic horror host – something further explored from 1945 until the series' demise in 1952 by replacement Paul McGrath.

Host McGrath brought an even greater sense of morbid comedy and dark graveyard humor to the role of the macabre horror host part and soon descended into the use of the lowest common denominator of comedy, the pun. Nevertheless, the "Inner Sanctum Mysteries" episodes of the late '40s, of which about one hundred still survive today and

Lon Chaney Jr., following in the footfalls of his versatile father, adorns the cover of a VHS release of two film entries in the "Inner Sanctum" series of the 1940s.

are obtainable within the old-time radio collecting world, are immensely entertaining. Both for their unpredictability and for the anticipation of what new macabre wordplay McGrath might engage in as "Raymond." He went on to voice-over the part again for a 1954 TV pilot episode of "Inner Sanctum," but no series developed from it. He was also in the daytime radio serial "Big Sister" (as a character named John Wayne). A sporadic film career included supporting roles in "A Face in the Crowd" (1957) and "Advise and Consent" (1962). He died on his 74th birthday in London in 1978.

Like "The Whistler," the radio version of "Inner Sanctum Mysteries" made the transference to the big screen in a series of lower-berth features made at Universal during the World War II years. An arrangement was made with the studio with Simon & Schuster Inc. which was then producing a line of Inner Sanctum mystery books. None of the titles gave away any connection to the radio show: "Calling Dr. Death" (1943), "Weird Woman" (1944), "Dead Man's Eyes" (1944), "Frozen Ghost" (1945), "Strange Confession" (1945), and "Pillow of Death" (1945).

Although these six "quickies" (all starring Lon Chaney Jr.) have a "host," he is like nothing to be found on the radio. Each film opens in a spacious library dominated by a long table. In the center of the table, in a pseudo-crystal ball device, floated a human head. The head belonged to a Russian-born actor, David Hoffman, who also made horror history with small roles in "The Beast With Five Fingers," "The Creeper" and "Flesh and Fantasy."

As his face wavers with slight distortion inside the bowl, this "Spirit of the Inner Sanctum" (as he was billed) intones:

*"This is the Inner Sanctum. The strange, fantastic world controlled by a mass of living, pulsating flesh: the mind. It destroys, distorts, creates monsters, commits murders. Yes, even you without knowing can commit murder."*

There would be two other "Inner Sanctum" movie projects over the years. In 1947 a 62-minute low budget effort starring Charles Russell and Mary Beth Hughes borrowed the radio show title but presented no sign of Raymond. The only story-teller became Fritz Leiber (the actor, not his son the science-fiction writer) who tells the narrative aboard a speeding train to other characters. Then there was Fred Olen Ray's 1991 horror film with an "Inner Sanctum" title but it had nothing whatsoever to do with the radio show.

In describing the macabre programs of radio yesteryear, there were two "hosts" who made unparalleled history by portraying only themselves, and talking to listeners from the creative heart. Even today both are considered to be among the best writers produced by the era of dramatic radio.

One was Wyllis Cooper who in 1934 created "Lights Out," described as "the ultimate in horror." The show opened with howling wind, clanging church bells and an intensely menacing voice: *"This is the witching hour. It is the hour when dogs howl and evil is let loose on the sleeping world. Want to hear about it? Then turn out your*

Horror story specialist Wyllis Cooper, the creative genius of "Lights Out" and the designer of the unsung largely-forgotten classic of Sunday afternoon radio, "Quiet Please."

Arch Oboler took over "Lights Out" from Wyllis Cooper and also created the memorable allegorical anthology series "Arch Oboler's Plays."

*lights."* Some listeners had been so shocked by early episodes that they made news in Newsweek magazine, which reported in April, 1935, that one listener had passed out unconscious by her radio and another had called police to her home to help her get over her uncontrollable fear.

Wyllis was an excellent writer in his mid-30s who loved to structure his stories on more than one level and make them allegorical, and Hollywood beckoned for his talents almost at once. He forsook his horrific radio creation to write three of the "Mr. Moto" movies starring Peter Lorre, and then produced his best work, the script for "Son of Frankenstein" (1940). And then he would vanish for the next few years, lost in creative obscurity with radio products that never rose above the average.

The second host who talked from the heart was the very fellow who had replaced Cooper when he left for Hollywood. He was a brash, enthusiastic, fast-talking writer named Arch Oboler who in just two years (1936-37) would write more than 100 "Lights Out" episodes. The series now became famous for its sound effects, and Oboler's reputation was enhanced when it was revealed that a glove was turned inside out to simulate a human body being turned inside out by an evil alien force. Need a human head chopped off? Just borrow a head of cabbage. Fingers being chopped off? Try carrots from the nearest produce market. "It sounds great," he told one interviewer. "It's delicious." Oboler would always bring a gentle macabre touch to his on-microphone moments.

When the series left the air in 1939 Oboler had already solidified himself as radio's prime author, and he now turned out show after show, week after week, under the generic title "Arch Oboler's Plays." No matter what the subject matter–wartime propaganda, horror, romance, comedy–he always found an allegorical level

Arch Oboler during the nights of "Lights Out," after Wyllis Cooper has left.

to work on, as Wyllis Cooper had so well taught him. Oboler was also instrumental in bringing a new kind of stream-of-consciousness to radio writing, so his characters seemed to have greater depth and perspective. Others tried to imitate his unique style, but he remained the master of technique and psychological exploration.

As Cooper had done, Oboler embedded social problems and life-and-death themes into each tale, making it richer than other programs of the period. And he remained in front of the microphone, setting up each story in an open conversation with the show's announcer, explaining where some of the ideas came from. And what one might expect from next week's episode. Often he would credit current events for inspiration, making the stories seem that much more timely. Modern problems had become dramatic fodder.

But listeners still hadn't forgotten "Lights Out" and demanded it be brought back. So in

1942 the horror series returned with a vengeance, with Oboler as writer and producer. For the next two years he would write some of the most memorable horror/sci-fi tales for radio, always intellectually commenting on them in his topical openings. He was an outspoken patriot of World War II, often fashioning fantasy tales around sadistic dictators and not afraid to make fun of himself on occasion – in one story some psychiatrists think Oboler has lost his sanity and he is subjected to psychiatric study. His wrap-around commentary gave the stories a completeness lacking anywhere else in radio. You understood the ideas behind each tale, and as a result Oboler's thought processes became as intriguing as the unfolding fanciful tales. With the demise of "Lights Out" in September 1943 (it would return all-too briefly in the summers of 1945 and '46 as a replacement series), Oboler began convincing the Mutual Network to allow him to revive

Character actor Jack LaRue was the first host (better described as a floating head) on the 1949-50 TV version of "Lights Out."

"Arch Oboler's Plays," which finally happened in March 1945. These were to be memorable pieces examining contemporary issues surrounding World War II, and the most memorable would be "An Exercise in Horror (A Peculiar Comedy)" on May 24, 1945. With Peter Lorre behind the mike, the program carried listeners into a macabre, dark region where Americans were being marched into sports stadiums and mowed down by machine-guns – in reference to the horrors of Nazi Germany that were just being uncovered in Hitler's concentraton camps.

As radio began to decline, Oboler turned his talents toward movie-making. Often working with a small budget independently, he made minor history in Hollywood with "Five" (1951), one of the first films to deal with mankind after atomic apocalypse, "Bwana Devil" (1953), the first 3-D movie of the fad that swept Hollywood for two years, and "The Bubble" (1966), another 3-D movie that attempted to revitalize the process but failed. Lesser remembered today are his other fantasy/horror films: "Bewitched" (1945), "Strange Holiday" (1945), "The Arnelo Affair" (1947) and "The Twonky" (1953).

"Lights Out" would be one of the few radio classics to transition to the new medium of TV with producer Fred Coe turning out 160 half-hour episodes. Arch Oboler was nowhere in sight, having gone to the movie world. Film actor Jack LaRue served as the first host – nothing more than a "floating head" in front of a table with a burning candle on it.

He was replaced in the second season by Frank Gallop, whose face was grossly overlit to make him appear ghoulish. Because of his distinguished, aristocratic voice Gallop will forever be remembered as one of the hosts on the New York Philharmonic radio broadcasts and as the comedy foil in the 1947-48 Milton Berle comedy series of radio.

But he did contribute his share to the horror genre, first by serving as narrator for the early "Casper the Friendly Ghost" theatrical cartoons, then as the "Lights Out" host for three seasons. Later he hosted "Great Ghost Stories," the last U.S.-TV series to be broadcast live in 1961.

Arch Oboler, however, would have his day in the midnight rays again. He returned to the old-time radio limelight in 1964 with "Arch Oboler's Plays," a revival of his old scripts with new casts and freshly cut opening and closing Oboler commentary. The revival continued in 1970 when many of the old "Lights Out" transcriptions were rebroadcast into syndication under the new title "The Devil and Mr. O," again with Oboler commentating. He would go to his grave in 1987, at the age of 78, still trying to keep the memories of old radio horror shows alive.

During all of those years when Oboler was having his greatest success, Wyllis Cooper, the man who had given Oboler his springboard, had struggled in the vineyards of Hollywood and radio without an equal amount of success. Whatever his problems, Cooper finally convinced the Mutual network in 1947 to give him a Sunday afternoon time slot for a series of half-hour macabre tales, "Quiet Please." There was little budget, even for a cast, so announcer Ernest Chappell often played multiple roles or did an entire script about only one character, as told by that one character. Sound effects were minimal, there was just the one piano (Albert Berman) . . . and yet the stories were strange and engaging. And utterly memorable.

Ernest Chappell, the announcer and leading actor on Wyllis Cooper's unforgettable "Quiet Please."

An episode opened with announcer Ernest Chappell gently saying "Quiet Please" . . . then another "Quiet Please" with just a touch more forcefulness. This was followed by a slow, melancholy piano rendering of "Symphony in D Minor" by Franck. None of it was intense or very dramatic. It was Cooper's way of telling a horror story with subtlety, without lightning or thunder, without howling wind or howling wolves. Let the horror of it seep through the cracks without slamming it into the face of the listener. Unlike Oboler, who would set up each story from the perspective of the creative mind, Cooper didn't appear until the end of the episode. And then not for long: He would describe the show for the next week, but he conveyed none of the showmanship that had helped to give Arch Oboler his radio identity. Ultimately, the poor time slot and diminishing ratings left Cooper without a showcase. He would keep active writing "Whitehall 1212," a series based on actual Scotland Yard cases, but it was a comedown after the high level of storytellling he had shown on "Lights Out" and "Quiet Please." He died forgotten in 1955 at the age of 56.

Robert A. Arthur and David Kogan, two New York-based radio writers, were keen listeners to "Inner Sanctum Mysteries" and decided in 1943 to create their own storyteller, a singular man in black who rode a train through the dead of night. Was it a commuter train or a phantom train?

The latter was suggested by a wailing whistle of a locomotive, steel wheels racing along steel tracks. "The Mysterious Traveler" was a genuinely macabre show, with none of the verbal tomfoolery of Raymond.

This sinister "traveler," on his way from Hell or going to it, meant business when he opened the show: *This is The Mysterious Traveler, inviting you to join me on another journey into the strange and the terrifying. I hope you will enjoy the trip and that it will thrill you a little and chill you a little. So settle back, get a good grip on your nerves and be comfortable . . . if you can, while I tell you the story of . . . "*

"Get a good grip on your nerves . . . "

His macabre tales were right out of the pages of a lurid pulp magazine, totally lacking even a hint of subtlety. And when the strange tale was over, the Mysterious Traveler returned to wrap it up: *"Oh, you have to get off here? I'm sorry. I'm sure we'll meet again. I take this same train every week at this same time."*

**Maurice Tarplin, otherwise known as The Mysterious Traveler, was a weird storyteller aboard a train that sped through a midnight world. He was also "The Strange Dr. Weird."**

The star of the series was Maurice Tarplin (1911-1975), a Bostonian who worked long and hard in radio. He also played Inspector Faraday in the "Boston Blackie" radio series, and spent his last years doing commercial voice-over work and dubbing foreign movies into English for Bret Morrison.

**Boris Karloff would host only one horror program in the 1940s: the short-lived "Creeps by Nights."**

Tarplin as "The Mysterious Traveler" was so popular (he would continue in the role through 1952) that Robert Arthur created a spin-off especially for the actor, again in a sinister storytelling role: "The Strange Dr. Weird." This time the yarn-spinner, sponsored by Adams Hats for the Mutual Network in a 15-minute format, sounded more like Raymond. And the show drifted off into a category we would politely describe today as "campy."

First, a door opens. Not a creaking one, just a plain ordinary door. Tarplin: *"Good evening. Come in, won't you?"* The door slams, feet shuffle. Tarplin again: *"What's the matter? Surely you're not nervous. Perhaps it would help calm you if I tell you a story I heard just the other day . . . "*

These stories were as lurid as those on "The Mysterious Traveler" but Arthur had less time to tell them and today they seem rushed and simplistic. When the tale was done, Tarplin closed with: *"Oh, you have to leave now? Too bad. But perhaps you'll drop in on me again soon. I'm always home. Just look for the house on the other side of the cemetery–the house of Dr. Weird."*

Meanwhile, Arthur was still busy with his collaborator David Kogan turning out yet a third horror-host radio series: "The Sealed Book," a 1945 effort for the Mutual Network. Like "The Strange Dr. Weird," it too began to deteriorate into newfound horror-host absurdities.

First a gong, followed by a burst of weird organ music, and then a voice: *"The Sealed Book."* More organ music. Fade under. The sound of a latch being lifted, a creaking door just like in "Inner Sanctum Mysteries." The voice again:

*"Once again the Keeper of the Book has opened the ponderous door to the secret vault wherein is kept the great Sealed Book, in which is recorded all the secrets and mysteries of mankind through the ages. All the lore and learning of the ancients, all the strange and mystifying stories of the past, present and future. Here are tales of every kind, tales of*

*murder, of madness, of dark deeds strange and terrible beyond all belief. Keeper of the Book, I would know what tale we would tell this time. Open the great book and let us read."* Organ music simulating something inching open. *"Slowly, the Great Book opens. One by one, the Keeper of the Book turns the pages. And stops. Ah, the strange story of . . . "*

While this opening made it sound as if the stories would be rooted in the long-ago past, they were not unlike "The Mysterious Traveler," being contemporary tales about modern people. Some episodes had a variation in the opening signature. In addition to the announcer there would be a second voice, that of the Keeper of the Book, who sounded as old as geezers get, a special talent of radio actor Philip Clarke. *"I must unlock the Great Padlock that keeps the Sealed Book safe from prying eyes. Now, what story should I tell you? I have tales of every kind . . . let me see, here's a tale for you. A dark story . . ."* They didn't come much cornier than this and audiences must have been wise because the show left the air before the end of the year, the Great Book never to be opened again and the Keeper of the Book consigned to poor-ratings oblivion.

Although a frequent guest on "Inner Sanctum Mysteries" in one-shot roles, Boris Karloff despite his excellent abilities at the microphone would host only one series: "Creeps by Nights," which played all-too-briefly from February until June 1944. Karloff stood out with the program's openings: *"This is Boris Karloff, inviting you to join us for another dramatic exploration into the unknown darkness of the human mind. Our theme tonight: revenge. We have chosen for you a story that plumbs the very depths of one of man's primary emotions: the eternal seeking of an eye for an eye, a tooth for a tooth."*

Joseph Kearns would be the first on "Suspense" to portray The Man in Black, one of the classier hosts of the mystery-horror radio age.

"The Man in Black" was to become one of the best-known introducers/story hosts in the radio era, on one of the most listened-to programs, "Suspense." The series, which ran for 20 years on the CBS Network (1942-62), consisted almost entirely of newly-written mysteries in the tradition of "The Whistler" but also occasionally delving into science-fiction and horror, as proven on the night that Orson Welles starred in "The Hitch-Hiker." And when Ronald Colman did "August Heat" and "The Dunwich Horror," the latter based on the H.P. Lovecraft book. Other favorites of the fantastique were "Donovan's Brain" (a two-parter with Welles), "The House in Cypress Canyon" (a werewolf tale with Robert Taylor) and "The Burning Court" (a supernatural yarn with Clifton Webb). Hollywood stars flocked to do the series for the first decade and the shows are as rich for their casts as for their well-produced and well-written stories.

The introducer known as "The Man in Black" would only last the first three years of the run (1942-45), but Joseph Kearns brought it a special sinister quality that makes him one of the most memorable of the radio host oddities. His personal favorite show was on the night of August 21, 1943, when he introduced Lucille Fletcher's "Sorry, Wrong Number" for the first time. (It would be repeated eleven times over the next decade.)

Here's how Kearns sounded that night: *"This is the Man in Black, here again to introduce Columbia's program, 'Suspense.' Our star tonight is one of the most compelling actresses in America today: Agnes Moorehead. Miss Moorehead returns to our stage in a new study in terror by Lucille Fletcher called 'Sorry, Wrong Number.' This story of a woman who accidentally overheard a conversation with death, and who strove frantically to prevent murder from claiming an innocent victim, is tonight's tale of 'Suspense.' If you have been with us on these Tuesday nights, you will know that 'Suspense' is compounded of mystery and suspicion and dangerous adventure. In this series are tales calculated to intrigue you, to stir your nerves, to offer you a precarious situation and then withhold the solution until the last possible moment. And so it is with 'Sorry, Wrong Number' and the performance of Agnes Moorehead we again hope to keep you in . . . suspense."*

Kearns, who had originally started out as a theatrical pipe organist, became so identified with the series that even after "The Man in Black" was dropped from the opening format, he continued to serve as the announcer for "Suspense" on and off over the next two decades, and frequently turned up in the cast as a supporting player. He continued to do hundreds of radio broadcasts during the '40s and '50s and finally made a transition to television in 1955 to play Superintendent Stone on "Our Miss Brooks." But his most popular TV role came in 1959 when he was cast as Mr. Wilson, the next-door neighbor on "Dennis the Menace." However, he died in the middle of the show's second season, having just turned 55. The show was never the same again.

As the war wound down, radio continued to offer new so-called horror hosts, although they seemed to be taking on less persona, and had no colorful names or identities. "The Weird Circle," an offering from 1943-47 that was syndicated by the Mutual Network out of New York, opened with waves pounding against rocks and a tolling bell. An echoey voice told us *"In this cave by the restless sea, we are meant to call out of the past stories strange and weird. Bell-keeper, toll the bell so all may know that we are gathered again in . . . The Weird Circle."* After much tolling and surf-crashing, the voice returned:

No actress portrayed neurotic women on radio as well as Agnes Moorehead—in this historic shot she is performing "Sorry, Wrong Number," in which she was a bedridden women pursued by imaginary and real demons. She would ultimately perform the role 12 times by popular demand on the great mystery series, "Suspense."

*"Out of the past, phantoms of a world gone by, speak again the mortal tale . . ."* Most of the shows were adaptations of famous short stories, such as Poe's "The Fall of the House of Usher" and "Murders in the Rue Morgue," Dickens' "Dr. Manette's Manuscript," Fitz-James O'Brien's "A Terrible Night" and Balzac's "The Niche of Doom."

Capturing a more contemporary note from 1944 to 1946 was "The Haunting Hour," which again failed to give the narrator any distinctive identity. After harrowing music, menacing footsteps of some nameless entity approaching along a echoing corridor and a tolling bell suggesting doom, a narrator announced:

*"No . . . no, stay where you are. Do not break the stillness of the moment, for this is a time of mystery, a time when imagination is free and moves forward, swiftly, silently. This is . . . The Haunting Hour."* The stories tended to be modern mysteries, some with supernatural overtones, most without.

The story-teller without a name was Berry Kroeger, a skilled film actor who specialized in out-and-out villainous roles. He conveyed a sense of sneering evil in almost all of his films (especially as a sadistic military officer in "Battles of Chief Pontiac" opposite Lon Chaney Jr.) and his contributions to the horror genre were many: "Young Frankenstein," "Black Magic," "Chamber of Horrors" and "The Time Travelers."

"Murder at Midnight," broadcast 1946-47 from radio WJZ in New York, featured an opening-signature by Raymond Morgan, a one-time minister from Long Island who had given up the cloth to do dramatic radio parts. In a threatening voice he told listeners:

*". . . The witching hour, when night is darkest, our fears the strongest, and our strength at its lowest ebb. Midnight, when the graves gape open and death . . . STRIKES. How? You'll learn the answer in just a minute . . . "*

The stories were directed by Anton M. Leader, who would distinguish himself again when he became director of the "Suspense" series in the late 1940s. Leader would have a distinguished career in episodic television and also directed the 1963 sci-fi feature "Children of the Damned."

"The Hall of Fantasy" first originated from Utah in 1947 in a syndicated format. In 1952 the show's creator, Richard Thorne, would move it to Chicago on the Mutual Network.

Thorne, who also wrote the scripts, went for the jugular vein of his characters and strived for downbeat shock endings. No cop-outs or happy endings here. The unidentified story-teller opened with:

*"The Hall of Fantasy! . . . Welcome to the Hall of Fantasy. Welcome to the series of radio dramas dedicated to the supernatural, the unusual and the unknown. Come with me, my friends. We shall descend to the world of the unknown and forbidden, down to the depths where the veil of time is lifted and the supernatural reigns as king. Come with me and listen to the tale . . . "*

**Bernard Herrmann, already a distinguished film composer by then, returned to radio composing for "Crime Classics" in 1953-54.**

In the later incantation, Thorne added echoing footsteps as if some evil thing was stalking down the ultimate Corridor of Doom.

Two radio series were hosted by fictional characters who seemed to be totally ordinary, and in no way related to the Nancy or Raymond extreme of casting—and yet, they carried an element of the macabre if you listened closely enough.

"House of Mystery" (1945-49) was an examination of the world of psychic phenomena simplified for a young Sunday afternoon listening audience. The expert in the supernatural who introduced the show was Roger Elliott, played by John Griggs, who opened each episode with: *"This is Roger Elliott, otherwise known as The Mystery Man, inviting you to join us for a story-telling session here at . . . The House of Mystery."* Usually Griggs would debunk the ghostly proceedings, revealing a trick or misinterpretation of the facts.

Also playing an expert—in the history of infamous crimes—was Lou Merrill, who posed as Thomas Hyland, a "connoisseur of crime, student of violence and teller of murders."

Written by the excellent team of Morton Fine and David Friedkin (who would go on to create the Bill Cosby-Robert Culp classic "I Spy" series for TV), the stories were based on actual crimes from historic records. Merrill/Hyland delivered the dry facts of each case with a macabre sense of humor that was unique to dramatic radio. Also unique was the use of sound effects for comic punctuation.

The unusual music was by Bernard Herrmann, who by 1953 was already an established composer in Hollywood, having written "The Day the Earth Stood Still" among other classic scores. He had started out writing for radio shows in New York in the late 1930s and thus was making something of a tongue-in-cheek comeback to radio.

Here is an example of a classic opening: *"Good evening, this is* Crime Classics. *I'm Thomas Hyland. I am going to tell you another true crime story. Listen."* (Hammer striking nail) *"The man is nailing a horse's picture to the wall. The horse is pawing the western skies in the classic attitude of pawing horses and is the top half of a calendar."* (The hammering continues nonstop.)

*"It's a hot April day in St. Joseph, Missouri, in the year 1882 and the man is hanging the picture in his living room because he has a fondness for the noble beast. Horses have got him out of many critical situations. Such as, one, holding up railroads, two, robbing banks, three, murdering fellows. His name is Jesse James. And as soon as he finishes hanging that picture, a friend of his is going to shoot the back of his head off."* (A pistol shot.) *"So tonight, my transcribed report to you on 'The Death of a Picture Hanger.'"*

As radio began to die a year at a time throughout the 1950s, ultimately succumbing at the end of 1962 when the last dramatic series "Suspense" and "Yours Truly, Johnny Dollar" left the air, another medium was rising up to take its place.

Old Nancy, The Mysterious Traveler, The Whistler and Raymond were about to inspire an entirely new generation of horror hosts. The Strange New World that would showcase these weird and ghastly personalities was television.

And the weirdos were just waiting for the chance to don the garb and persona of their horrific predecessors.

Garb? Yes, this time it was going to be *visual*.

WHO IS THIS MYSTERIOUS WOMAN WHO SITS ON A NOT-SO-DIVINE DIVAN SURROUNDED BY SKULLS AND LOOKING MORE THAN A LITTLE LIKE MORTICIA ADDAMS? HER IDENTITY WILL BE REVEALED ON PAGE 31 . . . BUT FIRST BRACE YOURSELF FOR THE COMING OF TELEVISION AND A NEW ERA . . . AN ERA THAT BROUGHT . . .

## THE WAR BETWEEN TWO COLOSSAL GIANT MEDIA-BEASTS

# THE BATTLE ROYAL BETWEEN
# TWO COLOSSAL MEGA-BEASTS

Before there could be a thing called the TV horror host, there had to be a fledgling business called television. And in the beginning there was a threatened, bloody ending—a showdown between the two mediums with all barrels blazing.

When the little 12-inch screens started showing up in American homes around 1948 (less than one per cent of the population had TV sets, but don't blink, that figure would climb very quickly) studio executives were afraid that Hollywood wasn't going to be big enough for two entertainment powers-that-be. "Gunsmoke" hadn't been created yet, but that damn box was gonna have to get out of Dodge—or hell was gonna break loose in front of the Longbranch Saloon.

The first thing the movie warriors did was create a slogan: "Movies Are Better Than Ever." In 1949 those words were scrawled all over the lobbies,  marquees and GIANT screens (not to be confused with those #$%&*@ smaller ones at home). Some gimmick had to lure audiences away from their living rooms where they now seemed to live 24 hours a day. Another form of movie-makers' disgruntled behavior was to keep one's distance from that lame stepchild, television. Shirk it. Demean it. Turn your back on it. Let it be known throughout the land: television was a lowlife, an inferior product, beneath the contempt of any self-respecting *movie* maker or *movie* actor.

So, movies were bigger and grander and greater . . .  Well, that's what Jack L. Warner, Harry Cohn, Darryl F. Zanuck and other moguls wanted audiences to believe, anyway. And so the studios stuck together and fought off this new force of evil—at least for a while. In 1953 the studios used three-dimensional movies as a lure, starting with "Bwana Devil," a jungle adventure starring Robert Stack that had been concocted by radio's "Lights Out" icon, Arch Oboler.

And again later that year with the introduction of CinemaScope, the first anamorphic widescreen process that attempted to make movies seem at least longer, if not taller. Merian C. Cooper, the real-life jungle adventurer who had audaciously helped to bring the first movie monster, King Kong, to the screen in 1933 by believing in the pioneering stop-motion techniques of Willis O'Brien, had also made his contribution with a newfangled curvature screen (broken into three parts onto which three separate pieces of film were projected) called Cinerama.

These were unique features to movies, but ultimately only the use of the anamorphic, widescreen lens would have any lasting effect. The process would take on various names, including Techniscope, another anamorphic system used to photograph European genre films.

As for all those old movies the studios had in their vaults, it was obvious that televison was a good way to make some dough off product previously though to be totally useless. (Theatrical re-runs in those days only happened with classics, such as "The Sea Hawk" and "The Wizard of Oz," which had hit theaters in the summer of 1948—the first summer of this newly fought war.) No longer did studios throw their negatives and prints into debris bins, as they had once done with the coming of the sound era. There was gold in them thar frills and thrills.

Now there was a market for film distribution, in the form of repackaging. Even so, the studios hypocritically held on to their best stuff. And so, while it was getting a lot of movies, TV wasn't necessarily getting the best of the movies.

The B-movie of yesteryear had become the A-movie of television. One desperate enough would settle for old Monogram studio packages, or the PRC low-budget quickies that had filled out the bottom-half of double bills for years. Old old horror films, old old oaters . . .

In the mid-'50s, when the studios finally realized there was enough business for movies and TV in the same town, caution and paranoia began to fall away. A truce was unofficially declared.

It was kiss and make-up time. Sworn enemies became friends. Executives from studios and networks began to take meetings. Hey, let's do lunch. Walt Disney himself spearheaded the change with a deal with ABC to make "Disneyland," a specialty series that debuted in Oct. 1954 as a mix of old cartoons, live-action adventures, documentaries and nature studies. (In exchange Walt would get the money he needed to build an amusement park in Orange County, in a place called Anaheim – ever hear of it?)

Meanwhile, Warner Bros. made a deal with ABC to produce an alternating series of TV versions of their box-office hits "Casablanca," "King's Row" and "Cheyenne," with actor Gig Young appearing as the wraparound host. He also walked viewers through behind-the-scenes vignettes at Warner Brothers. Only "Cheyenne" survived, but history was made.

As a result of these icebreakers, studios had greater trust in networks and began releasing bigger and better film packages to the stations. Many well-remembered and sought-after films finally became available and suddenly television was not a bastard child but a prestigious outlet through which the studios could make even more money by producing original product for the three networks. A production "gold" rush was on – as in, let's make millions.

And then 20th Century-Fox, which had jumped on the TV bandwagon in 1955 with its anthology series "Hour of Stars," often based on an old Fox picture, set yet another precedent in 1961 when it joined NBC in presenting "Saturday Night at the Movies" with the first-run offering of "How to Marry a Millionaire." This single showing was a major turning point in television history.

First-run flicks, never before shown on TV, were like gold nuggets. Now old and new films were profitable product for the market and the fledgling medium would enjoy a new growth. An explosion of better product sent television–networks and indie stations–into a new stratosphere.

Unlike today's vid-world of superstations, partisan-slanted news channels, animal and gardening kingdoms, and hundreds of viewing choices 24 hours a day, it was a primitive and simplistic business back in the 1950s. Try to image a viewing world in which there were only three major networks (NBC, CBS, ABC), an educational outlet, and a handful of independent stations, depending on the size of your market. The viewable numerals ranged all the way from 1 to 13. Wow! At least watching test patterns had become a joy of the past.

These independents had plenty of ample air time to fill and started to rely on syndicated shows, reruns and, of course, the staple that all TV stations fell back on in the time of need, movies: "The Early Morning Movie," "The Midmorning Movie," "The 8 O'Clock Movie," "The Late Show," "The Really Late Show" . . . "The Really Really . . . "

While this movie boom was booming in the mid-1950s, the more resourceful stations began creating in-house product. Often it was boring stuff – community affairs (which ultimately became a requirement) or cooking shows or sewing circles or kiddie gatherings.

Gradually these stations built up their news teams. Finally someone got the idea that a host might be suitable for a 1 p.m. weekday movie. Maybe the host could raffle off some prizes, talk a little about the film, take calls from viewers, and between commercials give the two-hour format a kind of cohesiveness it would otherwise lack.

Then someone noticed that within a package of syndicated movies were certain recurring themes. You know, genres. Five crime thrillers, six romances, five comedies, three service dramas, seven horror shockers and – wait! What if you could put together seven horror shockers from package #1, two sci-fi flicks from package #2 and six fantasy adventures from package #3. And maybe call it something special.

"The Witching Hour"?

"Fright Flicks"?

"Scream Playhouse"?

How about "Shock Theater"?

And what if the host was clad in a horror-character costume with ghastly make-up?

Vampire? Werewolf? Mummy? Zombie? Creep? Corpse?
And maybe standing in the center of a cemetery?
Maybe in a vault?
How about a dank dungeon set?
Maybe with a few torture-chamber devices scattered around?
Thunder for background sound, flashes of light simulating lightning?
Howling wolves in the distance, could be?
And a name like Son of Svengali?
The Creature From the Pit?
How about Dr. Hypnozombie?
Or The Thing at Midnight?
Do all that and maybe you'd have something special. A horror show!
With its very own horror host.
Wow! It was too good to be true.
And so it came to pass. And so now we open the coffin lid . . .

# SHOCK IT TO 'EM – THE BIRTH OF CREATURE FEATURES

**B**EFORE I can tell you the story of the very first TV horror host in American history, I must first tell you the history of a film maker named Edward D. Wood Jr., better known to his cult followers as Ed Wood Jr.

If there is one thing that all TV horror hosts share in common, it is the fact that at one time (or more) in their professional lives, their challenging duty was to introduce "Plan 9 From Outer Space," the single and singular film for which Ed Wood Jr. will be forever remembered (and dismembered). This low-budget movie, first unleashed on an unsuspecting public in 1957, was an instantly forgettable failure and did no business at the box office whatsoever. It just laid there for a few mercifully brief screenings, gasped for oxygen, and died–a fitting end in the eyes of the those working in the movie world, and those who attended movies during the 1950s.

Edward D. Wood Jr., at the precise moment he first saw the early rushes of special effects scenes from "Plan 9 From Outer Space," perhaps?

It might have been totally forgotten were it not for the fact that it came to TV in the early 1960s and would be seen by vast audiences that would be knocked silly by its ineptitudes and gross distortions of even a science-fiction sense of reality.

But the level of incompetence was so appalling, and the lack of respect for even minimal visual values so astonishing, that critics and fans alike began to garner an "enjoyment" (the term is bandied about loosely here) in examining what made the film so terrible.

Wood put together such an incomprehensible patchwork quilt when he made a movie that the film, in defying description, provided a remarkably colorful description – of incoherence, incompetence and utter failure. It has been said that you can accuse Wood Jr. of just about any film-making flaw, but you cannot accuse him of producing boredom.

So many unfathomable visuals are heaped on the viewer that one becomes grossly involved in the film's ability to reach new heights of cinematic crudity. Thus it becomes "entertaining."

Perhaps this explains why Ed Wood memorabilia is now among the most collectible, and expensive to buy. Go to E-Bay to confirm this.

I myself first introduced "Plan 9 From Outer Space" on my "Creature Features" program by extracting some of the graveyard scenes and laying titles over them, in the style of a "preview-of-coming-attractions" short. Then I wrote a fast-paced voiceover and timed it all so it came out to a 30-second promotion, designed to be aired at various times by the station to draw an audience.

The result were title cards that read "Yeeeccchhh," "Rotten Dialogue," "Crummy Set Design" and "Wretched Camera Angles" plus my breathless narration: *"Coming to 'Creature Features': 'Plan 9 From Outer Space.' Only one word describes this cinematic embarrassment* [here's where the "Yeeeccchhh" came in], *which catapulted its director into instant oblivion. A thriller with everything you seek in a rotten movie. So lacking in style and concept, it makes 'Three's Company' look like art. Inept handling, incompetent production. Not since 'Fire Maidens From Outer Space' has a motion picture been so horribly mangled. 'Plan 9 From Outer Space'. You will always forget it."*

Ed Wood Jr. has since been immortalized in the 1994 motion picture "Ed Wood," in which Johnny Depp gave fresh life to the director, dead from alcoholism since December 1978. This is how impactful Wood and his movies have been on the generations that grew up with TV horror hosts. How ironic that Ed Wood Jr. should be our conduit back through time to the beginning of TV horror hosts. For one of the "stars" of "Plan 9 From Outer Space" was Maila Nurmi.

Maila who? The world came to know her better as *. . . Vampira.*

# THE LEARNING CURVE: THE FIRST OF THE FIRST

*"I hope you were  lucky enough to have had a terrible week."*
*– Maila Nurmi*

The history of in-house TV horror hosts indeed begins with Maila Nurmi. And she begins with emphatic sexuality – a body curving in various directions to a statistical 38-21-35.

That body, which had been born in 1921 in Petsamo, Finland, was poured into a slinky, black dress with "shredded sleeves" and a bodice cut down to a V somewhere near the navel. Or so the photographs of the past now visually reveal to us so subtly.

This pliable body was no illusion. But the black hair was, because the woman in the plunging-neckline outfit was a natural blonde. How all this blonde-into-brunette business came about was on a warm evening in the year 1954. Maila had assumed the black wig as part of a costume for a masquerade ball.  But do not underestimate Maila.

This well-educated woman, steeped in American pop culture, had intellectually arrived at her costume by remembering the Dragon Lady of the "Terry and the Pirates" comic strip, and by remembering the Evil Queen in Disney's film version of  "Snow White and the Seven Dwarfs." Equally important a memory: the New Yorker cartoons by Charles Addams – especially the drawings of Morticia, who looked a lot like actress Gloria Swanson to Maila (it would be actress Carolyn Jones  who would ultimately give Addams' Morticia her sexual  look

Maila Nurmi as the first TV horror host Vampira. And now you know the identity of the divan-seated lady on Page 27.

in the 1964-66 TV series called "The Addams Family.")

Since the beginning of womanhood, Maila knew, there was the anima or the archetype of the evil, cool lady in control of men. A succubus, who came to helpless men in their dreams, an all sexually powerful, commanding figure.

So Maila took all these components and turned them into this remarkable masquerade ball figure. And what a figure. "I wore no Hollywood glamor make-up or fingernails," she recalled years later. "I bound my bosom tightly. I wore a dark wig." She also kicked off her spike high heels and went barefoot. Maybe Hunt Stromberg Jr. had a toe fetish – history does not attribute such a trait to the then-TV programming executive working at KABC, the Los Angeles ABC affiliate station. Nevertheless, he was there the night Maila walked in with her husband Dean Riesner, a one-time child actor who would later write the scripts for "Dirty Harry" and "Charley Varrick."

Most of the guys at the ball had reacted with an immediate *"boingg"* when she hove into view. Had Tex Avery animated the scene, eyeballs would have extended from their sockets. The legend goes that Stromberg Jr. had been searching for a way to jazz up in-house product at KABC and suddenly he had something in mind for Maila: Could it be that she was perfect to play the hostess of a Saturday night movie series, one that would show all the lousy Z-grade movies the station had picked up in a syndicated package? It was a crowning moment for Maila. She had spent the early

years of her life trying to establish herself as Maila Nurmi THE stage and film actress. But dreams kept failing. Forget the pin-up period and burlesque shows. Better to remember how Howard Hawks had thought her a worthy replacement for Lauren Bacall.

But it, like the other its, came to nothing. So now, after years of failing possibilities, she had unwittingly established an acting identity with an unexpected "it." In fact, "it" (as in "It Came to the Studio Out of Nowhere") was a unique acting identity that soon would have a name: Vampira.

She had never intended to be a horror host because she hadn't known, before 1954, that such a job description existed. Whatever its description, she wanted the job and told Stromberg so, but she also told him of her trepidations about duplicating her masquerade costume. It needed some changes.

She didn't want to steal Morticia from Charles Addams (because of lawsuit threats Stromberg agreed) but she still wanted to blend sex and death. That female anima had to remain in all its frightening femininity.

"I got trashy. Fishnet hose, black patent leather shoes with studs. Long phallic fingernails and phallic cigarette holder. Tight waist, uplift bra. Glossy make-up."

And *voila,* Vampira was vamping vigorously around KABC. She would play the part for only two years, making $59.60 a week take-home pay, but they would be, for the totality of her career, the two most important years of all.

And unfortunately, she would be destined to spend the rest of her life never completely shedding the plunging-neckline persona of Vampira.

Whether she loved or hated it, Vampira would be her.

And, forever more and into eternity, she would be Vampira.

# SHEDDING LIGHT ON THE MISTRESS OF THE DARK

Although no footage from her stint has survived (video tape was but a dream), Maili Nurmi is vividly remembered by her loyal fans for her tongue-in-cheek portrayal. According to various eyewitnesses, she established several of the styles that would come to stereotype later horror hosts. This "Mistress of the Dark," who soon had her own national fan clubs, came out of a swirling fog, screamed, and welcomed her fans. She employed a Victorian sofa embedded with human skulls (revisit Page 27) and had a coffee table that better resembled a tombstone.

Somewhere on the set was a pet spider, Rollo. Candelabra, cobwebs and dry-ice mist were among the gimmicks and sight gags. She often wandered the set, holding a lighted candle, as if trying to reveal things hidden away in the dark.

She seemed to realize that the unseen was as important as the seen when you were fooling around with horror. Other times she held that lengthy cigarette holder, in the Mata Hari style, and disdainfully blew off her viewers. With smoke, that is. Men must have dreamed of her personally blowing smoke into their faces, and liking it.

The packaged movies she played for KABC were lousy stinking rotten because the best of the horror films had yet to be released to television. But the important thing to her fans was her, not the lousy stinking rotten movies. They had seen nothing like her before and she was deemed Outstanding Female Personality by the local branch of the Academy of TV Arts and Sciences. She also made national headlines in Newsweek and Life magazines. (In only *a matter of weeks*, she would always stress.)

Then, doom and gloom of the real kind. Something evil decidedly happened at the end of her second year as Vampira. Exactly what did happen remains shrouded in speculative mystery. If you look carefully at a scene in the 1994 "Ed Wood" motion picture, there is a newspaper headline announcing that Vampira has lost her KABC job after being accused of affiliations linking her to the Communist Party. But Nurmi would later claim that she was blackballed because of a dispute between her and KABC about who owned the rights to the Vampira character.

Another legend (is it farfetched?) has Nurmi romantically involved with actor James Dean at the time of his death in 1955. It was Nurmi/Vampira, some superstitious types claimed, who put a death-curse on Dean. Whatever the truth is, she was denied a job at KABC and never worked there again. I suspect that a battle over character rights was at the heart of the dispute, if I know anything about the nature of TV executive beasts.

Bela Lugosi, as he appeared when he and Ed Wood first saw Vampira on TV. He was most impressed, according to legend, with her "jugs."

Vampira might have totally faded into oblivion after 1955 had it not been for the movie maker to whom I have already introduced you: Ed Wood. How singular, in retrospect, that the first horror host should become immortalized through her one and only Ed Wood movie role, identified simply in credits as "Vampire Girl." A movie role she accepted reluctantly. Against all better judgment.

Ed Wood is also remembered for his other horror monstrosity, "Bride of the Monster," which starred "Dracula" icon Bela Lugosi. And therein is the beginning link between Ed Wood and mystical, mythical Vampira.

The legend goes that Wood and Lugosi were watching Vampira one night as she showed Lugosi's old 1932 schlocker "White Zombie." After Vampira told her audience "You're watching our Halloween movie with Bela Lugosi, John Harron, Madge Bellamy and a bunch of other people I've never heard of," Lugosi is alleged to have said: "She's a honey. Look at those jugs." Ed Wood never forgot Vampira after that initial "meeting" and would contact her and ask if she would like to appear in "Graverobbers From Outer Space," retitled "Plan 9 From Outer Space," because the Baptist Church financiers felt "grave-robbers" was a sacrilegious word. Vampira was heart-broken at the time of "Plan 9." "Before the [breakup with KABC] I'd been wanted by many Hollywood producers for a film." She would never have worked for Ed Wood, "never in a million years." But now, broken in spirit and broke in the pocketbook, living on a lousy $13 a week, she needed the work as a "Vampire Girl." So she consented, being promised all of $200 for one day of zombie-bloodsucker thesping. But first, Wood had to rewrite her part

Tor Johnson, wrestler turned would-be actor, co-crept with Maila Nurmi (right) through the graveyard scenes in "Plan 9 From Outer Space."

without dialogue. "Allow me to do it as a mute, as a zombie," she pleaded, hoping to make herself as inconspicuous as possible. Was not silence in a rotten horror flick golden? Get in, get out. And then forget it as quickly as possible.

*Who, God forbid, will ever see this awful unmentionable atrocious revolting abominable condescending thing?*

It is true she rode on a bus to the rundown one-room studio in Hollywood, "in the shadow of the Hollywood Presbyterian Cemetery." She remembers: "I didn't know where my costume was. I had thrown them away or lost them."

She wore an old low-cut dress that had an inconvenient hole in the crotch. The whole thing unfolded so amateurishly on the graveyard set that she truly believed the movie would never be seen–perhaps never released. Her anonymity, she felt, would be preserved for the rest of eternity. Thank God for giant favors.

How wrong, how wrong. "Plan 9" may have died at the box office in 1957-58, but it came back years later with a vengeance to newfound reaction from TV viewers. Now it is "Plan 9" and the biographical feature film "Ed Wood" that Maila will be remembered for. In "Ed Wood" Vampira/Maila Nurmi was played by Lisa Marie, who captured a no-nonsense, cynical attitude as Maila. Seemingly very true to how Maila felt whenever she recalls the events.

Johnny Depp as Ed Wood and Martin Landau as Bela Lugosi in the 1994 docucomedy "Ed Wood."

Like Maila, Marie was typecast afterward. She was a Martian girl in "Mars Attacks!", Ichabod's mother in "Sleepy Hollow" and cave girl Nova in the 2001 remake of "Planet of the Apes."

But she has yet to become a TV horror host.

# BEHOLD: A SHOCK!-ING EVENT

As Vampira was fading away in 1957, Universal was taking the next big step. More than 600 pre-1948 features were unleashed from the vaults, and among them were the studio's classic horror films from the 1930s. These films had been especially set aside and packaged under the title "Shock!" The studio had produced these films in cycles, beginning with "Frankenstein" and continuing with "Dracula," "The Mummy" and "The Invisible Man." Out of each initial title an ongoing series had evolved.

These series – plus a new one spinning off from "The Wolf Man" – had continued into the 1940s, finally culminating with the comedy antics of Bud Abbott and Lou Costello meeting Frankenstein and other monsters. There had been plenty of one-shot titles along the way ("The Murders in the Rue Morgue," "The Black Cat," "The Raven" and "The Invisible Ray" among countless others). With so many titles new to TV, "Shock!" lent itself well to independent stations and the growth and development of the TV horror host.

Not only did "Shock!" fill hours and hours with new-to-TV material but a generation was to discover these

**A facsimile of a promotion sheet used to sell the "Shock!" series to TV stations back in the late 1950s**

films for the first time and a newfound interest in horror movies sprang up all over the country.

In England, Hammer was turning out new Frankenstein and Dracula versions and low-budget companies in Hollywood were discovering a younger audience was out there clamoring for more sci-fi and fantasy movies. American-International (see the Roger Corman story on Pages 166-167) would be at the forefront of producing new product. Before long, there were fanzines, Famous Monsters of Filmland and fandom conventions all over the country. What "Shock!" inspired was a whole new interest in the cinefantastique.

And waiting in the wings were plenty of freakish, costumed personalities to go around.

# They Crawled Out of the Woodwork – And Oozed Into The Video Ether to Haunt Us

Greg Bransom as Professor Cerberus

Larry Vincent as L.A.'s memorable Seymour.

After the resurrection of old horror classics in the "Shock!" package, several generations of horror hosts, most of them costumed and portraying tongue-in-cheek take-offs on monster movie characters, crawled out of the woodwork and oozed their way through video ether to make history.

"The dead" were entertaining "the living."

Philadelphia's Roland, one of the very first, was really actor John Zacherle, who moved to New York where he became Zacherley, a never-to-be-forgotten host who set a classy standard for the costumed entity with a sense of humor (see Page 90 for more). San Francisco had a Shakespearean actor, John Barclay, who hosted "Nightmare Theater." Another San Francisco-based variation was Russ Coughlin (later to become a leading news reporter and commentator in Bay Area TV) who portrayed Terrence, a host ensconced in a mummy tomb.

In Miami, Fla., viewers savored Chuck Zink perched atop a coffin. Seattle, Washington, showcased Warren Reed wearing an eyepatch, while his partner Our Boy Frankie was Paul Herlinger. Dallas had Bill Camfield portraying Gorgon the Gruesome. In Hollywood there was Ottola Nesmith, a one-time horror film actress ("Invisible Ghost," "Return of the Vampire") who now introduced films as a crazed old woman. Portland, Oregon, featured Suzanne Waldron's Tarantula Ghoul. New Orleans offered up Morgus the Magnificent, a mad scientist played by Sid Noel.

And so it went across the nation. Here are but a few who rained blood down on the viewers for some 40 years, and who live on in the memories of mind-numbed generations:

Nashville, Tenn.: **Dr. Lucifur** (Ken Bramming); **Phantom of the Opry:** Sir Cecil Creape (Russ McCown).

Cleveland, O.: **Ghoulardi** (Ernie Anderson, see Page 88); **Son of Ghoul** (Kevin Scarpino), **Big Chuck** (Charles Schodowski) and **Little John** (John Rinaldi); **Frank** (Christopher Allen) and **Drac** (Robert Kokai); **Mad Daddy** (Pete Myers); **The Ghoul** (Ron Sweed).

St. Petersburg, Fla.: **Dr. Paul Bearer** (Dick Bennick).

Indianapolis, Ind.: **Selwin** (Ray Sparenberg); **Sammy Terry** (Bob Carter).

Philadelphia, Pa.: **Dr. Shock** (Joseph Zawislak); **Maneater From Manayunk/Daughter of Desire Stella** (Karen Scioli).

Syracuse, N.Y.: **Baron Daemon** (Mike Price); **Dr. E. Nick Witty** (Alan Milair); **Epal** (Bill Everett).

Seattle, Wash.: **The Count** (Joe Towey); **Dr. ZinGRR** (Robert O. Smith).

Wilkes-Barre, Pa.: **Uncle Ted** (Ted Raub).

New York City: **The Creep** (anonymous).

Fort Wayne, Ind.: **Dr. Meridian** (of crossweird puzzle infamy).

Traverse City, Mi.: **Count Zappula** (Don Melvoin).

Tom Ryan as Count Scary or just plain Count.

Omaha, Ne.: **Macabra** (anonymous).
Peoria, Ill.: **Milton Budd** (anonymous).
Richmond, Va.: **The Bowman Body** (Bill Bowman).
Miami, Fla.: **M.T. Graves** (anonymous).
Baltimore, Md.: **Dr. Lucifer** (anonymous).
Los Angeles, Ca.: **Seymour** (Larry Vincent); **Elvira, Mistress of the Dark** (Cassandra Peterson, see Pages 83-87); **Jeepers Creepers** (Bob Guy); **Jeepers Keeper** (Fred Stuthman); **Grimsley** (Robert Foster).
Detroit, Cleveland.: **The Ghoul** (Ron Sweed); **Count Scary** (Tom Ryan).
Wichita, Ka.: **Host and Rodney** (Tom Leahy and Lee Parsons).
Omaha, Neb.: **Gregore** (Greg Dunn).
Pittsburgh, Pa.: **Chilly Billy** (Bill Cardille)
Milwaukee, Wi.: **Dr. Cadaverino** (Jack Du Blon); **Toulouse-Noneck** (Rick Felski)
Tampa, Fla.: **The Outsider** (John Burke).
Norfork-Hampton, Va.: **Ronald** (Jerry Sandford).
Detroit, Mich.: **Sir Graves Ghastly (**Lawson J. Deming).
Dallas-Ft. Worth: **Professor Cerberus** (Greg Bransom).
Atlanta, Ga.: **Super Scary Saturday** (Al Lewis, Grandpa on "The Munsters").
Washington D.C.: **Count Gore DeVol** (Dick Dyszel).
Kansas City: **Crematia Mortem** (Roberta Solomon).
Virginia Beach, Va.: **Dr. Max Madblood** (Jerry Harrell).
Chicago, Ill.: **Svengoolie** (anonymous)**; Son of Svengoolie** (Rich Koz).
USA Cable Network: **Commander USA** (Jim Hendricks).

Dick Dyszel as Count Gore DeVol.

Karen Scioli as Stella, aka That Maneater from Manayunk. Some yum.

The Attack of the Incredibly Creepy Horror Hosts happened in every major television market, and it would continue to expand and explode – until the coming of satellites and cable systems that eventually wiped out the art of movie packaging forever. Today there are few horror hosts left, as the syndication of old movies has become virtually extinct.

In the San Francisco-Bay Area you will find the decidedly erudite Doktor Goulfinger, portrayed by a soft-spoken gentleman whose real name is Michael Monahan. Sacramento's Mr. Lobo (Eric Lobo – yes, that's his real name) has been syndicated in scores of markets but is limited to playing only public-domain features, and hence finds it difficult. And let's not forsake Zomboo, otherwise known as Frank Leto, a creature of the night haunting Reno, Nevada (for revealing looks at these three contemporary personalities, see Pages 198-199).

But it's time to focus on one of the greatest of horror hosts. He never wore a costume. In fact, he was the antithesis of Svengoolie and Son of Ghoul and all the others. He was so ordinary, in fact, viewers wanted to un-scream.

And un-scream again. And again?

His ordinariness is legendary in the annals of TV horror hosts. Mundanity incarnate.

His name: Bob Wilkins.

**Rich Koz will forever be Son of Svengoolie**

Sid Noel as Dr. Alexander Morgus.

# THE HORROR HOST WHO WAS BETTER SUITED NOT TO WEAR A COSTUME – AND WHO BECAME THE BEST-ADDRESSED "MONSTER MAN" OF THEM ALL

Bob Wilkins the television personality might never have happened. But he did happen. Clearly, Bob Wilkins the horror host had to happen. And yet it all started by accident. The kind waiting to happen, perhaps?

He was as different from most other TV horror hosts as vampires are different from werewolves, as different as Boris Karloff was from Bela Lugosi, as different as Alien from E.T. He resembled nothing that slithered out of the world of horror. Or rocketed down to Earth from outer space. Ordinariness, not the macabre, was his trademark. Besides all that, Wilkins was not a trained broadcaster. His voice was too weak to come up to the level of a professional TV announcer.

And his facial features were not those of the high-powered, ruggedly handsome and authoritative spokesman we normally associate with on-air personalities–the mold that made Walter Cronkite and Dan Rather. Rarely allowing a smile to his face, he seemed tranquilized or on a downer sedative. He was clad in no costume or motif-accoutrements of any horrific kind.

His wardrobe was utterly mundane: business suits, striped ties, pointed-toe shoes. Was his blond hair a tangled mass or stick straight into the air? Heavens no, it was perfectly combed. Not a hair or wave out of place. You could almost imagine a hairstylist just off camera, comb in hand, waiting to rush in should a single hair become displaced.

Yes, by traditional standards, Bob Wilkins shouldn't have ever become a TV horror host. Yet he became one of the most popular of his kind. One of the most fondly remembered.

Through pure happenstance he emerged at a time when he was sorely needed by a major San Francisco-Bay Area independent TV channel for prime-time, and he was needed as an alternative to standard programming in the 9 p.m. time slot. Being ordinary in a situation that was decidedly extraordinary, being monotonous and mundane in a wacked out world of movie monsters and mayhem, Mr. Bob Wilkins

provided the ironic contrast the program (and the station) needed.

With a package of old horror and science-fiction movies, most of them ranging from bad to lousy to terrible to god-awful, and a handful definitely classics from the Universal library, Wilkins with tongue firmly implanted in rosy cheek looked condescendingly down on the product. In so doing he provided a breath of honesty and fresh air as alien to television as a creature from another world or an executive who didn't care about Nielsen ratings.

At first viewers were stunned and agape when they heard the satirical put-downs. Then, when they realized the uniqueness of the joke and the depth of the wry humor within which Wilkins couched that single joke, they suddenly realized they were seeing TV history in the making and came to appreciate it that much more. They channeled in, they saw and they enjoyed the wraparound commentary as much, if not more, as they enjoyed the movies. Suddenly it was the Wilkins touch that made it fun to see bad movies. In Wilkins' attitude descent, he simultaneously ascended to the top of the

By Tom Wyrsch

THE BOB WILKINS SCRAPBOOK

Edited and published by Tom Wyrsch in 1999, this scrapbook history of Bob Wilkins became the first major source of memorabilia for the "Creature Features" TV program and began an impactful revival of interest in the long-running show and its cigar-clenching host.

ratings and then – were you watching, Ma? – to the top of the world of localized TV. An icon had been born. Whether by accident or some grand design either on Earth or in Heaven, he became a trend, a habit, a weekly custom as pleasant and warm as going to church. Or as chilling as cuddling up with a good slasher flick.

In the final annals of TV horror hosts, Bob Wilkins will go down historically as one of the most unusual, rivaling the longevity of Zacherley, Vampira, Ghoulardi and Elvira, and still perched high on a pedestal in the pantheon of fame for TV personalities. Today there exists Tom Wyrsch's "The Bob Wilkins Scrapbook," collections of VHS and DVD highlights taken from his surviving TV shows (another Wyrsch enterprise), and literally thousands of photographs out there in fans' collection bearing his signatures.

He connected to his fans in a way that was unprecedented. He imprinted himself on a young generation of TV viewers in a permanent way, so that those who grew up watching him from 1971-80 still connect to him when they see him at conventions and personal appearances, no matter how old they have become. With no costume or fictional character standing between him and his fans, Wilkins has aged into an avuncular or father figure utterly approachable, who smiles when a fan draws near, who extends his hand, who willingly signs autographs or poses for photographs. Suddenly these adults are children again when they see Bob Wilkins, and they approach him, open-mouthed and agog, with the awe usually reserved for movie stars or British royalty. They tell Wilkins the circumstances of watching the show, of sneaking out of bed to see him against the wishes of parents, or of gathering around the TV with the whole family. Childhood memories stoked by nostalgia, warm and comforting memories. Wilkins became part of his fans' weekly lives, and they will never forget him.

He is a phenomenon hard to understand if you have never seen Bob or have never met him. He seems not to have a single TV personality's bone in his body, and maybe that's why he is so approachable and so admired. Humility does have its virtues. How a reserved, almost shy individual born Robert Gene Wilkins on April 11, 1932 became Bob Wilkins, TV horror host extraordinaire, is a Horatio Algier story of success created out of middle-class America values. Hammond, Indiana, was not a particularly glamorous setting for growing up. Steel mills were the principal sources of employment, and that is exactly where his father toiled, often 16 hours a day, to provide for Bob and his six sisters who had to share the same bathroom, 24 hours a day.

**Robert Gene Wilkins is all of 7 months old in this family portrait taken outside the residence in Hammond, Indiana, in the year of Our Lord, 1932.**

The memory of an exhausted man coming home to seven children, in Bob's mind, is that of a man who needed his space for a while. Once revitalized he would begin to warm up to his wife and kids. As for that one bathroom, "We would line up and take a number," Wilkins recalled, relying on that wry wit of his. "And if I had to wait too long, I'd give my number to the sister behind me and step outside and go behind the tree."

When you see your father establish a work-ethic standard the way Mr. Wilkins did, it was only natural that Bob early on began to take odd jobs, to help support himself if not the family. He became a pin setter in a bowling alley for a while, then churned out ice cream. "I was the original cone-head," he said, never one to resist levity. He even managed a car wash, an early demonstration of the entrepreneurial skills he would later refine into his own advertising-agency businesses.

Dad being a steel worker, Bob decided after graduating from high school that it should be his destiny. "You won't believe this," Bob once told me, "but I actually worked my way up to become a clerk in the crane shop. Not every kid growing up in Hammond, Indiana, can make that claim. But I had a problem. I didn't look too manly. Rugged I wasn't. Anyone with ears in those days was considered a sissy. So, to overcome that, I started smoking cigars on the job. We had a plant full of guys who looked like football players and Chuck Norris bodyguards."

He was making good money in those days and thought this was going to be it, a life just like his father's. "My sights needed to be raised," he added, "and a mentor came along, a fellow steel worker, who opened my eyes to other possibilities."

Those possibilities, especially the idea of getting a college education, were interrupted by the Korean War. "I got inducted. Drafted. I spent the next two years marching with an M-1 rifle."

Bob Wilkins' high school picture.

Korea wasn't a good place – he contracted tuberculosis. "It was a bad case of TB. I started to spit up blood. My lungs were gravely affected. A section in one of my lungs . . . I don't recall all that was done, but it was considerable. I was in recuperation for a long while. Thank God the nurses were good looking." No more steel mills after he got home. That mentor had told him to go to college and because there was a special program at the University of Indiana with little tuition, he went–and earned a marketing degree.

"I took the train to Chicago and almost immediately got a job with an advertising company, Post-Keyes-Gardner, one of Chicago's biggest. It was the degree that got me the job and I knew I had done the right thing, getting away from the steel mills. I never looked back. Never regretted anything."

The job, he admitted, was minimal, a mailboy in a mailroom ("Good thing I was a male.") "I started looking around for the important people. When I learned the company president wanted to publish an in-house newsletter I wrote up a nice piece about him and submitted it. 'Hey, this kid can write,' he said, and he gave me a better job in the copy department writing commercials."

He learned the advertising business from "the best guys in the business" and began to dream of having his own agency. On New Year's Day, 1963, he jumped into his old

A Wilkins family portrait (that's Bob in the background, standing to the left of his father).

Oldsmobile with aspirations to make a cross-country trip to California. "At first I thought I was taking a vacation. But when I got to California I loved the feel of things. Land of opportunity and all that. Fruit and honey. I started looking for a job in Sacramento. I landed on my feet at KCRA (Channel 3), an NBC affiliate owned by young guys, the Kelly Brothers."

Bob still isn't exactly certain why an executive called him into his office one afternoon and suggested that he host a late-night program, showing a package of old movies that had been gathering dust in the station vaults. "I had spoken at a farewell party for one of the sportscasters there, and I guess they liked the way I'd ad-libbed my way through it. Anyway, this guy from management told me to look at the films and pick something. One of them was this Japanese thing, 'Attack of the Mushroom People.' I knew absolutely nothing about horror films, or about Hollywood. The whole thing was an unknown to me. I guess you could say I was stepping into the unknown. Without even pondering much about the film, I thought it was a funny title and decided to have some sport with it." A key moment . . .

Now came an arbitrary decision that would prove to be almost fatal. "It was 1966 and in those days young people didn't trust anyone over 30. Remember 'Logan's Run'? I decided I couldn't lie to my audience. I'd have to tell them how I really felt about the movie. And I felt it was absolutely awful. Now in those times, most stations had the news, played 'The National Anthem' and went off the air. No cable, no all-night programming. Management at Channel 3 wanted to fill some of that post-midnight void just to see what kind of ratings would come out of it. Truly, it was experimental. I decided I probably wouldn't have much of an audience so I'd spoof the whole idea of a late-night movie host. This was like a one-shot thing to me, a novelty. When I cut the first show, I held up a copy of TV Guide and read what was playing on other channels. I told my audience that my movie was too terrible to watch."

"Attack of the Mushroom People" (original Japanese title: "Matango") is a 1963 Japanese sci-fi flick that launched Wilkins' TV career. It has become an example of cinema so bad it must be seen to be believed. It continues to plague the viewers of the world in DVD format. If you never saw it, you have been forewarned . . .

On Monday morning, as Bob recalled, "a fate worse than death" was awaiting him. "The bad stuff hit the fan pretty fast. My sponsors, automobile agencies, were on the phone ready to take my head off. 'What's the big idea, knocking the movie when we're trying to sell cars?' They had no sense of humor at all." But what seemed fatal quickly turned out to be providence. "The station pointed to the great high ratings

of that first show and the car dealerships instantly backed down. In fact, one called and wanted to take me to lunch. 'Let's sit down and talk about this, son.' They started patting me on the back. Suddenly I began to think maybe I really had something. A new formula. Paydirt. But, could I expand on that one show?"

And so "Seven Arts Theater" was born. A member of the KCRA art department created a sign for Bob's set: *"Watch Horror Films . . . Keep America Strong."* (It was a motto that would cling to him.) Bob decided to blend the put-down gag with his wry sense of humor by touching on local or national politics of the day, other local TV personalities and even jokes about some of the sponsors. "These were things I felt the average viewer would relate to." His unusual worldly views began to become part of the wraparound material more and more. He was growing as an on-air personality.

Although he openly admitted from the start that he knew nothing about movies, he would look at the 16 mm prints "just so I could say something about each one. I was always looking for the ridiculous scene or something I could spin my humor off of." Gradually, as he picked up more feeling for the movies, he opened the format by having special guests.

One of the early ones was Boris Karloff, at a time when the actor was 80 and in a wheelchair with a lung disorder. The twilight of a horror star . . .

Recalled Bob: "He was in the slow process of dying and we all knew it. Yet, I have never met anyone so courteous, kind and considerate. He kept apologizing for any inconvenience he might be causing." Bob also met John Carradine and Vincent Price as well as cheapie producer Sam Newman, who had made "Invisible Invaders" with so little money, Bob recalled, "he moved bushes to indicate an unseen being was near at hand."

The celebrities kept pouring in. Wilkins concluded his interview with "Star Trek" star Leonard Nimoy at an airport as the actor climbed into his own airplane and took off, leaving Bob in the propeller dust.

Comedian Jack Benny wasn't stingy at all the night he sat down to talk to Bob, but he did try to borrow some money after the show. One thing about Bob. He was *never* stingy.

Wilkins also began to show amateur films made by Sacramento-area wannabe movie-makers. It was a rich and

Boris Karloff, as he looked toward the end of his life. After a lengthy and successful career as a horror movie star, Karloff was interviewed by Bob Wilkins–one of the British actor's last on-camera appearances before death claimed him on February 2, 1969.

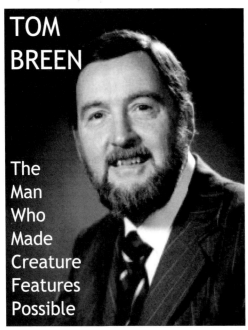

# TOM BREEN

The Man Who Made Creature Features Possible

Tom Breen, the unsung hero of "Creature Features" – the soft-spoken and much beloved TV executive behind the scenes who remained the unseen driving force and who would made the program possible for 14 successful-in-the-ratings years.

capital area had never been exposed to before, and the ratings of "Seven Arts Theater" (soon changed to "The Bob Wilkins Show") continued to climb.

This is about the time when I came in. Although I lived far from Sacramento, on the coastside of California about 20 miles south of San Francisco, KCRA miraculously channeled in on the limited Pacifica community cable system. (Talk about the Fickle Finger of Fate.) One Saturday night I saw this mild-mannered fellow knocking a horror movie (title long forgotten).

That week I zipped off a letter to Mr. Wilkins – mainly to point out factual errors in his commentary – only to be startled a few days later by a phone call, the now-familiar Wilkins voice thanking me for my encouraging comments and for the corrections. He wasn't offended, in fact, he sounded downright thankful that someone out there cared. It was the beginning of a friendship, and for the next couple of years we would exchange letters and phone calls. That friendship would ultimately become . . . well, more about that later.

Back in Sacramento, Wilkins settled into a weekly format. One of the management figures Bob respected was Tom Breen, a one-time Marine Corps volunteer of World War II who had served in the Pacific Campaign.

Breen, aware that Wilkins was a neophyte to the world of TV hosting, encouraged him to experiment, to reach out, and above all not to be afraid to try daring and novel things. Theirs was a good relationship. Eventually Breen signed off to take a brand new station

Wilkins at Channel 3 in Sacramento with one of his on-air pals, Harry Martin, who would also become an on-air talent, though briefly, at Channel 2 during the Wilkins' era, hosting evening movies.

management position in the San Francisco-Bay Area, a step that would soon have a major affect on the life and career of Wilkins. But for the moment, life went on for Bob with the KCRA Saturday night late show. Aware and even perhaps even subliminally fearful that the novel TV stint might be a flash in the pan, he became co-owner of a local advertising agency and began looking for his own set of clients. "I wasn't sure where the future would lead me, so I was covering all my bets, sticking to what I knew best, the advertising world. The TV thing, it was fun but I had to wonder: Was it just a lark maybe?"

At Channel 2 (KTVU) in Oakland's Jack London Square, in an old warehouse building converted to an independent station run as part of a chain owned by the Cox Sisters, Breen had settled in as program manager. KTVU was a popular Bay Area channel mainly for its movie packages, and for unusual in-house programming designed for children as well as adults. A fond memory that still hangs over the station today is Captain Satellite, a futuristic hero in a dark blue uniform with a lightning bolt emblazoned on his chest. Played by Bob March from the early 1960s into the early '70s, the superhero introduced cartoons from a rocketship, the Starfinder 2, one of the cheesiest sets around. The knobs on the control panel, March would confess years later, were nothing more than pie tins secured by nails. Yet the set's cheesiness is what made it fun and memorable, especially if you were a kid who would grow up to become a "Creature Features" fan. March also hosted "Dialing for Dollars," a daily afternoon movie slot with giveaways to listeners who called in and answered film trivia questions.

Bob March, in the role of Captain Satellite, was the first of the unusual hosts who would hallow the halls of Channel 2 for several decades.

"Who said I was off my rocker?"

Call Wilkins the Rocking Chair Kid – actually the rocker was designed to alleviate his nervousness in the early days of the show. It became such a well-liked addition to the set that Wilkins decided to make it part of the regular routine. Notice the casual dress and the impeccable grooming. All Wilkins' personal touches.

Another personality at KTVU in the Bob March mold was Pat McCormick, who picked up where March left off with "Charley and Humphrey," a hand-puppet show with McCormick giving us the fingers. Horse Charley and his not-too-bright dog Humphrey became delights for the kids as did their pal Pussyfoot, a piano-playing

**BOB WILKINS STILL LIVES!**

tomcat. McCormick was an in-house fixture who at one time or another also did the kiddie shows "TV Pow" and "Brother Buzz." And eventually he became the call-me-up host for "Dialing for Dollars," giving away money and prizes in between bursts of old movies. (Later I would share an office with Pat McCormick when he was serving as the station's nightly weatherman on "The Ten O'Clock News.") So, if any station in the Bay Area was ready to produce "Creature Features," KTVU was it, and the pioneering Tom Breen, showing the stuff that U.S. Marines are made of, was ready to explore new possibilities. Breen contacted Wilkins, suggesting that he come to the station with his horror-show format, which would now be retitled "Creature Features." The station would build him a creepy set but Bob could continue to be Bob, still in the suits, still doing his wry comedy.

# THE COMING OF THE ATOMIC AGE "CREATURE FEATURES" ERA

What had worked for Sacramento might go over even bigger in the Bay Area. As Breen explained it, he wanted to put the show into prime time as counter-programming. To offer a package of movies surrounded by the unusual Wilkins style. To give viewers a chance at something more than what the three basic networks were offering on Saturday night. Each of them knew it could be a bust, but there were potential advantages that the new location offered.

Unlike the Sacramento market, Breen felt, San Francisco was a hub for entertainment publicity and Bob would enjoy richer opportunities for media-driven guests. Motion picture producers and their casts were passing through town all the time looking for outlets to promote their products. Interviews with Hollywood stars and movie-makers would enhance the show's format.

And the Bay Area was well-known as a home to many science-fiction and fantasy writers. Then there were all the special events – the "Star Trek" shows, the comic-book conventions. Plenty of thematic fodder that Bob could tap into. And besides, Channel 2 had a lot of the old Universal classics in its library. More than enough stuff to keep him busy for a couple of seasons. (Well, for 13 weeks at least. That was the out-clause, the maximum the station would have to keep him if the shtick and the ratings failed.)

So, in the early days of 1971, "Creature Features" premiered with "The Horror of Party Beach"–and instantly found popularity in viewership. And that meant incredible success in the ratings, a fact unheard of for an independent station during prime-time hours.

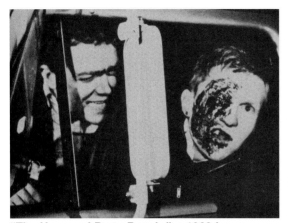

"The Horror of Party Beach," a 1963 horror non-epic about radioactive monsters attacking teenagers during a rock-n-roll party on the surf's edge, set into motion a party that would last 14 years – and be full of horrible moments like this.

Overnight, Bob Wilkins became one of the most talked about celebrities in the Bay Area. The very fact he was unlike any other broadcaster put him into a category all his own. ("A fish out of water," he once said, "can do a lot of jumping around.")

It was nervewracking, given his lack of experience in a major TV market, and he began displaying House of Windsor cigars – not because they were part of his lifestyle but because he was fidgety and nervous and needed something to hold on to and keep the jitters at bay. He also sat in an old yellow rocking chair–another anomalous prop he had chosen so he could disguise some of his nervousness behind the back-and-forth movement. It was one incongruity heaped on another. With a cigar in hand he would lean back into the rocker, offering what was the closest thing to arrogance and contempt for his surroundings and his lousy movies. A set that resembled a room you might expect to find in an old haunted mansion was adorned by the *"Watch Horror Films–Keep America Strong"* sign and a table on which the fans saw a skull and a burning candle. These things were to become weekly trademarks. He always kept it simple but effective. Incongruity was everywhere. And Bob's inner comedic spirit thrived on it all.

And that's where I came in–again. Wilkins and I met for the first time at a posh San Francisco restaurant (name forgotten) to do an interview and it was like old friends reuniting, even though we had never met face to face. After my story ran in the Chronicle just before "Creature Features" debuted, Bob walked into the station on Monday morning and was heralded as a new station star because of the journalistic recognition. How had an unknown commodity, sight unseen to Bay Area television, been given such spectacular coverage–in the pages of the city's leading entertainment section yet? "I just smiled that all-knowing smile I loved to flash in those days and told them true talent always rises to the top. They went away muttering to themselves. Even Tom Breen was flabbergasted when he'd opened the Sunday paper. If anything had helped me get established, it was that exposure in the Sunday Pinkie."

And here is that exposure, dated Jan. 24, 1971:

# THE FIRST BOB WILKINS INTERVIEW EVER . . .

While it may come as a jolting revelation to some, two schools of thought have spawned over what constitutes a suitable host for a series that specializes in reviving horrible old horror movies:

One well-entrenched school believes the host should mirror the nonsocial types in the films. He should be shrouded in capes, possibly even wear fangs or pointed ears for the close-ups, bay at the moon should it happen to be full, drink from a bubbling test tube for refreshment, and be as menacing as possible. Another less-entrenched school believes that subtlety is the keynote, that the host should wear ordinary business suits and smoke something as mundane as a cigar. He should project not ghastliness but intelligence and erudition. And while he should never snub his fans he should certainly gaze down his nose onto the product being served up on a blood-covered platter. He should, in short, be patterned after Bob Wilkins.

Wilkins is the new host of "Creature Features," a series of horrible old horror films which KTVU-TV instituted recently as an answer to other channels parading out those costumed nonsocial types of hosts.

Already some have branded Wilkins an imitator lurking in unfamiliar Transylvanian territory – a transgressor unworthy of serious attention. However, Wilkins did this kind of show for three years at KCRA-TV in Sacramento, establishing many trends and techniques unique to television. Unlike those other costumed horror hosts, Wilkins breaks the illusion of the Black Castle setting by interviewing "interesting, provocative and well-seasoned" guests and by periodically showing amateur short subjects. Unlike the Continental Ghoul or the Caped Monstrosity who constantly reaffirm their product, Wilkins goes out of his way to transcend everything his product should stand for.

But if the truth must be known, many of Wilkins' fans will certainly be mildly disappointed (if not downright shocked) to learn he is not a great admirer of horror films. As he puts it, chomping ever harder on one of his cigars: "I wouldn't walk across the street to see one of those [censored] [censored] films." Which reveals to us that in addition to being an intellectual, Wilkins is a mercenary.

To Wilkins, the Creature From the Black Lagoon is strictly an ecology problem.

Dracula is "one of those thirsty foreigners" and, he elaborates languidly, the Frankenstein Monster is one of the less fortunate who should be sent back to the laboratory for one more transplant.

"But," adds Wilkins in the next breath, taking a new drag on his cigar with gentility, "I have great

> "Good evening, fans. So sorry you tuned in tonight. My movie is pretty lousy . . . "

# ... AND THE KID CAME OUT OF SACRAMENTO TO DO IT

respect for the fans of horror films. They're my kind of people. They'll watch anything I show them, and love it. And in my business that's a sheer necessity, considering some of the films I'm forced to put on the air."

(Sample titles of upcoming shows: "The Navy vs. the Night Monsters," "Curse of the Werewolf," "Jesse James Meets Frankenstein's Daughter" and "The Evil of Frankenstein.")

Wilkins has learned that the horror fan, while usually capable of telling a good film from a bad one, still needs to be frightened if he/she is to be satisfied; quality has nothing to do with his criteria. "When that monster is finally zapped, and falls on its ugly face, the average horror fan feels a great, overwhelming sense of disappointment."

Hosting horror films is really an avocation for Wilkins, who is a Sacramento advertising agency writer.

"I've always loved to put people on in my approach to advertising," says Bob, "and I guess in my new profession that's exactly what I'm doing. God forbid anybody should ever take me seriously."

Wilkins admits that secretly he has always had the ambition to make people laugh, and his ultimate goal is to write comedy material for professionals.

He considers his own delivery and timing to be inferior– an attitude his legions of fans would no doubt take exception to. (And despite whatever he may tell you, there are legions of fans.)

On camera, Wilkins strives for a slow, meticulous effect a la George Burns, pausing between sentences to flick the ashes from his cigar so his sardonic wit can settle in. He is refreshingly honest about his films to the point some have branded him the Howard Cosell of horror movies. "Tonight's film stars absolutely nobody . . . tonight's most exciting moment comes during the third commercial . . . tonight there's an excellent film playing on Channel 13; you should try it."

Wilkins, who quit his KCRA gig about a year ago, conveys a likeable, gentle quality, and he has a boyishness that plays well.

The one and only negative thing about Wilkins is that he used to promise to give away a thousand dollars at the end of each show but when the shows ended, he was never there to give the money away.

Some guys will do anything for a better Nielsen.

In addition to the new KTVU "Creature Features," Wilkins is hosting a Saturday night series for Channel 40 in the Sacramento Valley, which means that in some areas (Contra Costa and Alameda counties) serviced by cable TV, you could spend a total of four hours on Saturday night watching horrible old horror movies hosted by Bob Wilkins.

Four hours?

As the good Dr. Frankenstein might have put it:

"It goes beyond the ken of mortal men."

*–John Stanley*

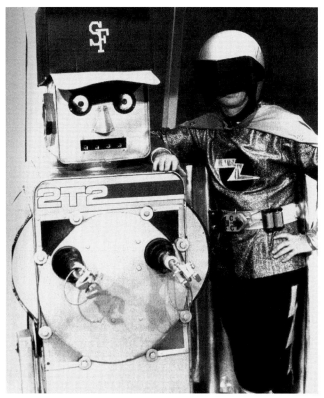

And so it would go for Bob Wilkins for the next eight years. Complete success symbolized by high ratings at Channel 2, first in prime time on Saturday night, then in an 11 p.m. follow-up time slot. Two doses of Wilkins. His popularity seemed bottomless. And eventually came an additional Friday night 11 p.m. gig. Add to that a job as weatherman for several years (always in the back of his mind a fear that the monster gig would come to an end, struck by thunder and lightning) and his continuing ownership of his own advertising agency – now moved to Oakland's Montclair District, where he and his wife Sally made their new home with son Robbie and daughter Nancy.

Another wrinkle but a happy one came along in 1977 when he finally was convinced to don a costume – to portray Captain Cosmic, the host of a late afternoon KTVU show designed for kiddies with its reruns of old "Flash Gordon" serial episodes. Along with his "wonder robot" companion 2-T-2, the familiar Wilkins' countenance was hidden behind the dark visor of a crash helmet and a costume one critic described as "longjohns from a Minneapolis rummage sale."

Despite having avoided wearing costumes for all those years on "Creature Features," Wilkins was to find yet another audience that came to idolize him. Captain Cosmic was introduced in a montage of scenes that included Bob in his superhero costume running alongside a BART train and in aerial flight ripping his superduds on the antenna atop the Transamerica Pyramid tower. With these comedic "special effects" sequences, this new role would appeal mainly to children. And because of that, the ratings were tops.

Whether Bob really enjoyed this part of his career or not, and I suspect it might have been a case of "grim and bear it," the "Captain Cosmic" series only added to the nostalgic adulation that would be his in later years.

It appeared Bob Wilkins and "Creature Features" (with Captain Cosmic lurking around the perimeter) and KTVU would be forever – until one evening in November 1978 when my phone at the San Francisco Chronicle rang. After I picked it up, life was never going to be quite the same again – for Bob Wilkins *and* me.

# The Trials and Travails, and Just a Few of the Terrors, of Auditioning to be a Horror Host

## or

# How You Planning to Fill Bob Wilkins' Boots?

Do we not live in a science fiction world?

When we look back on our lives, and we can clearly see the twisted and convoluted trails we took, for better or worse, there are those individually historic moments that seem to be completely contrived by forces beyond our control. We went left at the fork in the road instead of right, but why? Is it not as whimsical to contemplate as the Gods on Mt. Olympus, for example? Remember the ones depicted in "Clash of the Titans" and in "Jason and the Argonauts" which both featured the stop-motion special effects of Ray Harryhausen? Whimsical beings with powers who arbitrarily controlled the events of mortal men below. All for a laugh. Each

Like Triton saving Jason's ship Argo by holding earthquake-quivering cliffs in place, as depicted in Ray Harryhausen's "Jason and the Argonauts," are not our lives controlled by the whims of the Gods?

day, as we take a few more steps closer to the cemetery where finally we will be laid to rest, are we controlled by things we cannot see in a manner not unlike the Gods in Harryhausen's fantasy?

Or am I just being too fanciful? Perhaps not, for what once seemed inconsequential or capricious now seems consequential and uncapricious. In the context of what we now know, fortuitous outcomes and monumental events almost seem preordained . . . or somehow shaped by an unseen power wanting to bring sense to otherwise universal chaos. These "forces" can bring about great, wonderful things – or disasters that destroy us. Think of them as touches of irony, or "patterns of destiny," which can be as whimsical as those white-robed Gods we see depicted atop cinematic clouds.

For example, doesn't it seem completely unlikely that a fellow who only writes for a living should suddenly one morning, with no particular training or preparation, step in front of a TV camera and become a horror host?

In retrospect, that seems not only unlikely but downright impossible. (Dare one call it perverse?) Like something you would find only in a fantasy yarn spun by Ray Bradbury or Robert Bloch. No four years of study at the Institute of Advanced Technology for Zacherley Lookalikes. No diploma with a Shock Theater major. No Vampira how-to-look-sexy-and-slinky minor. No Son of Svengoolie cape-waving Bachelor of Arts Parchment or Count Scary fang-protrusion Master's Degree.

My first-ever appearance on Wilkins' show, introducing a fantasy 16 mm film I wish I had never made. But it was a beginning . . . of sorts . . . and proved there was a human side to Bob. On the other hand, is the pretty girl below (whose identity and phone number have been lost to the ravages of time) handing the film can back to me because it's so terrible? It happened the spring of 1971.

Here's another weird aspect to my story: One of the reasons, if not the most important one, that I got to that moment in my life is because I just happened to have made a friend of a guy who was a horror host for many years. Out of that rather tenuous union came a friendship–and a new professional path-way. Frightening, isn't it?

It had started that night when I was switching channels and accidentally discovered "Seven Arts Theater." That had led to letters to, and phone calls from, Wilkins. Then the Chronicle interview. Then I made this not-great 16 mm film, "Homecoming: A Fable," and Bob agreed to play it one Saturday night in April and let me appear on air (presumably so I could take the blame for the celluloid fiasco.)

The whole 15 minutes splayed out onto videowaves of the Bay Area. "Homecoming" was a beginner's cinematic blunder, a failed attempt to tell a parable about a commonplace man (Gene Blodgett, a high school friend not to blame, he did his best) who comes home to find his wife and child missing. As he examines his home, he ultimately finds their shadows etched on a basement wall, as if those images had been burned onto the wall's surface by a terrible apocalyptic blast. End of story, no further explanation. An alien abduction story? Who the devil knew. It was a cinema experience that taught me all about life, liberty and the (haphazard?) pursuit of art.

Two years later I was back as a frequent guest on "Creature Features" to promote a movie I was making, only this time in 35 mm Techniscope with a large cast that included Kerwin Mathews, the swashbuckling star of "The Seventh Voyage of Sinbad," "The Three Worlds of Gulliver" and "Jack the Giant Killer." He had a small but good cameo.

"Nightmare in Blood" (an object lesson in how and how not to make a feature movie and now available on an Image Entertainment DVD) would have two major sequences shot on

Kerwin Mathews as Prince Zaroff, a cameo role in the 1978 horror film, "Nightmare in Blood," directed by . . . me.

# IT WAS A TOUGH ROW BUT SHE PUBLICIZED CREATURE FEATURES LIKE NO OTHER PR LADY WHO EVER LIVED

She swam with the sharks of the public relations world and daily fought off barracuda and other slimy entities – yet Judith Morgan Jennings gallantly served "Creature Features" for eight glorious years, publicizing and promoting the series on such a successful scale that other PR guys and dolls were crazily jealous. Eventually Judith and husband Dean Jennings moved to Baja CA where she continued to serve Cox Broadcasting out of San Diego. Still fighting off the sharks with a whammy from her lovely eyelashes . . . until she retired in 2006 to live South of the Border with hubby Dean.

Wilkins' Channel 2 set, and Bob would even have a cameo in the film, smoking a cigar as he stood with a crowd of angry mothers protesting the coming of a horror-movie convention. (He also plays himself in the 1975 horror film "The Milpitas Monster.")

And then I returned to be a guest on "Creature Features" when I co-wrote with Malcolm Whyte a modest novelty book, "The Monster Movie Game," published by Troubador Press in 1974. Bob had put together a panel of media characters from San Francisco to play a monster-question game with Bob as moderator. Our acquaintanceship built again when my novel "World War III" came out from Dell in 1976–a fantasy war adventure that was a natural for a little shoptalk on Bob's show. And because of these eclectic events, we remained in harmonious touch.

And that brings us to Judith Morgan Jennings, a personable, charming woman who had become the publicist for KTVU-TV in 1977 and with whom I had worked on several stories for the Chronicle. Judith will always be remembered by her peers as the plucky young thing in the hats and long dresses who each weekday morning rowed her small dinghy from her Alameda houseboat across the Oakland Estuary to the shore front of Channel 2. Coming across she would dodge freighters, pleasure boats and other nautical handicaps, tie up to the dock and step into a fast-paced

I'm seated left of Bob Wilkins as he hosted a panel quiz with questions from my book "Monster Movie Game," published by Troubador in 1974. Right of Bob: George Tashman, Dan Faris, Al Gutthertz.

## A MARINE CORPS HERO WHOSE MANEUVERS HELPED TO WIPE OUT POCKETS OF ENEMY RESISTANCE AT KTVU

Ray Jacobs had served in World War II on the Pacific island of Iwo Jima, and was one of the first to reach the top of Mt. Suribachi as the unit's radioman. He helped to place a small U.S. flag atop the volcano–to be replaced soon by a larger flag, the one that became famous in Joe Rosenthal's award-winning photo. Ray was wounded a few days later and got off the island alive, but would have to face new dangers at KTVU as he cleared the figurative mine fields and obstructions so Bob Wilkins would have the creative atmosphere he needed to thrive. For the series' 14 year-history Ray Jacobs was always there to make sure nobody interferred with the show or its hosts. He has since retired and now lives on the edge of Lake Tahoe.

He Raised the U.S. Flag on Iwo Jima 23 Feb 1945

world of TV promotion and publicity. Judith and I had struck a professional chord – a writer needs creative contacts to get good stories and a publicist needs media contacts for exposing new products. In this case Judith had brought me many outstanding interview opportunities with stars associated with Operation Prime Time, a movement started by several independent TV stations across America to produce original two-hour movies that could compete with the major networks. Every few months the star of an Operation Prime Time project would drop into town and I would be there to check him/her out.

So now we get to that phone call in November 1978. It was Judith with a flash news exclusive to me: Bob Wilkins had just announced he was quitting the show and moving on to other pastures. Eight years of hosting at KTVU was enough. I immediately called Bob Wilkins at home, who confirmed that it was true. We were chatting away when abruptly Bob asked me, "Are you interested in the job?"

It was a question that almost knocked me out of my swivel seat. I hadn't consciously been thinking of any such madness. Me, a TV horror host? Impossible. To paraphrase mystery writer Dashiell Hammett, the stuff that dreams and only dreams are made of. I was a newspaper writer, and only that. Bleached white by a lack of sun, having spent years behind a typewriter (first a manual, then an electric, now a computer).

I used to break out into a sweat during speech class, and always dreaded the moment I had to stand up in front of a group and hold it enraptured. If all of these thoughts were pouring wildly through my mind, I somehow kept my end of the conversation going. The next thing I knew, Bob was telling me that he'd speak to the powers at the station, and that I was to call a certain Mr. Ray Jacobs. Gods on Mt. Olympus would take it from there.

Please believe me: I had not gone around muttering under my breath and trying to find a way to wrest the position away from Bob with some nefarious scheme or dastardly plot. I had always respected his popularity but had never coveted it. I had extolled his virtues in writing but I had never undergone an attack from the green-eyed monster. I was too

**Was Bob Wilkins really leaving the show? It was a question that dismayed and puzzled almost all of his fans. It was a nightmare come true for the Bay Area TV world.**

realistic a guy to daydream about having things I didn't feel I was capable of having, or deserved to have.

I had no idea how to prepare to be a TV horror host so I decided chutzpah was called for when I went to a luncheon with two KTVU executives: Ray Jacobs, who would be my immediate supervisor should I get the job, and program director Tom Breen, Wilkins' idol and the mastermind behind "Creature Features." As nervous as I was, I talked my way through the lunch as if I knew it all, pointing out all my achievements in journalism and fiction writing, never bothering to mention I knew nothing about TV hosting. But I achieved what I needed from that eating event. When it ended, Breen told me that he would like me to do an audition and to arrange it through Ray. I let out a sigh of relief (at least Breen hadn't told me to go jump in the Bay just down the street from the TV station) – and then panicked! I was overwhelmed by a wave of pure terror! How the hell was I ever going to do an audition and still beat out all the professional media names Judith had warned me would also be auditioning for the much-coveted job?).

Bob, sensing my uncertainty, congratulated me on getting the audition and suggested I hang around the station on the day he cut his next episode. "Try to pick up on how I do the show. Watch for the technical stuff. A lot of it is just getting familiar with what happens before the red light comes on. I'll introduce you to some of the players. And don't worry, once that red light is on, you'll know what to do. It always works for me."

True to his word, Bob led me around the station the next Friday morning, introducing me to the technicians in the control room, the camera men and other "floor people" who were visible while Bob cut his segments. Despite all the good stuff that day, I was almost stopped cold when I came out of the control room and a sound man stepped up and asked as bluntly as he could with a deep macho-tone in his voice: "What makes you think you can fill Bob Wilkins' shoes?"

"I can't replace Bob Wilkins," I said as humbly as I could. "I can only go out there and do the best I can being *me*. Nobody can be Bob Wilkins but Bob Wilkins." Yeah, it was an honest answer but he'd still stopped me cold by reminding me of what I was facing: I was an unknown coming out of nowhere, with no experience. How dare I think I could replace a station star. *Prove you're worth a damn, kid. Prove it.* That was what was on everyone's mind. I thanked Bob and scurried out of the station as fast as I could, feeling like an alien that had just been fatally trapped in the sights of Buck Rogers' raygun. There was no way, I told myself on the way home, I can make this happen.

Not when everyone is probably hoping I fall figuratively to my death.

The next two weeks, in preparing for the audition, were tense. On the next Sunday my Chronicle friend and movie-making collaborator Kenn Davis helped me film scenes in 16 mm for a proposed opening to my audition. Kenn photographed me walking down Market Street and entering the entrance to the Loew's Warfield Theater, a number of film cans precariously perched under my arms. Also scenes of me walking in and out of the main entrance to KTVU with the Channel 2 logo in view. In one of the scenes, to develop a running joke, I dropped some of the film cans. It was hastily shot, but I was hoping it would give the audition a professional kind of opening and impress Jacobs and Breen enough they might be more lenient about my in-studio presentation. I was still plenty worried. I got the footage edited and prepared an opening bit, in which I decided to respond to the very question that sound man had asked me:

On the day of reckoning would I burst out of my every day identity to become Super-Creature Features Man . . . like Christopher Reeve in "Superman"? Or was I destined to remain a non-Superduper Man for the rest of my life? Would the phone booth remain empty, with never any need for a place to change?

*How was I going to fill Bob Wilkins' shoes?*

No better way to defuse a situation than to respond to the very thing that might be on everyone's mind. On camera I would pose the question, hold up a pair of boots described as Bob's, and picking up a pitcher fill each one with water. Then I would do an interview with theater operator Alan Michaan, discussing a new movie that was scheduled to open.

Two nights before the audition I went to a premiere screening of "Superman," the one starring Christopher Reeve as the Man of Steel. I was so moved by the heroic score by John Williams that I went home feeling as if I was about to bust out of my Clark Kent suit. Did I have the "super" powers to pass the coming audition? I hyperventilated when I got home and went over every line in my script. I threw the script away and tried to remember it all from memory. I had it down so pat I was muttering lines in my sleep, or so my wife said.

Erica and I came to the station on a Saturday afternoon. Using Bob's standing set, I did the audition, opening with the 16 mm sequence, introducing myself and doing the boots routine, and the interview. I missed a couple of my cues from the floormen along the way. When it was over I swallowed my pride, gathered up my stuff and headed for the door. I turned to Erica and whispered, "Well, I blew that one. There's no way on earth I'll ever get this gig." All I wanted to do was immediately go home.

And immediately get drunk.

I left thinking it was a good thing I worked for the Chronicle.

I still had my day job.

# THE TRUE MEANING OF ... A TALE WELL CALCULATED TO KEEP YOU IN SUSPENSE

Nothing happened for the next two weeks. I crawled out of bed each morning not expecting anything to happen. I have never been one to set myself up on a high pedestal for a downfall, and I had assumed my audition tape had been glanced at and quickly forgotten by Channel 2 management. Judith had forewarned me that many professional Bay Area radio and TV personalities had been trying out for the job. I could visualize them coming through the front door in droves. Guys with years of broadcasting experience and expertise and acumen. What chance could I possibly have to nail down the job? More likely if there was any nailing it was to drive nails into my "coffin."

Christmas Eve, 1978. I had been away for a few days with my parents in Napa Valley. We had celebrated the holidays prematurely because I had been scheduled to work on Christmas Day and that meant being back home in Pacifica the night before. I had no sooner walked into the house when the phone rang.

It was Judith Morgan Jennings, her voice low but urgent, as if she was speaking from some secret place that might be wiretapped. "John, I was at the Channel 2 Christmas party a few nights ago and overheard two executives talking. I wasn't supposed to hear this so please you can't tell anyone I called you. But one of them said you have the job. You're going to be the next 'Creature Features' host."

I was so stunned I thought I had been fired upon by a phaser in the hands of Mr. Spock. I must have muttered a few incoherent retorts, such as "Are you playing with my emotions?" or "You can't be friggin' serious" or "This must be a practical joke, right?" Whatever I said, I concluded with thanks to Judith and hung up to spend the rest of Christmas Eve in a strange place of mixed emotions. On the one hand, I was elated that I had risen above all the contenders to nail down a highly-visible media job. On the other hand, I felt pure fright and uncertainty in myself. Now I really had to face the question: How was I going to fill Bob Wilkins' shoes without getting all ten toes painfully pinched?

I didn't sleep much that night and wandered to work that Christmas Sunday morning in a distracted state. I didn't tell anybody because I knew it wouldn't be official until I heard it from the station. On Monday morning, before I had even left home, the call came from Ray Jacobs. "Come on down to Jack London Square. We want to talk to you." That was it. No promise of a job, just come on down. I did.

Ray told me I had the job. A contract was offered for two years. Tucked away in the fine print was the traditional "13-week clause." It was the station's way of dumping me if I didn't have the stuff to replace Bob Wilkins. That meant I had limited time to prove myself.

And suddenly it hit me like a ton of bricks. I had another problem I hadn't considered: What about the Chronicle? I hadn't said a word to anyone in management about my audition, thinking it would be a waste of their time to discuss it, given the odds working against me. Now, with the KTVU offer at hand, I would have to inform my managing editor, Gordon Pates, a cigar-chomping, no-nonsense guy who had always treated me decently. He could say no, which would bring the whole thing to a wasteful close.

On the other hand, wouldn't it be good for the newspaper – one of its entertainment writers hosting a highly visible weekly TV show? Which way would he view it?

Now I knew the true meaning of the phrase "Cliffhanger Suspense."

# My Psychoid Career in Horror Begins

I T WAS THE WORST of times, it was the hardest of times. Certainly it was never the easiest of times. And certainly it was the most challenging of times. And now, in retrospect, I can see that it was the best of times. The greatest of times. And I will never forget those greatest of times.

This was the issue: Filling Bob Wilkins' "shoes" had not been as easy as pouring a pitcher of water into my old 1957-issue G.I. combat boots.

In January 1979 I began an uphill struggle that I knew was going to challenge my dazed, overwhelmed brain. Not only was I faced with replacing a Bay Area icon and ratings hero, but I knew I had to do it with my own style. I had to dredge up whatever I had that would make me different. I had to be me, not Bob Wilkins, and me had to be as good if not better than Bob Wilkins, and I had few thoughts about being better, given my tendency to underestimate myself and fear the worst.

F irst, I straightened out the Chronicle issue, knowing it was my one real stumbling block. Gordon Pates, chomping on his ubiquitous cigar as if to remind me of the man I was replacing at KTVU, listened to me describe the job offer, nodded and – to my astonishment – wished me well. There was no issue about it that bothered him nor did it bother Scott Newhall, the paper's now-legendary executive editor. There was even the feeling that Newhall and Pates, who had helped in the '50s and '60s to turn the Chronicle into one of the most popular and entertaining newspapers in America, seemed a bit glad. I had come to the paper in 1960 a total fledgling, wanting to be a reporter. Both of them laughed out loud at my neophyte ramblings. The only job open, they had told me, was copy boy, and I had taken that position despite a stern warning that the paper didn't promote copy boys. Expect a dead-end job. Endsville for you, kid. However, in less than a year I had landed a writing job on the Sunday staff, had reviewed a handful of first-run movies, and had worked my way up to become one of the Sunday Datebook's writers and editors. I was free to pursue my new TV job as long as it didn't interfere with Chronicle business.

AT KTVU, in an old one-time nondescript warehouse that had been turned into a nondescript TV station building ("falling down around us" as one employee put it), Bob Wilkins benevolently took me under his wing. We had a very serious talk about my lack of on-camera experience. In a figurative way he called me to attention: I sensed that he was assuming the role of the noncommissioned officer, the field sergeant, whose assignment was to shape a greenhorn, me, into at the least a competent TV host.

I was a raw recruit who needed to be shown the ways of TV "combat," and "top kick" Bob was going to get tough to make sure I didn't bungle and die on the infiltration course. I was walking through a video minefield and I could potentially blow myself up with each step. I decided I had better listen because Bob was the one and only person there guiding me. He was my voice of

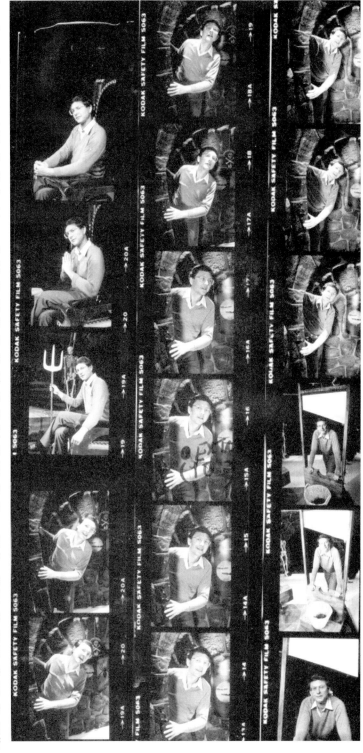

experience. He had his own reputation to consider and I felt certain he didn't want "Creature Features" to fail just because he was leaving, so he shared with me everything he had learned.

Bob even began to talk to me in an officious, no-nonsense way, but it didn't bother me or affect our relationship. I realized what he was doing and I have thanked him more than once in later years for sticking by me. And so my "basic training" continued for the next two weeks, until my NCO "sarge" introduced me one night in January 1979 and I officially took over the show.

I had never prepaped for anything so much in my life. I had memorized, word for word, my opening comments, and had brought in a snake handler and a ten-foot python to emphasize the theme of my film, "Cult of the Cobra" (1955). Except for the moment when the curious snake crawled into my lap and I leaped up in my chair, my face blanching white and the director demanding a retake, the taping went even better than I had hoped for in my panicky state of mind. Bob congratulated me. I didn't hear a word from any of the executives and life went on as if nothing had happened. Me, I was on a high. That same afternoon I took my cameraman Ron Willis to shoot my first interview at an alleged haunted house in Oakland with its owner John Slaughter. I called the report "The Slaughter House" and it turned out to be an exciting, baffling beginning. I knew about the house because I had gone there the previous fall to cover the filming of an episode of "In Search of . . ." hosted by Leonard Nimoy. I had done interviews with a parapsychologist and had a story ready for the Chronicle so that afternoon I had asked for Chronicle photographer Vince Maggiora to join me and take pictures of the house. He called me excitedly that night to tell me he had found strange splotches on the negatives of one of the photos he had taken of the house exterior from the street. We ran the strange, blotchy picture as it turned out but nobody ever came up with an adequate explanation. (See the story on Pages 178-182.)

This was exactly the stern look that Wilkins gave me as he prepped me in the art of becoming a TV horror host. You should be so lucky.

> I FELT I HAD A TRUE FAN'S APPRECIATION OF THE WORLDS OF SCIENCE FICTION AND HORROR, CINEMATIC AND LITERARY

There were several reasons why I was able to replace Bob without "Creature Features" losing its audience or dropping in the ratings. For one thing, I felt I had a true fan's appreciation of the worlds of science-fiction and horror, cinematic and literary. Bob had relied on others to provide research background for his segments, namely Bob Shaw, a one-time revival-house film theater manager/owner who had joined KTVU as a film editor (years later Shaw would become KTVU's permanent in-house Emmy-winning film reviewer for the 10 O'Clock news staff and today spends much of his time attending junkets in Los Angeles and New York.)

As the new host, I was able to do my own research. I had grown up reading E.C. horror comics, pulp magazines and novels of every kind, and respected the leading writers in the fields. In other words, I could start talking about many of these folks off the top of my head. One of my prize collections was August Derleth's Arkham House books, special editions of macabre fiction that were collectors' items and considered rare gems by critics.

# I CREATED AN OFFSHOOT ABERRATION OF THE REAL JOHN STANLEY, CAUGHT UP IN THE UNSEEN WORLD AROUND US

I had reviewed scores of sci-fi books for the Chronicle's book editor, Bill Hogan. I had hundreds of non-E.C. horror comics as well as countless other kinds of four-color frolics, and would be able to use my collection on camera for interviews and commentary segments. I had a mini-library of movie history books and show-biz biographies that would also help me fill in what I didn't already know. Viewers could sense this when I talked about the films with actors, directors, producers, or about the productions themselves. While Bob had gone off on other non-horror tangents with his barbed wit, I used my sense of humor to poke fun at the world of science-fiction and horror, a world I knew firsthand.

I began to create a character for myself, an offshoot of the real John Stanley. I thought of this host as a curious, open-minded fellow who wanted to learn about "the unseen world" around us. Such "terror topics" as unidentified flying objects, alien abductions, psychic phenomena, cloning and other modern sciences that walk a fine line between what we know and what we don't know, ghostly or spectral sightings, the existence of supernatural creatures such as vampires, werewolves, zombies and other hideous beasts of the night.

This was the thing all actors looked for – motivation. And what is hosting a show but acting? I decided this newly created chap would be as ordinary as Bob Wilkins in appearance. Since I too was characterized by blond hair and a certain youthful look, I dressed in suit and tie on some occasions, collegiate sweaters and slacks on others, trying to keep the image as youthful as I could for what I envisioned to be a youthful audience. Let my guests be the ones in the costumes, if they chose it. Once shaped, I found I was able comfortably to take this special character through any phase of "Creature Features." There was another special experience I brought to "Creature Features": the art of interviewing show biz folks. For two decades I had been profiling major Hollywood movie and TV stars for the Sunday Chronicle.

Top stars such as James Stewart, Fred MacMurray, Barbara Stanwyck, Mae West – and many others I had grown up watching on the Silver Screen. And I was as fascinated with other kinds of talent during my Hollywood odysseys – from directors like Stanley Kramer to producers to composers to writers to cinematographers.

I had met these professionals on movie locations all over the country, on Hollywood

Bob Shaw started out at Channel 2 helping Bob Wilkins each week with research and preparation. Knowledgable about genre movies beyond the norm, Bob eventually became the station's movie critic and today is considered one of the Bay Area's leading experts on movies and their histories.

# RUBBING ELBOWS WITH CELEBRITIES FROM ALL WALKS OF LIFE – NOT JUST THE SWEET, LOVEABLE HORROR FOLKS

They came from all parts of the entertainment universe – mainly to have a little fun selling their products. In the case of Misty Rowe (left) I went to Nashville to the set of "Hee Haw" for the fun. It was quite an event there in the haystacks, cutting promotional tapes to use back at KTVU. Kenny Rogers (middle left) had some fun in Las Vegas by dealing me four kings, not telling me he had dealt himself five aces. But five of a kind always beats four of a kind. Doesn't it? Mamie Van Doren (lower left) loved talking about being a "sex kitten" and still had plenty of purr-able qualities to make the idea zing. Frank Gorshin (top right) did great impressions of Kirk Douglas and Burt Lancaster, not to mention John Stanley. He loved performing in San Francisco at the Fairmont Hotel's Venetian Room. Ricky Schroder (second right) was all of ten years old when he made "Last Flight of Noah's Ark" – and made a lasting impression on my nine-year-old daughter Trista. As for Angelique Pettyjohn, of "Star Trek" fame, she fittingly wore her costume from the episode "The Gamesters of Triskelion" (see third right). Tragically she died of cancer shortly before her 49th birthday. Al "Jazzbeau" Collins was always a delightfully loveable disc jockey and music expert who loved being on "Creature Features." The fella at bottom right with the "hands" on his shoulders is Barry Newman, who was there to promote "Amy."

Carroll Baker (top left) came to San Francisco to be honored on a theater stage, only to discover I was her interviewer. Still, she said it was a memorable evening. Karl Malden (second left) came for a show dedicated just to him in honor of "The Streets of San Francisco" starting in reruns. Professor Toru Tanaka (middle left) squared off against me in 1984 while promoting his new comedy "Chattanooga Choo Choo." Such a charmer! Then Rodney Dangerfield (fourth left) in 1983 was enjoying his first starring role in "Easy Money" and was one self-admitted neurotic mess of a guy–but he was the funniest ever. And you couldn't help but love him. Bottom left is Harry Dean Stanton who said he hated "Alien." He didn't seem to get it. Buddy Ebsen (top right) was nothing but fun and engaged in the "Stan Scan," a report that my brain wasn't functioning very well. He agreed. Ken Murray (second right) was a colorful showman I had enjoyed on TV in the '50s and it was an honor finally to meet him. Polly Holliday (TV's Flo) was appearing in "Gremlins." Terry Carr is the guy surrounded by me and all those countless sci-fi paperbacks he had anthologized. Bottom right is Cloris Leachman, who re-did her Frau Blucher from Mel Brooks' "Young Frankenstein." What folks!

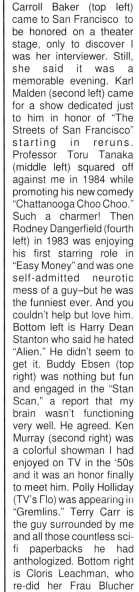

soundstages, in posh and not-so-posh restaurants. Over the years I had learned that you first gain the interviewees' confidence by knowing a few esoteric things about them. Surprise an actor by knowing about an obscure film long forgotten, and suddenly that actor comes to life thinking you've done you're homework and this is going to be a decent experience. Later you can hit them with the harder, juicier questions once they have built a trust in you. Rarely did this technique *not* work. So when the professionals came to "Creature Features" to sell their wares I was ready for them.

Among those who would pass through the Channel 2 studios were not always obvious

This is how things looked the night a roving band of harem belly dancers dropped by the set. At far left the station's chaperon kept a close eye on things–if you know what I mean.

icons. Carroll Baker came to talk about being a sex goddess in the movies, for she had never been a sci-fi goddess. The only person who ever complained about my occasional emphasis on the subject of sex was Harlan Ellison, who once questioned whether or not I was "chauvinistic." No doubt in my mind, but I felt it was appropriate for the commercialism of the show. The station never complained about my choices–any and all celebrities (sexy or otherwise) tended to make the show look that much better. (I wonder if Ellison was watching the night a harem of belly dancers dropped in; or the night a harem lady spent most of the evening fanning me with a huge "leaf.")

Memorable moments: Joseph Bottoms, while talking about Disney's "The

Black Hole," was almost like a child, he was having so much fun on my set. Roger Corman was his articulate self and knew he was squarely in his element with his audience. Nobody was better at intellectualizing crappy movies than him. Buster Crabbe, as much as I loved him, talked too long about any one subject so I wasn't able to cover as much of his career as I wanted. But you couldn't help but love the man.

Dr. Demento took a walk with me down a hallway of the Fairmont Hotel, then we did more interview out on the street with the Doc throwing novelty records

Buster Crabbe, Flash Gordon himself, and I appeared at a special fantasy show in San Jose.

into the air like a juggler. Whoopi Goldberg appeared on the show a year or so before she became a movie star so I was a little too early for her to impact my audience. However, she had been an enthusiastic fan for years living in the East Bay. Frank Gorshin was a gas, doing an impression of John Stanley, and epitomized the witty guests I loved to find. Charlton Heston was an utter gentleman and was willing to talk about all his sci-fi movies, pointing out why some weren't so good. I appreciated his honesty.

Another utter gentleman was DeForest Kelley, who spoke more elegantly about what "Star Trek" meant to a young generation than some of his co-stars. He loved that show like no other. Local sci-fi writers Fritz Leiber and Richard Lupoff appeared often because they were so colorful and articulate and personable.

A childhood TV idol, Ken Murray, who specialized in "home movies" of Hollywood stars, was a highpoint even though he had nothing to do with my genres. A fast-talking, cigar-flicking comedian, he fell into the Frank Gorshin category of showmanship. Anthony Perkins proved to be as weird as Norman Bates, egocentric, eccentric and downright moody (see Page 158 for proof). He would make some innuendo that suggested he didn't like you, then would go on to the next thought as if nothing had happened. No wonder Hitchcock had cast him–he had found the living equivalent of an actor who could totally

Figures of Darkness: Jimmy Doohan, Scotty on "Star Trek" (left), never seemed happy with the way things turned out for the TV cast; Anthony Perkins of "Psycho" fame was a brooding soul who wouldn't hesitate to offend. Success doesn't always open up the heart to total happiness.

capture the essence of Bloch's fictional mass murderer. Harry Dean Stanton was a disappointment. He hated his movie "Alien" and said so, knocking the very thing he will probably be best remembered for. Some people never get it. It got a little quirky with Patrick Wayne who was still upset eight months after the death of his father John Wayne. He asked that I replace the coffin on which my guests usually sat with a regular chair. It was too macabre for him. We complied, and nothing more was said. The interview went well.

Max Von Sydow seemed as wise as an owl and totally usurped the role (Ming the Merciless) and movie ("Flash Gordon," 1980 version) he came to sell. One of my favorite guys became George Takei who always called up when passing through town to ask if he could appear. I'd reshuffle my schedule to accommodate him. James Doohan was always brooding and talked as if he had a chip on his shoulder about "Star Trek"–how come Shatner and Nimoy became so popular when he didn't? (Or was I misreading his inner angst?)

Another thing: I had learned something about the techniques of film making from my experience making my own film, "Nightmare in Blood." I could understand some of the hardships and heartbreaks these creative people went through. I could be empathic. I wasn't putting myself on some lofty pedestal, but I was coming down on their side of the experience. I felt I could talk to these people on a level that not even Bob had attained.

Max von Sydow

Movie music has always been a great love of mine and I decided to introduce this into the show, for Bob had never used music. KTVU paid a fee to the music unions and hence I could freely use commercial tracks as I saw fit. From my LP collection at home I could locate thematic pieces I felt were appropriate for different kinds of interviews. (Much of this came from memory since I had been collecting and listening to soundtracks for years.)

I began taping selections from LP soundtracks (CDs were still an experimental dream in the early 1980s) to be played behind my sequences. For interviews I usually played slow, lyrical  selections low-key enough not  to be distractive, but  still providing a proper

Edy Williams . . . she did seem to have some kind of inexplicable appeal to a certain segment of my audience.

theme and level of emotion. Each taped segment ended with a superimposed wording about next week's movie or some special event coming up and I would have a musical track ready, usually something fast-tempoed and exciting (such as "The Asteroid Field" from "The Empire Strikes Back") or something horrific (such as "Alien"). I feel these musical pieces brought an unusual texture to the show and gave me another identifying feature not associated with Bob Wilkins.

I also came up with the idea of preparing special material for promotions whenever a celebrity guest dropped around. I had to cut one promotion each week for the next show, so I would show the material to the guest and ask if he would like to participate. I was never turned down.

Buddy Ebsen, for example, did a promo in which he steps up to me and shoves a pistol into my face, proclaiming I'm under arrest. "Under arrest?" I cry. "What for?" "For posing as a TV host," he replies, ordering me to get up against the wall as he frisks me. "Oh," he adds, "you know the routine. You've been through this before." Then in Buddy Ebsen voiceover: "It's a crime what John Stanley gets away with every Saturday night on 'Creature Features.'"

There was also the show when Hollywood sexpot Edy Williams slipped into a skin-tight minidress and proceeded to squirm around in her chair while suggesting fans should watch John Stanley for what appealed most to her, his intellectual qualities. These made great promotions which I used over and over again in the years to come.

As nice as all of these "me" things sounded, I fully realized they still needed to be enwrapped in the most important element of all: entertainment. I was talking to an estimated 800,000 viewers per show and I needed to keep as many of them awake and mentally active as possible. I wanted to show them my sense of humor (completely different from Bob's) while still wanting to inform them. And all through that other "curious guy" John Stanley.

There was something else Bob had never done. Soon, very soon, it would cause waves from within my viewing audience:

## ... AND THEN SUDDENLY IT CAME OUT OF NOWHERE, THIS THING THEY CALLED ... THE MINIMOVIE

# IT SLITHERED FROM THE DUNGEON AT
# CHANNEL 2 . . . IT WAS UNSTOPPABLE

The first of these things called "Minimovies" was entitled "Meeting at Morningside" and happened when Don Coscelleri came to San Francisco in early 1979 to promote his miniclassic "Phantasm." Because a hearst driving through a graveyard was a memorable visual in the film, I decided to find such a wagon not currently in service and have the driver bring it to a cemetery in Colma, a small community of graveyards outside of San Francisco. Coscarelli and his primary star, Angus Scrimm, a one-time Shakespearean actor

portraying the film's menacing villain known eerily as The Tall Man, met us there, curiously pleased I had brought them to this setting. ("I feel at home here," said Scrimm. "It has all the comforts of home.")

The story line had me mysteriously called to the graveyard where suddenly the hearst pulls up. Scrimm throws me into the back and off we go for a wild ride through

the tombstones of Colma, a thriving haven for the dead.

I conducted the interview in the back of the hearst, with Scrimm and Coscarelli up front, apologizing for the ruse but now ready to talk.

Coscarelli and Scrimm were in a hurry to catch an airliner back to L.A. so I had my cameraman shoot their scenes first, answering my prepared questions. After they were gone, I had the hearst driver take me back through the cemetery while my cameraman Ron Willis (see his picture on Page 198) photographed me in close up asking the questions. My music for this had been an appropriate organ track from Bernard Herrmann's score for "Journey to the Center of the Earth."

Angus Scrimm greeted me at the entrance to a Colma cemetery and introduced me to his "Phantasm" director Don Coscarelli (above left) by throwing me into the back of a hearst waiting nearby. The pair would do sequels–without me.

This unusual interview – for a well-received movie – went over so well that I continued this concept with "The Adventure of the Persian Slipper." As Sherlock Holmes, in Inverness cape and deerstalker's cap, I solved the mystery of an item missing from the Sherlock Holmes Exhibit Room at the San Francisco Holiday Inn. My co-star was Patricia Baetz, a beautiful public relations woman for the hotel, and my music selection was the main theme from Miklos Rozsa's "The Private Life of Sherlock Holmes," which emphasized Holmes' use of the violin – a fitting motif.

The fun continued with a decidedly tongue-in-cheek meeting with Chuck Norris and his brother Aaron at the Kuk Sol Won martial arts training school on Van Ness Avenue in San Francisco. Garbed in a karate workout suit provided by the Koreans, I had Chuck toss me to the mat at the end of the interview when I asked a leading question about the cruelty he showed to the villains in his then-new movie "Good Guys Wear Black." I did part two of this interview, "Revenge of the Channel 2 Dragon," two years later when Chuck and Aaron returned to the Bay Area to make the excellent martial arts actioner "An Eye for an Eye." (My music on that occasion was Miklos Rozsa's "Blood on the Sun" filled with Japanese motifs appropriate to the presence of Mako and Professor Toru Tanaka in the mini-movie as karate-chopping characters.) Fans loved the scene in which I was held at gunpoint by Richard Roundtree (playing a cop) who was suspicious of my presence on the movie location. He admonished me when I "misidentified" him as "Shaft!"

"Patrick's Day" was a promotion for the Australian film "Patrick," in which I did my interview with the film's American distributor at a hospital in Daly City. An ambulance arrives with the film's villain "Patrick" (actually a public relations man named Tony Cuneo)

on a stretcher, covered by a sheet. We photographed it at the emergency entrance behind the hospital. (I borrowed some music from Bernard Herrmann's "The Trouble With Harry," which was appropriately humorous and mysterious.)

"The Mummy Rises" was an attempt by myself and Ronald Fong, the manager of the Wax Museum at Fisherman's Wharf, to resurrect the exhibit's mummy. Substituting my neighbor and good friend Ingrid Cali as a gauze-enwrapped creature of the dead, I try the resurrection using tanna leaves and then the recitation of an ancient Egyptian Scroll of Toth. When it appears I've failed and I'm walking out the door, chastising myself for failure, the mummy suddenly springs to life – but I'm too busy brow-beating myself to notice. (Music: Hans J. Salter's score for "The Mummy's Tomb")

One of my favorites was "The Stanley Cage" shot at the San Francisco Zoo's monkey cages. I enter an empy cage and get locked in when the wind blows the door shut. Just happening by are Carol Kane and Lee Grant (below), stars of a film about experiments with monkeys, "The Mafu Cage." While Carol goes for a key to get me out, I interview Grant about the film. Then Carol returns unable to find a key, so I question her for a while about the film. Finally the two rush off, thinking it more important to talk to the zookeeper than to worry about getting me out. Fade out on me screaming for help. No music. I went to natural sound effects, dubbing in elephant and lion roars.

These pieces continued over the next three years, but Channel 2 would only allow me limited editing time each week and we were still filming in 16mm which was a slow process, so the number of minimovies remained small. I still managed "Return to Casablanca," shot in a Moroccan restaurant called the Casablanca and located next to the Daly City BART station (today it's a parking lot). I had a belly dancer in a sexy costume, a public relations man named Dick Arnold who affected Humphrey Bogart's accent (and knew from memory

all of Bogart's lines from the film), some other good-looking women and a waiter from the restaurant dressed like a Moroccan policeman. I filmed all day and night to capture a production quality I had never quite managed before. It ended up being quite a tribute to Bogart. (Naturally, the music was Max Steiner's score for "Casablanca"). Larry Larson, who helped me do some of my in-house promotions at the station, and who was especially creative at designing inexpensive special effects for the promos, portrayed a slightly different version of the Peter Lorre character who went more than a little beserk. He went on to produce-and-direct a film in Africa, "The Secret Force" (1995).

Certainly one of the best of the minimovies and one of the oddest was "Attack of the Incredible Killer Scarecrow," photographed one Saturday in October 1982 at the Nut Tree in Vacaville, CA, during that now-defunct establishment's annual Scarecrow Contest. An actor named Jamie Tvrdik, in an excellent scarecrow costume and wearing superb facial make-up, portrayed an "evil Scarecrow God of Vengeance" who attacks my lookalike (designed to free me from my legions of fans so I can sightsee at the scarecrow contest) and murders him. So I hire "private investigator" Don Herron (he was conducting the Dashiell Hammett Walking Tours in San Francisco) to determine which of the "lifeless" scarecrows at the contest is the killer fiend from another dimension. Good effects and music (borrowed from Les Baxter's excellently weird 1969 supernatural score for "The Dunwich

Horror") made this very effective, despite a few production problems trying to film around a contest being heavily attended.

A return to the Wax Museum at Fisherman's Wharf gave the world "Nightmare in the Chamber of Horrors," in which the Jack the Ripper exhibit comes to life and pursues a scantily clad young woman (chosen for her busty endowments) down the museum's corridors. I encountered a problem with the San Francisco actor (I won't mention his name here) who had volunteered his services to play the Ripper and had serviced the part with an excellent Cockney accent.)

He had helped himself to a few "feelies" during the shooting, which the brave young thing hadn't bothered to tell me about – until we met a few weeks later in the station's control room to dub voices for the soundtrack.

"Jack" helped himself to another "feelie" during the dubbing session but this time the buxom young thing let loose with an angry reaction, and I had to step in and quiet things down, apologizing for the chap's abysmal behavior and promising my starlet I would never use that awful man again in a minimovie.

Another disaster occurred in the summer of 1980 when I took my old writing and film making partner Kenn Davis as cameraman to the Great America amusement park in Santa Clara to ride a new roller coaster called "The Demon."

My resulting minimovie, "The Demon Strikes Back," brought me to the very brink of utter disaster with KTVU.

Because when my roller coaster-car  was passing beneath an archway, the camera Kenn had mounted on the front was clipped and the magazine completely destroyed.

I was actually able to put together a professional cast for "All Heart," which I filmed in a San Francisco medical center's chief operating room one Saturday morning when the real doctors weren't in a cutting-up mode. This was designed as a promotion for a 1980 minor-league San Francisco-produced movie, "Cardiac Arrest," directed by Murray Mintz, about the extraction of body organs for sale on the retail black market.

Garry Goodrow, a member of San Francisco's famous improvisational group The Committe, had starred in the film and he agreed to play a crazed doctor in our operating room tomfoolery with the help of an equally crazed nurse played by the wonderful Nancy Fish, also an alumnus of The Committee.

**A PHOTO TO REMEMBER**
I'm between Allen Case (left) and Christopher Jones on the set of "The Legend of Jesse James" at 20th Century-Fox in 1965. But for 20 minutes Jones had tried to avoid me, he was so uncertain of himself. It was his first interview with the press and he was hating it. I came out of it with a pretty good interview.

These two improvised some zany dialogue as they prepare to operate on me to remove my vital organs for resale purpose. Their lines made this one priceless, even though "Cardiac Arrest" was not a big hit and quickly vanished. Producer Richard Salzberg steps out just before Goodrow and Fish cut into me to explain it was a set up just to make me aware of his new film. The patient lived but, I think, the minimovie died.

We used pig organs to simulate the body parts. I'm happy to report that "All Heart" did not destroy Goodrow's career for he went on to star in "Amazon Women on the Moon" and "Circuitry Man." And Nancy escaped absolute chaotic career disaster and destruction too by living to have  a role  in 1991 in "Terminator 2: Judgment Day"

as a "Roadside Woman" and also "Exorcist III: The Legion" as "Nurse Allerton." Typecasting, I guess.

There was a memorable night in 1979 when I introduced "Private Eye Night," as I am a devoted fan of mystery novels and films. Gorgeous blonde Gloria Masters portrayed the femme fatale and I played around with the tough-guy image on a special set. It was my way of introducing "Little Shop of Murders," in which I paid a visit to the San Francisco Mystery Book Shop on the corner of Diamond and 24th Street. There, a couple of "dames" came out as I was going in. Inside I met tough-guy owner Bruce Taylor, who had first opened the store in 1974, and a Sherlock Holmes-garbed character played by Dean Jennings, husband of aforementioned PR gal Judith Morgan Jennings. My son Russ, all of 13, was garbed in trenchcoat and soft hat and played a "stakeout" guy, "Louie the Kid."

In mid-1981 the station threw away all the long-standing 16 mm editing equipment and cameras and transferred over to the new video tape format. This facilitated faster editing and I began to do some of my standard sit-down interviews with tape, which could then be quickly prepared back in the editing room. We all became proficient at blending edited interview footage with studio inserts (close ups of stills, book covers, general memorabila) and background music chosen from my ever-growing LP library.

Over the years there were moments when things didn't always go so right.

One of the biggest potential disasters I ever had to face was with Leonard Nimoy. It began in the spring of 1980 when Nimoy was starring in a one-man play "Theo" (about the brother of Dutch painter Vincent Van Gogh) and I convinced his agent that Leonard should come on "Creature Features" to discuss the future of "Star Trek," which had just enjoyed a rebirth a few months earlier with the release of "Star Trek–The Motion Picture."

My big mistake was in announcing on my show that my guest the next weekend would be Nimoy. I thought nothing more about it – until I arrived at the station the next Friday morning to cut the show. A large crowd of uninvited fans had gathered at the front door in hopes of seeing Nimoy in person. There had never been a policy to invite an audience to the show but I figured I'd accommodate the group by putting chairs up in the studio for this small and appreciative gallery of onlookers. While I was fussing around with the floor department to set this up, Nimoy pulled up to the front of the station in a stretch-out limousine. He saw the crowd in the front and, rejecting the idea of going through the front door as planned, ordered the driver to pull around to an unloading/parking area in the back of the building.

My wife Erica, who acted as my producer in those years, rushed up to tell me Nimoy had arrived–and was very upset about the crowd outside. He was refusing to do the show unless I sent the crowd away. Puzzled over a star not wanting to be appreciated by his fans, I found Leonard in the "green room" totally agitated. He told me he had seen a certain woman in the crowd he did not like. She was a hardcore "Star Trek" fan from San Jose who had apparently bugged him on and off over the years. She bought a ticket for every performance of "Theo" and sat in the front row, so that with each performance she was staring up at Nimoy, and this had disconcerted him. "I walk through alleyways in the deserted part of town," Nimoy told me, presumably in a satirical moment, "and she pops up." There was nothing funny when he added: "She's uncanny. I don't want her around."

I went outside and told the group that the station had a policy about not letting groups in to watch shows being taped. There was no way I was going to break the heart of the woman who had offended Nimoy by sending her away with the complete truth. (I did manage to sneak a couple of the guys into the control room where they could watch on monitors, but everyone else dissipated away.)

Once Leonard saw that I had lasered the group, he smiled and calmed down, saying he was more than ready to do the show as planned. And what a show. Two hours of "Star Trek" TV reruns interspersed by interviews with Nimoy, and a segment about Vincent Von Gogh, showing off some of his famous paintings to Miklos Rozsa's music for "Lust for Life," the 1956 biographical drama in which Kirk Douglas played Vincent Von Gogh.

Nimoy even agreed to do some comedy with me for a 30-second promotion tape that I was able to use for months afterward to promote "Creature Features." He became the articulate, gracious man I always knew him to be. But for a brief few minutes, I feared I had lost my star.

When Leonard Nimoy was my guest for a two-hour special, I used a "book" entitled "The Trek of Leonard Nimoy." But no such book really existed. It was a "prop" prepared by the talented KTVU artist Jim Minton. He was one of the great supporters of the show during my years as host.

Another actor I almost lost was British horror star Christopher Lee, who found himself booked for my show in the fall of 1979. Usually I asked my guests to show up an hour or so before taping so I could brief them on what I had planned and handle any make-up problems they had.

On this Friday Lee was late and arrived after I had begun to cut my opening segment. At that time I was still using Bob Wilkins' old set, but had been making announcements for several

weeks that I would soon have a new set–an under-construction "old dark" dungeon with cell, guillotine, severed head in a basket, a skeleton, and other accoutrements to suggest a hellish environment for my weekly excursions into the realm of the weird.

I had asked a local "Star Wars" club to come over that morning to serve as a "construction crew." They were armed with hammers and saws and carried pieces of lumber, milling around me in a pre-choreographed routine. I sat in my chair, ducking 2 x 4s, while introducing the movie and my line-up. For effect, I had a soundtrack of hammering and sawing playing in the background.

When Lee walked into the studio with my wife, he didn't like what he saw. All the slapstick tomfoolery didn't set well with him and he turned to tell Erica that this was not the kind of program he wanted to be associated with – and literally turned to walk out the door.

And leave "Creature Features" behind forever.

At that very moment I had finished introducing a five-minute filmed interview I had done a few weeks earlier with fantasy writer Ray Bradbury (see Pages 142-148). As Lee walked toward the exit door, he stopped when he saw Bradbury appear on the monitor literally positioned above the door. Bradbury was speaking in his usual poetic rhetoric and Lee stood there to watch the full five minutes unfold.

When the lights came on, he turned to Erica and said, *"Well, I guess if it's good enough for Ray Bradbury, it's good enough for Christopher Lee."* And he stayed to do two excellent ten-minute segments on his career as Britain's leading Dracula in a series of Hammer pictures.

Christopher Lee, just minutes after deciding not to walk out on the show, thanks to the fact that he had seen my Ray Bradbury interview on the TV monitor just as he headed for the nearest exit.

So as not to upset me, Erica had kept the story to herself until we were on our way home that afternoon (for that interview with Lee, see Pages 185-186).

Another guest I almost lost was Hollywood sexpot Edy Williams. How does one lose a sexpot? Well, it's like this. She was appearing in an X-rated dancing club and pornie movie house run by the Mitchell Brothers, her film career having tanked. Somehow she ended up on my guest roster. I had gone out on a shapely limb, thinking this could end up being a most unusual interview in which I would be talking with a "creature" of a totally different kind. I decided to write some very colorful and sexy material for a promotion sketch and also prepared a tongue-in-cheek segment for her to do solo.

When the limousine arrived and Edy came into the studio, she was absolutely livid. She told Erica that the limousine driver had made a pass at her while crossing the San Francisco-Oakland Bay Bridge and she really didn't want to appear on the show in light of what had happened. Erica ran and found me. By the time I got into the studio Edy was madder than ever. I calmed her down by showing her the special material I had written for her, and her attitude drastically changed from pissed-off to delighted-to-be-here. Where have you been all my life, you fool you. Oh, John, what a dream boat you are. Mmm.

I was disappointed she was wearing unflattering jeans and a sloppy shirt, but as soon

as she perked up she grabbed a small carrying case and rushed behind a nearby studio screen "to change." She emerged a few minutes later in a skin-tight yellow minidress that showcased all her assets–and then some. We did an unusual sex-related interview (purely an exchange of words) and then I turned my chair over to Edy.

She started playing a promiscuous, no-holds-barred vamp as she read the material I had written for her, twisting seductively in the chair and provocatively sucking on her finger at one point. (This segment was preserved on a special tape and passed around to the male executives and other curiously-minded staff people for the next few weeks and was the talk of KTVU in the spring of 1984.)

There were times when guests didn't show up at all, due to some misunderstanding over dates, and finally there was one time when I did lose a guest who showed up and then walked out on me. He was the star of a stage version of "The Elephant Man." When he arrived on schedule, I explained he would be in the third segment. He objected and wanted to be in the opening of the show, because he was in a hurry to get back to the theater to rehearse. Usually I didn't have a guest in the opening, preferring to talk about the movie and the evening's line-up.

Before I had a chance to re-evaluate things, the actor walked out and I never saw him again. I had a premixed interview on a shelf that I had been holding and that got me off the hook.

By 1984 I knew that "Creature Features" was living on borrowed time. The ratings had begun to dwindle away and management was not happy with the new movie packages that were beginning to feature the slasher flicks of the time. Finally, it was decided to drop the show and I left the air September 1, 1984. One of my guests that night was Bob Wilkins. On camera, I asked him why he had given up the show. "Because," he answered, "I didn't want to be the host of the last show." A wonderful six-year experience had ended. Yet the memory of the show has lived on in assorted incarnations. I have now written six editions of "The Creature Features Movie Guide." Tom Wyrsch has published "The John Stanley Scrapbook" and also prepared

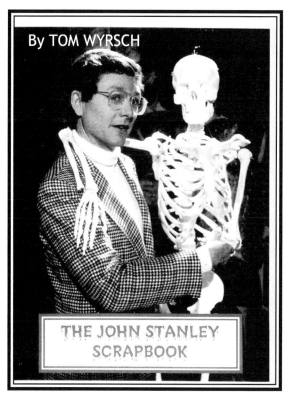

By TOM WYRSCH

THE JOHN STANLEY SCRAPBOOK

On the final "Creature Features" show (Sept. 1984) Bob Wilkins returned to reminisce about his good old days. And one of his fans returned to him the skull that had adorned his set during his eight years on the job. For me it was a nostalgic and more than a-little-sad evening as I was forced to bring down the final curtain.

special CDs and DVDs highlighting the best moments of the series.

So when I am contemplating all of this in my "silver years," I find it so ironic that Bob Wilkins had given up hosting "Creature Features" because of a misunderstanding. George Lucas had asked Bob to be his new marketing guru that fall of 1978. And Bob had accepted the job. But when he learned after the fact that he would have to move to Los Angeles, thereby giving up his advertising business in the Bay Area, he had recanted and turned the job down. By then it was too late to return to "Creature Features."

So Bob had stayed on at Channel 2 for another year as Captain Cosmic, but I could tell that it was not a happy year. Because of that one misunderstanding, my life and Bob Wilkins' had been altered onto new pathways forevermore.

Bob returned to running his advertising businesses in Orinda and Sacramento, and was successful for many years, with Chucky Cheese pizza parlors being one of his largest accounts. "Chewy," he told me.

Then, in the early 1990s, he was offered a job as advertising director by John Ascuaga at the Nugget, a major showtime/casino/restaurant in Sparks, a suburb of Reno, Nevada. He remained there for a few years but when he suffered a heart attack he was advised by his doctor to get out of such a nerve-wracking business. So he retired and with the eventual help of Tom Wyrsch began selling his old TV shows through mail order. He also saw thousands of copies of "The Bob Wilkins Scrapbook" sold by Wyrsch through the Bob Wilkins website. The fans still remembered him and adored him. Until 2006 we made many personal appearances together. I guess the old adage is true: some things never die. They fade . . . well, maybe just slowly. Oh so slowly . . .

# WHY DO YOU GROOVE ON THE STUFF IN THIS BOOK?

## HERE IS THE POSSIBLE ANSWER AS I DESCRIBED IT TO MY VIEWERS ON THE NIGHT OF MY LAST SHOW IN SEPTEMBER 1984

D
o you know who you are? Are you familiar with the strands of DNA that decide you from top to bottom? Do you understand the chemicals that flow through your system to make you what you are? Do you know why you enjoy horror, fantasy and science-fiction things (human and otherwise) that stalk deadly through the dead of night?

Why have you perched expectantly on the edge of your seat subjecting yourself to forms of entertainment and torture that some people would dismiss as utter trash? What is there about monster menageries, space spectacles, werewolf wailings, vampire vignettes, nocturnal narratives, lagoon leviathans, alien abominations, campfire curdlers, E.T. entities and ghostly guests that touch your appeal button?

Are you perhaps an adult seeking escape into your past, or are you perhaps an adolescent seeking escape into your future? Why do you want your worst fears and trepidations challenged by the images that regurgitate through the media of your world? Are you perhaps seeking a stimulation to your wondrous zone? Are you bored with your 9-to-5 life style and want situations and things beyond your own humdrum mundane montonous boring non-stimulating God-awful snore-filled reality?

Perhaps you have a perversity in your soul. Hmmm . . . do you enjoy seeing others suffer or being frightened to death? Or do you simply want a bill of fare you can't find on the menus of other channels? Does the sight of blood thrill you? Does the bloody edge of a butcher knife send a tingle along your curving spine?

Perhaps as we go not so gently into that evil night, it is all of those things so far mentioned. Each reaching out to a segment of you, clutching to you, clinging to you, refusing to release you back to the world of ugly norm until the channels of your soul become like a television signal that turns to pre-dawn video snow.

To be part of Creature Features is to be part of something special. Someone unique. Are we not a caring band that marches to the offbeat of another drummer? If so, if this is the DNA of your soul, then appreciate that uniqueness, cherish it, just as you cherish the mayhem, the mystery, the magic and melancholia that is our world together. Yours and Mine. The world of Creature Features.


I
t is now time to visit a "haunted" place in the heart of Hollywood. That seems appropriate since Hollywood has brought us so many haunted images. It is a place of mystery but it is especially a place of magic. Within this establishment dedicated to illusions you will meet four of the most unusual horror-host characters of all time. Five if you wish to count me in. So please, step out into the unknown with me. You won't regret it . . . I hope.

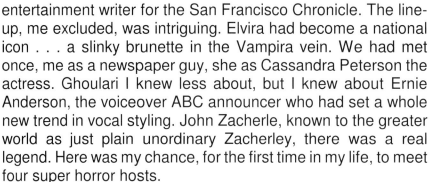

# HOP ALONG, PARDNER, AND BE PART OF A ROUND-UP OF MY FAVORITE HORROR HOSTS

*If you hate what you're seeing, you call it sex and violence. If you like it, you call it "romance and adventure."* – **Joe Bob Briggs**

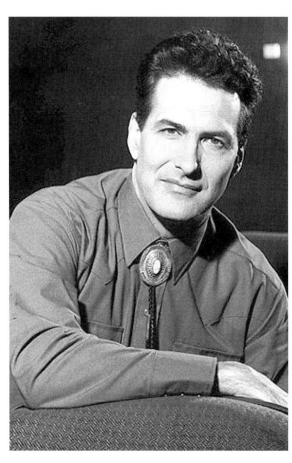

Joe Bob Briggs – no kidding, the one and only – was making me an offer over the telephone. "Come to Hollywood. You'll be one of The Big Four."

Intelligently, I responded: "Huh? One of the . . . Big Four? . . . ?"

Joe Bob went on to explain that he was cutting special material for a series of TV programs featuring four of his favorite horror hosts of all time. *Of all time.*

"I'm a favorite horror host of yours?" I was still trying to catch my breath. Were my ears functioning okay?

"Say, you bet. And you'll be in good company. Elvira, Ghoulardi, Zacherley. Each of you' will tape the opening segment for my TV show. Four hosts, four openings."

I was finally beginning to get the idea. And it was an offer I couldn't refuse. Not because my ego dictated I go, but because of the names Joe Bob had dropped. It was 1991 and I was long retired from the horror hosting business, working as a dedicated, very serious-minded

Come along, Stanley, you good ole boy

entertainment writer for the San Francisco Chronicle. The line-up, me excluded, was intriguing. Elvira had become a national icon . . . a slinky brunette in the Vampira vein. We had met once, me as a newspaper guy, she as Cassandra Peterson the actress. Ghoulari I knew less about, but I knew about Ernie Anderson, the voiceover ABC announcer who had set a whole new trend in vocal styling. John Zacherle, known to the greater world as just plain unordinary Zacherley, there was a real legend. Here was my chance, for the first time in my life, to meet four super horror hosts.

Yeah, I sure wasn't gonna miss this gol-darn major important event in my life history . . . no sirree, Joe Bob . . .

# THE SUMMIT MEETING OF THE GREAT ONES HOSTED BY JOE BOB BRIGGS – IN A MYSTIC MANSION TO MESMERIZE

@The Academy of Magic Arts Inc.

I expected to see the light in the third-floor tower window wink out suddenly, as it always does in those Gothic horror thrillers, and which it did so suddenly in the Xanadu mansion of Orson Welles' Charles Foster Kane in the opening moments of "Citizen Kane." Given the nature of early morning light, and the somber, depressive effect that comes from sluggish dense-gray Los Angeles smog, the Victorian mansion, built in 1908 but looking as if it had been pristinely erected only yesterday, stood like some sinister castle on the moor, generating an oppressiveness with its turrets, minarets, cornices, stained-glass domes and window casings shrouded in deep black shadows.

And yet to break this doom-like spell, all I had to do was turn my head a few degrees left to see the top of Grauman's Chinese Theater (or what was at one time Grauman's – by 1991 it was more mundanely known as Mann's Chinese, but I'm the kind of guy who will forever call it Grauman's and there it will stay cemented in my brain, minus the footprints.) I was standing at the foot of the Hollywood hills, just a couple of blocks back from

@The Academy of Magic Arts Inc.

Hollywood Boulevard, in front of a landmark known as the Magic Castle.

How fitting that such a realistic haunted-house exterior sits in the heart of tourist-laden, fantasy-driven Hollywood.

Its innards, however, are not so much devoted to horror as to illusionary fantasy and trickery. The Magic Castle is the home of the Academy of Magical Arts Inc., which is home for a few thousand magic mavens from all over the world.

Even today it still serves as a showcase for magic, a melting pot for magicians, a bastion for legerdemain and card manipulations, and a museum for the memorabilia of such greats as Houdini and Howard Carter.

Would-be David Copperfields and David Blaines still come from all over the country to perform there. And now today, in the year 1991, it had become a "dead zone" for some legendary TV horror hosts of the past three decades. An appropriate location, since horror hosts are, like magicians, built on illusion. A fictional character garbed in thematic dress and surrounded by the props of the profession.

At the head of the pack, serving as producer for the day's event, was John Bloom, better known to the schlock movie-viewing world at large as Joe Bob Briggs. I had known John for almost a decade. We had first met through the pages of the Chronicle's Sunday Pinkie, where his Dallas Times Herald "Drive-In Movie" column had run daily since early 1982 on a syndicated basis. We'd talked on the phone many times and had found a mutual interest in lesser movies, which was how Joe Bob was now making his living. Keeping abreast of things. If you know what I mean, and I think you do.

He had once expressed his admiration for my work as a horror host, and then he had suddenly but not unexpectedly gone on to become a TV host himself on Showtime's Movie Channel, hosting "Drive-In

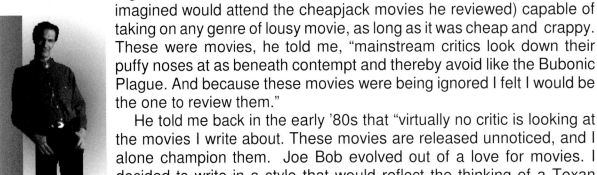

The kind of poster that appeals to Joe Bob Briggs, showcasing movie schlock that he loves to talk and write about, films that have a definite impact on our culture and change how we view the world at large.

Theater." Joe Bob was not a TV horror host in the traditional sense. He had instead affected an original concept.

This was the image of a redneck Texan character (not too unlike the movie-goers he imagined would attend the cheapjack movies he reviewed) capable of taking on any genre of lousy movie, as long as it was cheap and crappy. These were movies, he told me, "mainstream critics look down their puffy noses at as beneath contempt and thereby avoid like the Bubonic Plague. And because these movies were being ignored I felt I would be the one to review them."

He told me back in the early '80s that "virtually no critic is looking at the movies I write about. These movies are released unnoticed, and I alone champion them. Joe Bob evolved out of a love for movies. I decided to write in a style that would reflect the thinking of a Texan who'd go to see 'Night of the Living Dead' and other sleaze classics. I remember that Janet Maslin of the New York Times condemned these movies as too violent–but without ever seeing them. You had to go to drive-in theaters or 42$^{nd}$ Street in Manhattan to find them. In Texas, it was solely the drive-in."

This looks like a hunk posing for Vanity Fair advertisements but in reality it is nothing more than a casual photo of Joe Bob Briggs, aka John Bloom.

And it was at the drive-in that Joe Bob was born.

The cruder (or cruddier) the motion picture, the better the job that Joe Bob could do flaying its miserable, worthless hide. He would throw those suckers to the ground and stomp on 'em until they screamed for mercy. He'd keep a count. How many bare breasts, how many stabbings, how many shootings, how many alien feastings. You not only got this through the show but through the books that periodically have surfaced–compendiums of bountiful Briggisms. We were like brothers, me and Joe Bob. Two pods in a pea, I believe is the term.

The bar at the Magic Castle, where I was to encounter three of the greatest horror hosts of all time. And I'm not talking about looking at myself in one of the mirrors!

Joe Bob and his camera team from Showtime were already gathered in the Palace of Mystery, a large showroom complete with stage and curtain. We met at a bar patterned after a 17$^{th}$ Century London pub. The top of the bar, I was told, was made from pieces of floor taken from the gymnasium at the old Hollywood High School. The three other horror hosts were there: Cassandra Peterson, Ernie Anderson and John Zacherle. Each of us would perform an opening for Joe Bob's TV show on the stage that afternoon so there was plenty of time to get acquainted.

# THE MISTRESS WHO NEVER KEPT ME IN THE DARK: ELVIRA'S HAUNTING MEMORY–WHAT A LAYOUT

@Queen B Productions

Elvira and I hung out for a while in the Corridor of Stars, a hallway lined with handbills and photographs of some of the great magicians. I could immediately tell she had been careful to slither her 5-foot-7 frame into her clingy low-cut black outfit. Having survived a $10-million federal lawsuit in the pages of which Maila Nurmi had accused her of plagiarizing the Vampira character, I couldn't help but admire her for her obvious legal ramifications and intellectual mind-set.

Her blues eyes may have had something to do with it, too. But then I'd admired this mixture of beauty and brains before. We'd met once in 1988 at her home–only then she had been dressed inconspicuously in the persona of Cassandra Peterson, a Hollywood actress who was lesser known to the public at large and who would always be forced to live in the shadows of her altered ego.

Dressed in Elvira's get-up, I wasn't always sure which persona was talking to me. Was it the succulent and succinct Cassandra, or the seductive and subversive Elvira? It didn't matter--I decided to scribble my notes dutifully.

Elvira/Cassandra started talking about how she had felt about her life ten years before the success of her horror hostess. "I'd been hanging around Hollywood already for ten years and had absolutely nothing to show for it. Ten *tough* years, too. The highlight had been an audition for 'B.J. and the Bear,' which I walked out on. I couldn't pay my rent. When my car broke down I had no money to fix it. That's when I decided it was time to give up this futile acting existence and find a real job. September 17th was my 30th birthday – that's the day I would quit. On September 1, something odd happened. Overnight, I became someone new. *Something* new. The *thing* known as Elvira."

In her new incantation, Elvira was this sexually slithering seductress who hung out

@ Queen B Productions

@ Queen B Productions

once a week on "Movie Macabre" on KHJ-TV in Los Angeles. Ms Peterson was totally unrecognizable, having disappeared into a black wig, low-cut high-slit black gown and spike heels. She usually sprawled on a couch flashing her black fingernails and wise-cracked about some awful horror movie that was her fare for the evening. For "Queen of Outer Space" she quipped: "See Zsa Zsa Ga-bore us to death." For "Plan 9 From Outer Space" she flipped: "The producer shoulda stuck to plan 1: make a Western."

Now, in 1991, Cassandra Peterson had

developed into a money-making machine that wouldn't quit camping and vamping. And she hadn't climbed to the top just on her sparkling personality and sex appeal. She had done it with the help of her business agent, record entrepreneur Eric Gardner. Each had a clever head for business, proven by the incredible marketing skills they had shown since Elvira's unexpected birth. She was syndicated to more than 70 markets and her name was borne on 35 VHS boxes in the "Thriller Video" series.

She also has collaborated with her husband Mark Pierson on managing her affairs, and he helped her with her '88 New World feature film "Elvira, Mistress of the Dark" (160,000 VHS units had been sold). A fan club of 35,000 strong was still rallying its support around her, she had T-shirts, greeting cards, a Halloween record album from Rhino, a model of her Macabre Mobile car (a 1958 Ford Thunderbird), posters, key chains, buttons, a calendar, porcelain plates, sunscreen, a perfume called Evil, and accessories that included the best-selling Elvira Gown, the Macabre Makeup Crayons, Nightmare Nail Enamel and Midnight Kiss Lip Color.

"Cassandra Peterson works for scale," she told me, "and Elvira works for big bucks. So I lose money every time I take off the wig." She had repeatedly refused to cover up her cleavage or water down the double entendres or compromise the essence of Elvira. Some producers wanted her to tone

You know someone has arrived when the Hollywood Wax Museum puts up your effigy in wax. But can you tell the real Elvira from the effigy? . . . from the what?

down Elvira for the '88 movie, but "I wanted to have a larger life outside of being a TV hostess. I was finally free to be more risque, sexier. I got away with everything in the film."

At heart Cassandra is a farm girl (born September 17, 1949) who grew up outside Randolph, Kansas, and later got hooked on wearing outlandish outfits when her mother opened a costume shop in their second home in Colorado Springs.

The dress-up fetish clung to her like a thong made of satin and silk. It would be the spangles and glitter that ultimately lured her away to Las Vegas–that and seeing Ann-Margret wooing Elvis Presley in his 1964 musical-comedy extravaganza "Viva Las Vegas." Cassandra was 17, just days from graduating from high school, when she joined the chorus line at the Dunes in Vegas. "I was," she said proudly, "the youngest show

*Cassandra Peterson . . . She's More Beautiful Than Any Horror Host Will Ever Be*

girl in the town's history." She actually landed a date with Elvis, who gently told her to get out of town before she rotted away and became just another chorus gal. (At least that's what Cassandra told me. There is another story–apocryphal?–that Elvis told her she had a great singing voice and she should become a singer.) Whichever story you want to believe, she did take Elvis' advice. She got out of Las Vegas. "I went to Paris and went right back to the chorus line at the Folies Bergere." She was barely 21, and she was barely covered. "The French girls," she recalled, "didn't like me, they made life miserable for all Americans, not just me." So she took off to tour Italy as a rock band singer. "And then," she elaborated, "I met [Italian movie director] Federico Fellini and played a motorcycle girl in his movie 'Fellini's Roma.'"

All the international job-hopping ended when she returned to America to travel cross-country with her own revue, Mama's Boys. She hooked up with an improv group, The Groundlings, and shaped a talent for writing her own comedy. Then she settled into Hollywood with dreams of being the next Great American Actress. But instead, "I became nobody instantly and stayed that way for ten years." She did get work in a "Happy Days" episode playing a character identified in the script as "Girl." This namelessness continued in her scant roles. In "Cheech & Chong's Next Movie" she was "Hostage," in "Coast to Coast" it was "Dinner Party Guest"; in "King of the Mountain" just "Neighbor."

The late make-up and costume designer Robert Redding helped her create the Elvira outfit in '81 after the station told him they didn't care how she was made up. Just look sexy enough to make all male viewers drop dead. Recalled Cassandra: "Robert had seen Sharon Tate in 'The Fearless Vampire Killers' and had been taken by her ghostly pale makeup and see-through dress. But then when KHJ saw our outfit, they started to get more specific. They insisted I be in black, like an update to 'Dracula's Bride.' Robert went back and redesigned this wild dress. I told him they'd never allow that much cleavage on TV. But all the executives said was to put a slit up the side so more of my legs would show. We were flabbergasted, but happy." There would be a beauty mark under her right eye, a ruby ring, snake-shaped earrings, black fingernails, black pumps, a dagger in her belt ("I was definitely on the cutting edge of things") and ultimate measurements that added up to the succulent and succinct numbers 34-21-34.

How does she feel about the character? "Elvira's dumb but honest. She says what she feels. Real people don't do that. Me, I'm always tactful. And she has a certain childlike quality." And the voice? "There's no difference. I don't project or consciously play with it or change it. It's the attitude I assume when I slide into the wig and gown. I can't be with her without them. I have this wicked little laugh."

Does she ever get embarrassed by the bountiful cleavage? "I forget about the boobs until I start to talk to someone and their eyes are bulging and I get the feeling they're not really paying attention or even listening. It's the price you pay . . . John, are you listening to me? . . . John, you haven't heard a word I've been saying."

Hmm . . . does she really love or hate those "awful" horror films? "I've loved them since I was a kid. There's no way I could do this job without loving horror. When I was 7, I'd watch three or four movies a week. During dinner I'd insist on watching 'Blood Feast.' I don't mind goriness when it's in 'The Fly' or 'The Hunger,' or when it's in a fantasy context and doesn't reflect any sense of reality. It gives you an adrenaline rush. You know a vampire isn't really hovering outside your door, dying to get inside your house to make you die."

What she didn't like, and what she had refused to play on "Movie Macabre," were the slasher flicks wherein men attacked women. "It's a sick commentary on our society. We have too many psychotic sociopaths here in Hollywood anyway."

That's Elvira . . . on the left, I mean. As Cassandra Peterson, she is a totally different kind of individual who would never be mistaken for Elvira on the street. This photo was taken in 2003 when Bob Wilkins and I met Cassandra at the San Francisco Wondercon, where she was screening her new film "Elvira's Haunted Hills." At no time during the convention did she appear in the Elvira costume, but she was still as beautiful as ever . . .

One of the ironies that we both laughed at that morning is that Peterson and her Queen B Company control all the merchandising and character rights to Elvira. (KHJ-TV, it seems, didn't want to get involved in a fan club and felt there was little interest in Elvira outside the immediate market and passed on controlling the rights.)

As we finished up and she reported to the stage at Joe Bob's beckoning command, I could almost hear that wicked little laugh of hers. Yeah, as in "The beautiful, seductive woman laughed all the way to the blood bank."

UPDATE: When last we spoke in late 2006, Cassandra had separated from Mark Pierson and was raising their daughter Sadie singlehandedly. Yes, she admitted, at 57 her Elvira outfit "still slides across my body with considerable ease, although there is a small dimensional drop in a strategic place or two." Although the fan clubs and calendars had fallen by the wayside, her product line still thrives: make-up, Halloween T-shirts, a new video game called "Elvira's Match and Stack" and reissued "Movie Macabre" DVDs still flood the market. "I'm very much living in the land of the dead," she said.

She still frequently dons the Elvira costume (an estimated 35 times a year) although she utterly hates "the getting ready" process. But once in character, she undergoes a mental transformation. "I feel that I am Elvira – *and Elvira is me!*" An animal activist and a crusader for gay rights, she feels a horror host "becomes a conduit that takes all the fans into a special world. It's often a dark world, but it's a fun world. As long as I can maintain my figure, Elvira will be clinging to the edge of the darkness, there to entertain her fans."

## The Thing That Almost Gobbled Up Cleveland -And Then Set Sail on . . . 'The Lovvveeee Boat'

While Cassandra Peterson would always be identified with Elvira, no matter what else she might try to do, Ernie Anderson enjoyed a difference. He could be purely Ernie Anderson the TV announcer and enjoy every living moment of it, as he did on the day I met him at the Magic Castle. He had so identified himself with this offcamera persona from two decades of working in the medium that his horror-host identity dating back to the 1960s had become all but forgotten. Unless, of course, you had grown up watching his arcane characterization of Ghoulardi.

It was fascinating to hang around Ernie Anderson. Not only was he a fun-loving guy every moment but he seemed to be just waiting for someone to pop *the* question. And the question waiting to be popped was the same: "Can you do it for me, Ernie? Can you do it just once? Please, Ernie. Just for me? This one time?"

Each time he would pause, smile a wry smile that worked its way around the corners of his mouth, pause again (as if contemplating whether he should or not) and then allow the three little  words to roll languidly,  lingeringly off his tongue.  "The . . . Lovvveeee . . . Boat."

Stretching out "love" to "lovvveeee" had become an hourly way of life for Ernie. Each word, he told me, "has made me very rich. Those three little words have made me so rich I can laugh at it all." He could laugh at it all because he was one of the highest paid announcers in Hollywood. "Yeah," he said, "voiceovers, commercials, that's where it finally was at for me. You want 'Lovvveeee . . . Boat,' you get 'Lovvveeee . . . Boat.' Why should I deprive you of hearing it. . . . 'The Lovvveeee . . . Boat.' "

Commercials hadn't always been where it was at, as Ernie told me when we ducked out of the Palace of Mystery to hang around the Parlour of Prestidigitation, a small theater within the greater Magic Castle. It featured a handsomely carved proscenium from a lodge hall and seats taken from the original Santa Monica Opera House. It was a classic place to talk to a classic horror host. Please, Ernie, tell me about Ghoulardi. "At one time in my life," Ernie said, "Cleveland was where it was all at." And there had been a monster in his life, one that almost ate all of Cleveland . . . in a positive  way. Ernie Anderson in 1962 had become Ghoulardi, the mad ghoul of Cleveland,  when  he  first  began  hosting  Friday  night  flicks  on  a local channel. The character was memorably funny when he donned a laboratory coat, fright wig, goatee and mustache. The new thing hit Cleveland like a tidal wave, and all but gobbled it up.

"By the summer of 1963, 'Keep Cool with the Ghoul' was my motto. The motto of all Cleveland, if not all of Ohio. Four thousand letters a week. Postcards. Sweatshirts." He even did a second show, wrapping his gruesome comedy around Laurel and Hardy short subjects. Ghoulardi loved superimposing his face within the movie scenes and shouting "It's awful, it's terrible" over the soundtrack. "What a dog!" and "What a bomb!" were other taglines.

"You have no idea how I hit that town," Ernie said, "and how the town hit me. I had no idea there would be anything like that in my life." Born in Massachusetts, he had served in the U.S. Navy during World War II and worked at numerous East Coast radio stations as a commonplace disc jockey. Well, commonplace until he started slipping in novelty records that didn't always go over so well with management. It was only a tip of his sense of humor and gradually that sense of humor started to show

That's Ernie with his old partner Tom Conway (top) who later became Tim. They once did a duo comedy act.

more of itself. Along the way Ernie met a livewire named Tom Conway and they performed comedy together. (Tom would later change his name to Tim and move on to Hollywood.)

With the coming of Ghoulardi, the world opened up at his feet and never closed again. "All the world's a purple knif" became Ghoulardi's catch-line, "knif" being fink spelled backward. Everybody in town was hep to "knif" talk and Time magazine wrote him up as an Ohio oddity, a Cleveland cut-up whose ghoulish antics were gobbled up by viewers.

Finally, in 1966, he decided to give up the delightful tomfoolery. "I knew it wasn't going to last forever," Ernie told me that morning. "Besides, my popularity started fading after a couple of seasons. I knew I'd have to get a 'serious' job, so I headed for Hollywood, and I've been a 'Lovvveeee' happy guy ever since."

Having known Tim (aka Tom) Conway when they were both struggling would-be comedians, Ernie went to work with Conway in sitcoms.

Eventually Ernie became the announcer for "The Carol Burnett Show," and began developing a style that set a new standard for network announcing. He became known as "The Golden Throat" after he did "Winds of War," "Roots" and, yes, "The Love Boat."

"All I can tell you," said the happy-go-lucky horror host cum TV series announcer, "is that my ship finally cammmmeeeee in."

POSTSCRIPT: Ernie Anderson died in 1997 at 73. But, and this gets macabre in a Ghoulardi way, his voice isn't dead. You can buy lines Ernie recorded years ago for a fee – tag lines once used for promotions. If he were alive, he might scream "What a dogggg!"

# WHEN ZACH LET OUT A WHACK, YOU HAD VULTURE WITH CULTURE

At the Magic Castle that day was a dish of what I will forever call Vulture Stew. My little pet name for the one horror host who has stood out above all others, and who has survived with a gentle smile on his lips and not a hint of larceny in his heart. I refer you to the endurable John Zacherle. You can call him "Zach"–that's the nickname he prefers–but fans first knew him as Roland, when he debuted as a host for the first time in 1957 at Philadelphia's WCAU-TV, in charge of showing the "Shock!" package.

His "life changed forever," he would claim later, when one night he asked viewers to pluck three human hairs from their bodies and send them to the station. He told his audience he needed these hairs for a new pillow he was making "for his wife's coffin."

Even before he could pluck a hair from his own head, to make sure he wasn't dreaming, "Zach" was a "sin-sation" and found himself at WABC-TV in New York where he boosted the ratings for "Shock Theater" to all-time highs. But who needed a crummy title like "Shock Theater" when you could call it "Zacherley at Large." (Roland was nowhere in sight.)

Dark humor was his specialty, visualized in imaginative costume and make-up. He carried out all kinds of experiments with food *(gulp!)* and electricity (shocking what he did as a live wire) and hence he was the first horror host to carry out special effects right there in the studio before the disbelieving eyes of his audience.

Once his station held "an open house" and an estimated 12,000 fans showed up to idolize their anti-hero. "We spoofed the daylights out of the commercials and on-air mistakes became part of the fun [and the shtick] of the show."

There at the Magic Castle, I listened as this legendary character told Joe Bob Briggs how he came to be known as "The Cool Ghoul" after Dick Clark had dubbed him with that appendage. "One of the running jokes was my wife under the counter," a wife viewers never saw, only heard about. "I would talk to her jovially and sometimes chase her under the table with a knife that some came to see as a kind of sex thing. Ha ha ha." Zacherley's prolonged laugh was at first jovial, then took on a sinister touch. I sensed that it was this ability to seem menacing as well as charming that made the Zacherley characterization so memorable.

He told how eventually his character became a mini-franchise business with a record hit ("Dinner With Drac" in 1958) and an album of novelty songs, "Spook Along With Zacherley." One of his best hits became "Come With Me to Transylvania." (On my shelf are two paperback short-story anthologies that reflect this merchandising era, "Zacherley's Vulture Stew" and "Zacherley's Midnight Snacks.")

Ballantine Books brought out in 1960 two classic horror anthologies I covet as major collector's items: "Zacherley's Vulture Stew" and "Zacherley's Midnight Snacks." Each contains nine classic tales of undeniable shock.

He told Joe Bob that although Boris Karloff was performing in "Peter Pan" while he was doing his horror series, they never met. "However," elaborated Zacherley, "one day one of my producers ran into Karloff and apologized, thinking he might be offended by all the spoofery. 'Not at all, my dear,' Karloff replied. 'You brought me back to life.' "

His show moved to WOR-TV in Los Angeles but by then "Shock Theater" was winding down in popularity and he became a disc jockey for the next 15 years. In 1990 he made an appearance in "Frankenhooker" as a TV weatherman, and then in "Brain Damage" was the voice of a worm. "It bites into the back of your neck and sucks your brains out," he explained. And Joe Bob added: "The worm sings Cole Porter besides."

For his Joe Bob guest appearance that afternoon, Zacherley proceeded to create a huge green amoeba out of store-bought Jello. It was stuffed with spaghetti strands (standing in for intestines), grapes (for eyes) and several unidentifiable objects. It was a marvelously gooey mess – it made you want to laugh and regurgitate in the same breath. It was a "culinary treat" of a kind only Zacherley had a reputation for creating. "My boy, this is what it's all about," he shouted, running his hands through the crumbling "amoeba" and pulling out "things." He barked out another hearty laugh. One could only hope none of the pieces were falling onto the wife, down out of sight hidden under the counter.

# A "Profoundly Disturbing" Update About Joe Bob

In the intervening years since our meeting in 1991, Joe Bob Briggs has updated and redefined himself to meet an ever-changing media technology. With the coming of the DVD age, he has done numerous movie commentary tracks for Elite Entertainment and he has written his ultimate Joe Bob books, "Profoundly Disturbing: Shocking Movies That Changed History" and "Profoundly Erotic: Sexy Movies That Changed History."

About these unusual book, which revisit movies that in Joe Bob's eyes changed history,

HANGING OUT
AT THE MAGIC CASTLE
WITH ELVIRA, MISTRESS
OF THE DARK

**AN HISTORIC MOMENT CAPTURED** on Oct. 11, 1991: This is the day Joe Bob Briggs (left) gathered his favorite TV horror hosts at the Magic Castle in Hollywood to tape guest segments for his TV series: I'm standing next to famed "Drive In Critic" and on-air host Joe Bob (aka John Bloom), "Love Boat" announcer Ernie Anderson (Ghoulardi) is below me, and that's John Zacherle (Zacherley) abreast of Cassandra Peterson clad demurely as the Queen of Midnight Movies, Elvira, aka Mistress of the Dark.

"I wanted to do a fresh reading on movies that were originally misunderstood or not appreciated for what they have ultimately brought to our culture. It was this eclectic collection of flicks, considered beneath contempt and yet surviving for years, that did indeed change our culture but which we do not view in that light. These are not classics, but they had an impact on us whether we realized it at the time or not. Nowadays it has become commonplace for critics to look at crappy movies as social artifacts of our culture and re-evaluate them.

This is what I most admire and respect about Joe Bob Briggs. He always tries to surround himself with intelligent, uplifting guests who are designed to improve the minds of his viewers. Here he has wisely surrounded himself with some of the best scream queens of B movies: (left to right) Michelle Bauer, Melissa Moore, Julie Strain and Vivian Schilling. My own ten-gallon sombrero is off in Joe Bob's honor.

"The more we know about these movies and why we love them, the better we come to understand ourselves.  Nowadays we have professors of pop culture at universities who offer courses on the same movies that were all but ignored years ago except in my columns. A generation under 30 now writes about these movies of the '50s and '60s and '70s with a newfound fascination. 'Wild Angels' and 'The Last House on the Left' and other grindhouse cinema once judged beneath contempt."

John Bloom feels that Joe Bob Briggs hasn't changed much over the years. "I still celebrate the sleaze movies in the same style. Maybe I don't spin as many redneck stories as I used to. And I don't always stay within the bounds of just exploitation fare. I'm doing commentary tracks for movies considered a little more mainstream, such as 'The Wild Bunch' and 'The Cabinet of Dr. Caligari.' I try to make the commentary tracks as intimate as possible. Even though I'm trapped in a concrete room with a few sound engineers, I try to make the audience feel as if they're watching the movie with me. I even leave mistakes in the tracks because they create a feeling of immediacy."

And so the greatest anomaly within the genre of movie hosts, Joe Bob Briggs, lives on in new ways without John Bloom losing his booted stride.

## PREPARE TO BE GOVERNED . . . A GUTSY GLIMPSE AT AN ACTION AND FANTASY FILM STAR BEFORE HE BECAME HISTORIC . . . WHEN HE WAS STILL FRAMING PECS INSTEAD OF BILLS

I got this call one day in early 1977 from an ABC publicist who used his PR muscle to build up a body he wanted me to meet. The body belonged to a muscleman nobody had heard much of, but this strong-arm guy was muscling his way into Hollywood. He'd made a picture, "Stay Hungry," and now he was the guest-of-the-week in a "Streets of San Francisco" episode being shot that week with Karl Malden. This guy, he even had a picture then playing in San Francisco, a body-building documentary called "Pumping Iron." If I pumped some of my own leg muscles over to a classy hotel at Fisherman's Wharf where he was staying maybe I could build the body of a story. So I went. And so it was, in February 1977, that I managed to exercise my better judgment and pump journalistic iron:

# A CLOSE ENCOUNTER OF THE SINEWY KIND WITH THE BODY OF BEAUTIFUL BRAWN ... ON SECOND THOUGHT, MAKE THAT THE TERMINATOR OF BODY BUILDING

With vainglory and panache, The Best Built Man of All Times flexes the muscles of his 22-inch arm for the young woman behind the cash register. She radiates a warm, inviting smile in return, drinking in the sight of Arnold Schwarzenegger and drowning herself in the 230 pounds of beefcake encased in a 6'2" body with a 58-inch chest, 32-inch waist, 28-inch thighs and 20-inch calves.

If this Body of Beautiful Brawn wasn't so eager to devour his dinner, he might take up the young and shapely woman on whatever promises lie behind the incriminating smile. But the appetite of The Austrian Oak, even if no leaf should remained unfurled, cries out to be satisfied. So he looks just slightly disappointed as he leaves her behind and leads the way into the darkened dining room of a leading San Francisco motor lodge located in the heart of Fisherman's Wharf.

The 36-year-old Strapping Specimen walks in giant strides, glancing at the diners who are glancing at him and perhaps feeling slightly on the pruny side. Some might be recognizing him from his photographs (he is a five-time Mr. Universe and a six-time Mr. Olympia and is the best known bodybuilder anywhere in the world, or so his press release reads) or some might have seen him as Joe Santo in the 1976 film "Stay Hungry." Whatever the source of recognition, The Man of Might and Magnetism revels in the joy of identification in a public palace of dining, drinking and overnight staying.

No sooner has he slid into a booth than a waitress in a short skirt, and with a low-cut bodice to make the short skirt all that much more noticeable, hurries to the tableside–obviously she is not here to refill the pepper and salt shakers. But she does prove to be a shaker and mover, and a bit salty: "Arnold," she says with considerable anxiety, and with a certain familiarity bordering on total lack of formality, "I can't come to your room tonight. The management frowns on its employees visiting the guests."

"*Well*," says The Prince of Powerful Pecs looking indignant and rejected, his Austrian accent cutting the air like a bayonet slicing into human flesh, *"if you don't come to my room tonight then I guess you won't get laid."*

This "now or never" approach throws the well-endowed waitress into near-panic. The Director of the IFBB's Professional Bodybuilding Committee proposes a solution. "Not to worry. I will go to my room. I will open the window. I will throw a rope to the ground, holding one end. You will go to the rope, grab onto it, and I will pull you up into my room. I will close the

**Arnold Schwarzenegger, all of 23 years old, poses in front of a poster for a Hercules movie. It's a movie-within-a-movie because this is a scene from his very first movie, "Hercules in New York" (aka "Hercules Goes Bananas"). But don't look under Schwarzenegger to find this movie: He was billed as "Arnold Strong" alongside a comedian named Arnold Stang, who once co-starred on TV's "The Milton Berle Show." Everything's a joke.**

window. No one will be the wiser." But this nicely structured woman does not respond to the offer, more concerned with keeping her job. "Too bad," says The Austrian Mountain, "you could have helped me study my script tonight."

Script? "I'm doing a 'Streets of San Francisco' episode in which a . . . " Schwarzenegger pauses to watch as the befuddled, sad-faced but still curvaceous young woman scurries away.

"I think she'll come up with something yet. She strikes me as being an imaginative girl. As I was saying, I play a bodybuilder in this show ["Dead Lift"]. It's an unusual script. I have a bigger role than the stars. Quinn Martin the producer saw me in 'Stay Hungry' and he wanted me. We just filmed a scene today. I play a schizophrenic personality who goes psychotic and smashes up the furniture in a mansion."

The Muhammad Ali of Bodybuilding talks briefly about his newest film, "Pumping Iron," a pseudo-documentary that depicts how ten muscle heroes prepare for the Mr. Olympia contest in South Africa, the "superbowl" of bodybuilding. ("I don't have any weak points," says The Maximum Bod in the film. "My goal always was . . . that everything is perfect." )

"This is quite a movie [a 25th Anniversary Edition is on a Warner Bros. DVD] that shows the hard training, the personal sacrifice and the victory and defeat of competition. If a bodybuilder is involved with himself, he is easy to beat. If he is involved in the competition, he is harder to beat.

"Some bodybuilders get nervous. Me, I never get nervous. I've worked out a therapy of mind. It releases tension and aggression. I work out and feel like a new person with a new mind."

Lapsing into momentary modesty, The Mighty Man of Muscle compares himself to Burt Reynolds. "I'm going to be playing his roles in one year. I'm leading man stuff. I'm not going to be around as a co-star for long.

"I take acting seriously and see myself as a great actor and I see this image. I see it clearly. I am going to be a star. Just as I used to imagine myself as a bodybuilding star.

"Bodybuilding is a mixed form of art, sports and show business—get all three down pat and you've got it made. In two years, you will see me up there on the giant screen, a [motion picture] star."

The King of Weights glances around the dining room for some sign of the flustered cocktail waitress in the short skirt, but she is nowhere in sight.

The Powerful One assumes a stance that can only be interpreted as self-parody and winks at me.

"Ah well," says Statuesque and Unforgettable, stretching to His Maximum. "There's no time for fooling around with girls tonight. I have to study my script. There are many lines to be memorized."

That might depend on the kind of "lines" he's referring to.

**Arnold Schwarzenegger in his greatest role: The Terminator!**

# NIGHT OF THE CONAN REVELATION – NEVER UNDERESTIMATE THE MIGHT OF A MUSCLEMAN

I filed and forgot the Schwarzenegger story – until five years later. It was a night in April 1982. I was taking a jet from San Francisco to Burbank to attend the premiere of a new motion picture. The film: "Conan the Barbarian." Its star: Arnold Schwarzenegger. He had told me that in two years he was going to be up there on that big screen.

Well, it had taken him a little longer, but there he was that night, bigger than life, up on that 50-foot screen, living up to what he had promised he would deliver. And bigger was always, always going to be a way of life for Schwarzenegger, just as it had been that evening in that San Francisco dining room. I decided that Arnold Schwarzenegger, if nothing else, was a man who always carried with him a dream, and who lived up to his word.

He would go on to prove it in "Conan the Destroyer," "Red Sonja," "Commando," "Raw Deal," "Predator," "The Running Man," "Red Heat," "Total Recall," "Kindergarten Cop," "Last Action Hero," "Eraser," "End of Days." But mainly he would find his place in The Pantheon of Stars Who Say the Unforgettable Words. For Clint Eastwood those words were *"Are you feeling lucky, punk?"* and *"Go ahead, make my day."* For Schwarzenegger the words came from his most remembered film "Terminator" and its two sequels. And they were short -- if not sweet: *"I'll be back."* And back he came, time and again, ultimately thunking down into a very special place in the world of politics by claiming the governor's seat in the state of California. When Arnie says he'll be back, you better believe he means it.

*A*nd now it's time to take you back through time to tell you one of the most important science-fiction stories through which I had the opportunity to live. It began at a studio in Hollywood called Desilu and it ended in the backyard of a beloved comedienne-actress. Along the way I met some influential folks who created and acted out a space fantasy-adventure that would bring excitement and unforgettable entertainment to generations of TV viewers and ultimately to movie-goers as well. The subject of this story was to become the most profitable and most famous sci-fi franchise of all time. So come with me and . . .

## TREK WHERE NO MAN HAS GONE BEFORE

# BOLDLY TREKKING OUT TO MEET THE ALIEN WITH THE POINTED EARS

***"Insufficient facts always invite danger."***
*– Mr. Spock in "Space Seed" (Stardate 3141.9)*

**M**Y GREATEST and longest trek began with a journey to Desilu Studios in Hollywood. But back then, I had little hope it would be a good trek or a good story.

Not after the invitational phone call from an NBC publicist urging me to cover a new show debuting in September. Some thing called "Star Trek."

I figured the network salesman pitching me was overcompensating. It was commonplace for networks to serve up newspaper guys like me overstuffed turkeys.

I'd munched on more than my share of drumsticks and last-parts-over-the-fence covering television.

A "new, thrilling" series set aboard a starship traveling through the Universe? Yeah, sure. With "Lost in Space" currently blasting through the galaxies, this sounded like a star-studded extraterrestrial con job.

The pitch had included the name Spock. "He's a non-Earthling. From the planet Vulcan," said the tinseltown tinhorn hawker. "His skin's a pale-green color and his ears are pointed. But listen, this isn't kid's stuff. *This is the first adult space adventure.*"

Pointed ears not kid's stuff? Okay, but I didn't care if I was falling for a line or not. I loved covering science-fiction shows.  I'd visited "Voyage to the Bottom of the Sea" a

year earlier and walked through the stomach of a whale built on the 20th Century-Fox lot. Besides, at Desilu I would meet the show's creator. A guy named Roddenberry. Gene Roddenberry. "He's something. I mean, really something."

Warning! Warning! It Does Not Compute! Danger! Danger!

It was the summer of 1966 and most TV science-fiction was juvenile stuff. Irwin Allen's "Voyage" had the atomic submarine Seaview encountering the Monster-of-the-Week in the deep six. Allen had also created "Lost in Space," which had that ridiculous Dr. Smith (played by Jonathan Harris) and the Robby the Robot-like character ("Danger! Danger, Will Robinson!") that had spun off from "Forbidden Planet" (1956) and the lesser remembered "The Invisible Boy" (1957).

Then there were the ridiculous sitcoms cashing in on fantasy themes: "My Mother the Car," depicting a 1928 Porter automobile that yattered away with the voice of Ann Sothern, and "I Dream of Jeannie," with Barbara Eden as a genie in a harem costume (sorry, no belly button showing) straight out of a bottle soothingly granting wishes to Larry Hagman in his pre-J.R. "Dallas" days.

The better sci-fi shows, Rod Serling's "The Twilight Zone" and ABC's "The Outer Limits," were now but pleasant memories but still gave one hope for more good things to come.

There was a couple of spy series with sci-fi elements, "The Man From U.N.C.L.E." and "Get Smart," both very popular, and a sci-fi Western, "The Wild Wild West," but this newfangled "Star Trek" sounded like another Irwin Allen *wunderdisaster* waiting to explode.

Visiting Desilu Studios had always filled me with a touch of awe during my years covering Hollywood. Previously known as RKO, the Hollywood-based studio during its 30-plus years had turned out grand Fred Astaire-Ginger Rogers musicals and dark film noirs

I would meet the vivacious, frankly-speaking Joan Collins years later, in 1977, but not on the set of "The City on the Edge of Forever," which went on to win a Hugo award and is still considered a superb "Star Trek" episode with Collins as Edith Keller.

starring Robert Mitchum and Victor Mature. It was here that Orson Welles had arrived as the new *wunderkind* on the block to make "Citizen Kane." This was the studio that had produced "King Kong" and "Mighty Joe Young" with Willis O'Brien's trend-setting stop-motion frame-at-a-time animation work. So there was a lot of rich history to think about as I walked down the back-lot streets. Such as how, with declining movie attendance, RKO had sold out in 1957 to Desi Arnaz and Lucille Ball's Desilu Productions, and now the old faithful studio served primarily as a TV factory that would be most remembered for creating "The Untouchables." With Lucy herself, in those days, divorced from Desi and running the place as the head of the board of directors.

I didn't know it then but fate had picked an historic week for me to visit the "Star Trek" set. The episode being shot was "City on the Edge of Forever" with guest star Joan Collins. I never saw her on the set but the first person I did meet was the guy who had written the script, Harlan Ellison. I'd find out in later years, during my odyssey through the world of science fiction, that Ellison was Peck's Bad Boy of the literary intelligentsia. He's a superb writer of short stories, often with fantasy premises (although you could get your head knocked off for labeling him a sci-fi or fantasy

writer). Just call him a good fiction writer and media critic and leave the rest alone.

And I had loved Ellison's two excellent books about television: "The Glass Teat" and "The Other Glass Teat," based on his columns for the L. A. Free Press. In one of those classics he describes how he punched producer Irwin Allen in the nose during a story session for "Voyage to the Bottom of the Sea." In fact, Ellison's personality tended to be over-confrontational on numerous occasions. He was forever looking for the simplest reason to become argumentative. And get into your face about it. Catching you offguard was part of his technique. The more he disagreed with you, the sharper-edged he could get.

I would have my only encounter with him years later (mild compared to what others have gone through) when he accused me of being "chauvinistic" in my use of sexy women on "Creature Features."

I readily admitted to him this was completely true, as I considered myself an entertainer first and a philanthropist or crusader for women's rights second. But I also had good moments with this brilliant if unpredictable writer/personality. Several friends warned me never to do a TV show with him, he was a bull-headed Hollywood liberal who would rip me apart if I got on the wrong political side.

But we did do a show in 1982 and he turned out to be a totally charming, no-problem guest. We didn't argue once and at the end of

"I'm watching you, Stanley"

**Be wary when the chips are down and Harlan Ellison decides to look you straight in the eye. You could be in for it, brother.**

the taping he called me a "solid brick" (good thing I am not hard of hearing).

On the "City on the Edge of Forever" set, Ellison might have passed for one of the background players dressed like a vagrant. He was clad in a yellow sweatshirt with orange stripes and wore grimy tennis shoes. He struck me as short and frail, and he spoke with such enthusiasm about "Star Trek" that he reminded me more of a farm-bred fan, fresh from pulling the teats on farm milk cows, than a writer of fantasy . . . oops, make that fiction.

Rather than answer my questions directly, Ellison said he preferred to type out his thoughts on his "axe" (typewriter). He rushed away to a corner of the set and began slamming the keys frenziedly, producing a full page of prose that he later gave to me.

After categorically listing his many awards and accolades as a writer, Ellison got down to the gritty: *"The delight of working for and with Gene Roddenberry defies semantics. His respect for the writer, for the philosophy of writing–when it's being done by a craftsman who gives a damn, and not just a hack–is unique in my experience with Hollywood producers. Roddenberry won't settle for less than the best, and if that means great bursts of inventiveness, then it's up to me . . . That's the challenge that makes writing this show a kick in the head, and not the mere money-drudgery of the bulk of scriptwriting."*

(Some of this would turn out to be misdirected praise, because Roddenberry and D.C. Fontana would make drastic changes to Ellison's original teleplay and Ellison would remain angry and bitter for years afterward.)

***"Most legends have their basis in facts."***
– Captain James T. Kirk in "And the Children Shall Lead" (Stardate 5029.5)

Finally, with the ego-driven, in-your-face Ellison out of the way, I was introduced to the show's producer and creator, Eugene Wesley Roddenberry. This was a surprise. I hadn't expected a producer. Usually these TV interviews consisted on going onto a busy set, finding quiet blocks of time with the subject, getting a few solid quotes, and

Gene Roddenberry, who died in October 1991, will always be remembered as the brilliant creator of the original "Star Trek" TV series – but there would come a time when Paramount would wrest control of the film series from Roddenberry and hand it over to other producers. Thus "Star Trek" would become the boon and bane of his lengthy and creative career.

leaving. At least watching TV production was more exciting than lunch in the commissary.

Roddenberry had been waiting patiently and escorted me away to a quiet place. As if he knew I was thinking about "Voyage to the Bottom of the Sea" or that talking car, he said: "I want to blast the hour-series above the level of juvenile fare. I'll be honest. I'm working with familiar pulp-magazine material but I'm also injecting an unusual human element into the stories. We're taking the weirdest stuff and making it as believable as possible."

His purpose was twofold: "One, to show that science fiction is an incredibly rich body of literature as yet untapped by TV. And two, to show that the genre can be more than 'The Monster That Gobbled Up Tokyo' or 'The Thing

That Swallowed Cleveland Whole.' This is the distorted view most Americans have, thanks to a lot of cheap, unimaginative movies. Producers for too long now have been playing to the 15-year-old mentality. I say to hell with that. I refuse to believe an audience is that stupid. Doesn't it make sense to give them something that truly stimulates their imaginations?"

Roddenberry, with growing enthusiasm, went on to tell me he had some good "stimulation from well-known fantasy writers" and he mentioned "Ellison, Robert Bloch, Richard Matheson, Robert Sheckley and even Ray Bradbury, once he's free of his prior commitments."

**Early to Rise: Leonard Nimoy in his first incantation as Mr. Spock, during the TV season of 1966-67.**

*"Fascinating is a word I use for the unexpected." – Mr. Spock in "The Squire of Gothos" (Stardate 2124.5)*

At last I was introduced to Leonard Nimoy. If Gene Roddenberry had already begun to change my mind about the worthiness of my being there, Nimoy clenched it. Right away I felt something unusual was happening as he greeted me with a warm albeit intense smile and for the first time in my life I saw a half-human, half-Vulcan being: "Mr. Spock" was wearing the Starfleet uniform fans would soon be introduced to, and for the first time I saw those ears receding upward into a point, the heavy make-up and the uplifted eyebrows all giving his elongated face an appropriate alien look. This was no silly creature-of-the-week on "Lost in Space."

I sensed an intensity in Nimoy that would always be there in our later meetings. He was taking his TV role very seriously, and he wanted me to know that immediately. I could also sense he was worried about this character being taken seriously and so he pitched me harder than most actors on first meeting.

"I'm not a straight-man computer to Captain Kirk, blindly following orders," he began. "In fact, the Captain often asks Spock for his advice. He is his own man—or should I saw humanoid. I'm trying to give this unique being a hard edge, a no-nonsense attitude that goes beyond being purely human. A calculating mind without interference of human emotion."

For the first time I learned of an unscreened pilot made in 1964 with Nimoy in his first incantation as Spock and with Jeffrey Hunter as Captain Christopher Pike.

The show had not passed the acid test with NBC and had been put into turnaround, with William Shatner cast as a new captain, now named James T. Kirk.

(The first pilot with Jeffrey Hunter would become known individually as "Star Trek: The Cage" and then footage would be used for flashbacks in the re-edited two-part "Star Trek" adventure "The Menagerie").

On seeing the initial pilot, Nimoy told me, "I felt Spock was not complex or interesting enough. He spoke too loudly and quickly. I felt he needed to have a control of his own, almost a coldness. So I told Gene that I felt the pilot was a failure. And I told him I wanted to be released from my contract.

"But somehow, and this is an indication of how seriously Gene is taking all this, he talked me into staying with the series, with the out that I could undergo plastic surgery after 13 episodes and become more human-like. However, I thought it over and decided I'd be a fool to lose these ears and eyebrows. The more I've submerged myself into Mr. Spock, the better I've come to admire him for his personality and his looks. No one else in television is going to look like me."

Nimoy, seeing that he had me hooked, leaned in closer as if what he was saying was purely confidential: "I tell you, Spock is intriguing. To begin with, a Vulcan considers emotions in bad taste. His kind are a logical, sophisticated people who have bred feelings out of their blood. It interrupts clear thinking. Scientific and probing, that's a Vulcan.

"In one of our shows ["The Naked Time"], a virus [Psi 2000] intrudes aboard the USS Enterprise and strips crew members of their defense mechanisms and forces them to act out their repressed desires. Spock is equally affected and goes into hiding to begin an intended battle with himself to ward off the threat. He must re-establish his values, and in so doing breaks down and weeps. He also feels love and parental instinct toward a woman passenger. What I want 'Star Trek' to have are equally bizarre internal conflicts for Spock."

He pointed out that besides having green-colored blood, a 212 pulse count and an anatomical make-up totally different from any Earthman's, he knows how to pinch the neck to render an ordinary human being

**"BEAM ME UP, SCOTTY"... "ENERGIZE"... "TRANSPORTER ROOM"... ALL PART OF A NEW LEXICON**

unconscious.

I asked Nimoy if he had always had an interest in science-fiction. "An interest and a respect," he answered.

"Though I've never been an insatiable reader. But I was always aware of science fiction's contribution to literature and I remember Ray Bradbury influencing me a great deal as a young adult. I sincerely believe 'Star Trek' to be an equally significant contribution—our stories touch on the imagination and intrigue it in a way no contemporary drama can."

I wanted to find out more about this unusually articulate actor, who had just described a most unusual character for television. He told me he was a native of Boston brought up in a family of barbers. Born March 26, 1931, in a low-budget tenement house, he first appeared on a stage at the age of 8.

"When I decided to become an actor the first thing I did was lose my Bostonian accent. I was at the Pasadena Playhouse when I went through a lean period driving taxis on weekdays and pushing chocolate sodas on Sundays. My career has not been phenomenal. I went many years waiting for lots of small breaks to bring me one big break."

That career started with minimal roles in "Queen for a Day" and "Rhubarb" (both made in 1951). When he did land a starring role, the titular one, in the low-budget film "Kid Monk Baroni" (1952), nothing happened. "The critics liked it," recalled Nimoy, "but it never got the distribution it deserved."

He identified with the tough street-gang kid Baroni who grew into a professional boxer to escape New York's "Little Italy." Hadn't he escaped from Boston to pursue better things? Then he portrayed his first outer-space being,

# STAR TREK: THE NEW BUSINESS USS ENTERPRISE

. . . . Where No Man
Has Gone Before

Narab, in Republic's turgid 12-chapter serial of 1952, "Zombies of the Stratosphere," but there was nothing in his portrayal to suggest better outer-space beings to come. Nor was his career helped any by the excellent "Them" (1954) for he was squashed like an insignificant ant. Movies became scarce as a result and he turned to episodic TV: "Navy Log," "West Point," "The Man Called X," "Sea Hunt," "The Silent Service." He found repeated exposure as villains in Westerns: "Colt .45," "26 Men," "The Rough Riders," "Rawhide." Nothing helped. "I seemed to be in a rut as either a Spanish character or an Indian. It was a real stigma. They never wanted me to play a straight-man leading role."

Nimoy thought he had finally made a breakthrough when he was cast in John Frankenheimer's "Seven Days in May" (1964) but the part became fodder for the cutting-room floor. Then came a "Wagon Train" episode that in turn brought him a "Dr. Kildare" role.

He also spoke of the importance of his role as Jules LaFranc in a theatrical version of Jean Genet's "Deathwatch" directed by Vic Morrow, whom he had met while making the "Combat" episode "The Raider." He laughed when he quoted one critic who wrote that Nimoy had displayed a "laudable sensitivity" in his performance.

"You might say that I've come full cycle–that I'm playing a freakish character once again. But I don't look at it that way. Spock could be the start of something wonderful and new. Who knows, it might become a prestigious thing to play an alien as it's become a prestige thing to play a villain on 'Batman.' But whatever, I'm expecting entire new worlds to open up to me after 'Star Trek.'"

It's as if he wanted to end the interview with words most prophetic. For this was indeed only the beginning for Nimoy.

His words now seem strangely "all-seeing" as I read them off my old clipping, preserved all these years in one of a dozen fat scrapbooks in my library.

*"No problem is insoluble." – Dr. Janet Wallace in "The Deadly Years" (Stardate 3479.4)*

Before I would meet Nimoy again, I would beam back to the Desilu Studios for a second meeting with Gene Roddenberry. By the time I got to Desilu I discovered it had been bought up by Paramount and "Star Trek" was now a Paramount property. It was a fortuitously timed interview. It had been set up so Roddenberry and I could discuss the demise of "Star Trek" but suddenly, just a few days before we met, an announcer had cut into a "Star Trek" broadcast on the night of March 3, 1968, to announce the series, previously cancelled, would return for a third season. In a medium where shows came and went with the acceleration of unidentified flying objects, this was an unprecedented gesture, for never had a network axed or reinstated a show with such vocal and news-making hoopla.

On the other hand, NBC had "a million reasons" for making that unique announcement. That was the estimated number of fans who had written in to protest the fact that the series had been death-rayed out of the line-up in late 1967. This corps of irate and unsettled fans had demonstrated in several ways. Five hundred Caltech students had marched on NBC in Burbank; the Oregon Rocket Society had filed a formal protest, and even the Andrew School for Girls in Willoughby, Ohio, had petitioned its protest with 1764 signatures.

So intense and fervent (and sometimes threatening) had the mail been that NBC's statistical and audience survey experts had been shaken up as never before. (Especially shaken was their faith in the Nielsen ratings which had placed "Star Trek" low on the so-called popularity charts.)

The Gene Roddenberry I met a few days after the announcement was a man on top of his many alien worlds, ready to launch his starship for a third season.

"From the outset I tried to treat science-fiction not as 'Lo, the Wonder of It All,' but as having a tie-in with scientific possibilities. No matter how outrageous the storylines got, I asked the writers to please put a theory behind the premise to make it work.

"I built the show on high believability. For science-fiction to succeed it must first create a world of reality within its fantasy elements. This is achieved by establishing a few standard principles and remaining consistent with them from week to week in all the episodes, however farflung.

"We seek all the authoritative and authentic advice and aid we can get, so that what we present to our loyal audience is a normal, logical progression from what we have today. Not only in technical science but sociology as well. The human element is as important as the confounded machine."

I was surprised when Roddenberry estimated that everything he had just told me "goes right over the heads of our 20 million 'Star Trek' viewers." Most of these "logical" human beings, he continued, "have never read a sci-fi story and have not even a modicum of appreciation for such sophisticated refinements or intellectual insights."

The show, he felt, "has created quite an environment–quite a family of characters, quite a system of gadgets, and the fans don't like any fooling around with them. They want the phasers to shoot a blue beam, not a red one. One viewer noticed a computer blinking four times one week, six times the next. He wrote to ask if we had perfected the system.

"Another espied that when Kirk ordered deflectors up, Sulu the navigator hit the phaser button . . . you wouldn't believe the fan mail. Literate mail from the young in mind chronologically or mentally. We get advice, suggestions, even character analyses from professional psychiatrists."

*"Conquest is easy. Control is not."* –Captain Kirk in "Mirror, Mirror" (Stardate Unknown).

I had read Roddenberry described as "a driving force" behind the series, but on the surface he always struck me as becalmed as a starship without warp-factor power. He spoke gently, soothingly, without a note of urgency and affectation. Nor did I sense any resentments at NBC for the now uncancelled cancellation. He told me his "urge for authenticity" began with Jack Webb, with whom he had worked on "Dragnet" scripts. "I

## BEFORE 'TREKKIES' EXISTED, THE FANS CLAMORED FOR RENEWAL –AND SAVED THE SERIES FROM ANNIHILATION

watched Webb taking photos of robberies and duplicating the sets down to the pinholes in the wall. An audience smells authenticity, damn it, it's smarter than most producers will give it credit for being."

Roddenberry finished up our interview by telling me he had rejected suggestions of adding a "space cadet" or Lassie-type pet to the cast–suggestions the network had made in all earnestness. "The show has to stay on the straight-and-narrow spaceline it has designed for itself. It's definitely opened the door into the sci-fi genre, which is becoming more readily accepted by the public. The public is becoming conditioned to better quality sci-fi and this is evident in some movies coming out, 'The Illustrated Man' and 'Planet of the Apes.' I'll let 'Voyage to the Bottom of the Sea' and 'Lost in Space' continue to appeal to the juvenile mind. I'll let 'Star Trek' continue to contribute to adult entertainment and the maturity of science-fiction in general."

than #52 in the ratings, almost always beaten out by competing shows (even horrendously lousy ones like "Mr. Terrific" or mediocre ones like "The Iron Horse"), Nimoy had enjoyed incredible recognition, so unique was the character and his interpretation of the Vulcan. If you remembered anything about "Star Trek" after its cancellation, it was the Nimoy touch. It was the re-run episodes in the 1970s (on more than 140 stations worldwide) that would bring "Star Trek" its most popular following that ultimately resulted in a cult of fans labeled "Trekkies" or "Trekkers."

And they had pursued Nimoy with a vengeance – until all the out-of-control adulatory reached a saturation point.

As if to tell the whole world he'd had his fill of the Vulcan spaceman he wrote "I Am Not Spock" (Celestial Arts, 1975) to remind "Star Trek" fans and anyone else who happened to be reading that he was his own man, he was still Leonard Nimoy the actor. He could be a

# THE NEW (IMPROVED?) LEONARD NIMOY

*"Change is the essential process of all existence."* – Mr. Spock in "Let That Be Your Last Battlefield" (Stardate 5730.2)

Stardom is a finicky form of success for the human psyche. Fame is precious but also precarious. All performers dream of attaining celebrityhood and recognition in their days as aspiring neophytes or ingenues, but there is that old saying: watch out, you might get what you wish for. Handling stardom is far different from just wishing for it, as Nimoy had learned over 14 years.

Although "Star Trek" had only lasted three seasons on NBC and had never ranked higher

poet, he could be a renaissance man, he could be anything he wanted. But he did not have to continue to be Spock. Spock was a role in a defunct TV series and one that he wanted to see fade away as quickly as possible. The role had brought him recognition and fame and now he wanted to have a generic, non-Spock career out of it. But Spock refused to fade away or die after the book's publication. If anything, "I Am Not Spock" only fueled fans' needs for their star.

But "Star Trek" refused to die or even rest comfortably six-feet under in the syndication years and beyond. Scores of books covering every aspect of Gene Roddenberry's creation

Robert Wise, director of the first "Star Trek" feature film – it marked the beginning of the end for Gene Roddenberry.

reflected the zealous, undying attitude of fans. Thousands of these "Trekkies" were persistent in writing to Paramount to demand a new version in any form – movie, TV series, how about a set of books in Braille?

So it was that "Star Trek" lived on in re-runs and scores of fan conventions held all over America and England persisted. And Paramount became determined to cash in on its dormant property with a movie. Credit must be given to DeForrest Kelley, better known as Doctor Leonard "Bones" McCoy, for he was the first to suggest a movie version of "Star Trek" as far back as 1967, during the second season. His idea had been rejected by the studio on these grounds: "Whoever heard of a full-length movie based on a dead TV show?"

Despite the continuing success of "Star Trek," however, the movie version didn't come easy. There were false starts, cancellations and the squandering of $5 million on undelivered special effects before Doug Trumbull ("2001: A Space Odyssey") and John Dykstra ("Star Wars") were brought in to salvage the mess.

While Philip Kaufman had been the first choice for director, primarily because of his excellent remake of "Invasion of the Body Snatchers" in 1978, he and William Shatner had fallen out over story ideas and Kaufman had abandoned the project. Eventually Roddenberry settled on Robert Wise, whose contributions to cinema fantasy included two classics: "The Day the Earth Stood Still" (1951) and "The Haunting" (1963). Even the Aeronautics and Space Administration, including its Jet Propulsion Laboratory, was called in for advice in designing phasers, photon torpedoes, communicators and tricorders. Finally, at a reported cost of $40 million, in December 1979 "Star Trek–The

Motion Picture" streaked across the film Heavens. Box office was great but reviews were lukewarm, and the one question on the lips of fans was: Why had the well-remembered, beloved TV characters been largely ignored in favor of the hardware? A second question: Why had nonregulars Persis Khambatta (navigator Ilia) and Stephen Collins (Commander Willard Decker) been given more story to handle than the regulars?

My assignment that December was to interview Collins, who admitted to me he was not a great fan of the TV series and had been picked by Roddenberry because of his work in a film called "The Promise" opposite Kathleen Quinlan. After admitting he had little feeling for the TV version, he couldn't resist telling me of his great respect for Roddenberry. And for the next hour waxed enthusiastically about this "hero" as if he was the greatest fan of all.

Collins: "Gene cares tremendously about everything 'Star Trek' and he wanted to appeal to hardcore science-fiction fans as well as those not familiar with the TV series. He wanted this film to have a life of its own. Gene has a part of his mind that exists 300 years in the future. This was his attempt to portray the world as he'd like to see it. By nature, his concept is an optimistic one because it presupposes we're going to exist 300 years from now. He wrote a full-length history of

Taken on a day in December 1979 when Stephen Collins came to visit me on the "Creature Features" set to discuss his role as Captain Willard Decker in "Star Trek–The Motion Picture."

A Triumphant
Two-Hour Special
Stardate 3-28-1980

While I quoted from "The Trek of Leonard Nimoy," a book that didn't exist (except for a cover created by Jim Minton in KTVU's Art Department), Leonard Nimoy got over being upset and enjoyed himself immensely that afternoon during the taping of an honorary two-hour "Star Trek" special.

Decker's character, "which helped me in settling into the part and feeling at ease around actors who already knew their roles. I would look around and see this wonderful interrelating among the regulars. I believe these characters have made the show so popular for so long."

I would finally see Nimoy again a few weeks after the film's opening, on March 28, 1980, while he was in San Francisco doing the one-man play "Vincent: Story of a Hero." He would be quite different from the Nimoy of 1966, as demonstrated by the incident I have already described in which he balked at doing the show until I had dispersed a small group of fans gathered outside the TV station, one of whom from San Jose was constantly bugging him. Instead of a movie we played the two-part episode "The Menagerie" and it would be one of my favorite shows. I found Leonard to be the consummate professional, eager to cut

comedic promotion pieces with me and ready to talk about whatever I wanted to touch upon.

Nimoy's intensity and sincerity were as I remembered them from our first meeting on the "Star Trek" set in 1966. I had always sensed that acting was the center of his universe and he seemed to be one of the busiest of men. Since "Star Trek" he had completed two seasons as the master of disguise Paris on "Mission: Impossible," he had starred in the 1978 version of "Invasion of the Body Snatchers," he had done 18 weeks as the deductive Sherlock Holmes with the Royal Shakespearean Theater and he had appeared in sundry summer stock and regional theater. Not to mention writing five books that had included "I Am Not Spock" and a book of poetry.

Nimoy had devoted three years, off and on, to the staging of "Vincent," and he had turned it into a deeply emotional experience with a mixture of humor and pathos.

He had done his own personal research on Vincent Van Vogh while making (and narrating) an episode of the documentary series "In Search of . . ." in Europe.

"I discovered," said Nimoy, "that the Dutch painter had suffered epileptic seizures that had terrified him and yet he had still been able to paint as many as two masterpieces a day. He was a gifted and caring man even though some considered him a freak. I laugh and I cry when I do the play."

Another accomplishment had been "Star Trek–The Motion Picture" based on ideas taken by screenwriter Harold Livingston from two of the TV episodes: "The Doomsday

Machine" and "The Changeling." "There's a misunderstanding I want to clear up. Because I was the last to sign with Paramount to make the film, a lot of fans think I was holding out for more money or perhaps didn't want to do the film. None of that is true. As long ago as three years I was going to be involved. The rumors started flying because I was doing a play on Broadway, 'Equus,' when Paramount informed me that a TV series would start immediately. I was contracted for the play and had to say no. Then suddenly the series idea fell apart and the movie was on again. And then I was available."

Nimoy was in basic agreement with the critics: "The film was well-made technically with careful and precise set design. But personally I have a different taste in 'Star Trek' stories. If you were to ask me which episodes were my favorites, I would favor the ones that involve character rather than hardware."

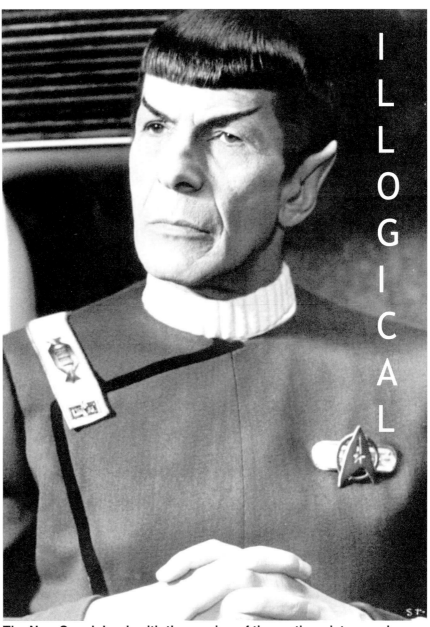

The New Spock Look with the coming of the motion picture series.

That criticism aside, Nimoy said he had felt very comfortable with the rest of the cast and about his place in the greater structure of "Star Trek."

"It was like we'd never stopped making episodes, as if the intervening years had never happened. I felt very much at home. I had a good feeling about being Spock again. In fact, I've written some ideas for Spock that I want to discuss with Gene and the writers. There are avenues not explored yet. Given the box-office take, there very likely will be another motion picture of perhaps even a TV series. I would be very much shocked and surprised if there was not.

"I think the most important thing about the followers and fans of 'Star Trek' right now is that you do an honest piece of work for them. They are entitled to the best. I take that very seriously. "I'm going to try and see to it there's good entertainment values in any 'Star Trek' work I do in the future." ❑

# WITNESS A UNIQUE VISION AT PARAMOUNT...

*"There are some things worth dying for."* – Captain Kirk in "Errand of Mercy" (Stardate 3201.7)

Spring, 1982. My flight from San Francisco arrives late at the Burbank Airport. There isn't time to get to the hotel in Beverly Hills where I'm supposed to meet the rest of the media who will then come by bus to Paramount Studios to attend a national media screening of "Star Trek II: The Wrath of Khan," the second feature in the movie series.

Good thing I'm late because it will give me, in a few minutes, the opportunity to witness a unique vision. The kind you never forget.

A cab gets me to Paramount ahead of everyone else so I'm alone as I stand in front of the studio screening theater. I suddenly realize that the nearby parking lot is where the Paramount Western Street used to be with its saloons, general stores and church. Torn down in 1979, the street had been used in scores of movies as well as the series "Bonanza" and "Little House on the Prairie." I had walked down that dusty street on many a visit.

As all these old memories wash over me, William Shatner arrives and stands alone at the unopened front door. He sees me waiting alone over by the corner and walks across to shake hands. He is soon joined by Leonard Nimoy, who throws his arms around Shatner as one greeting a long-lost friend. Their chatter reveals they haven't seen each other since filming ended late in 1981.

"Have you seen the finished cut?" Nimoy asks Shatner.

"No," says Shatner. "Have you?"

Nimoy shakes his head. No, nothing. He's seen nothing.

"Hey," says Shatner, "I wonder how it all turned out?"

Suddenly it hits me: these two science-fiction icons are as excited as any fan about seeing "Star Trek II." They are like two children standing in line at a department store, waiting to sit in Santa's lap. Like two kids seeing their first Martian. Their first UFO.

It's a strange feeling to see these two internationally known stars seem just like two more "Star Trek" fans waiting in a line outside a theater.

It was an exciting beginning to a two-day adventure of covering a major movie for media. This is the story that came out of it. So join me. . .

# ...AND STAND WITH KIRK AND SPOCK UNDER THE STARS

# "STAR TREK II": LAST VOYAGE OF MR. SPOCK?

**Hollywood**

THE LIGHTS in the sky are stars and, from places where no man has ever gone, they shine down on Paramount Studios. The smiling people emerging from the studio's screening theater have every reason to feel a sense of cosmic excitement. As the cast and film makers of "Star Trek II: The Wrath of Khan" they have just seen for the first time – in the company of press and friends – their $12 million epic space adventure.

"At last," comments sagacious, gentle-mannered DeForrest Kelley, known in some quarters as Dr. McCoy or Bones and respected by others as a self-appointed philosopher and self-named romanticist, "we've finally recaptured the values of the original TV series and lived up to its potential. This has been fulfilling for all of us, for doing exciting films and for having created this cult of fans. They and they alone are responsible for us being here. I think 'Star Trek' showed the youth of this country that there was an optimistic future out there. 'Star Trek' passed on a positive legacy for that future. It came in 1966 when the youth of this country was very confused. It was the hippie generation and the Vietnam War had to be contended with. What the youth of America finally saw was a universal federation. In 'Star Trek' there is hope and a place to go that is beyond the confines of our Earth."

DeForest Kelley saw in "Star Trek" the hope for the next generation.

"Wrath of Khan" is interstellar action at its purest, leaving strong impressions of its clean-lined spaceships locked in laser combat, and a deadly mind-controlling bug creature crawling into Ensign Chekov's ear. Even stronger are its human conflicts. At the center of these is Khan, a renegade Earthman with a psychotic obsession to destroy Captain Kirk. He screams his wrath across the galaxy with the memorable line: "I'll chase him [Kirk] round the moons of Nivia and round the Antares Maelstrom and round Perdition's flames." At the center of humanity are Kirk, Spock and McCoy discussing life, death and their fears of growing old; especially touching is Kirk fumbling with his bifocals as he reads "A Tale of Two Cities."

Later, at a "Star Trek" party in the Paramount commissary, the happy imagery reaches warp-drive velocity. Harve Bennett, having taken over the bridge control panel from Roddenberry, is looking distinguished, as a producer should . . . Jimmy Doohan, Scotty of the engine room, is unable to restrain a grin of triumph . . . Kirstie Alley, the most beautiful woman in the room,

**Where the hell was Gene Roddenberry?**

smiling warmly . . . William Shatner tells me this experience is "boggling my mind. We've gone from a cancelled TV series to two very expensive motion pictures and it's boggling my mind."

Standing over there, by the hors d'oeuvres table, director Nicholas Meyer is dressed in blue jeans, plaid shirt, black tie, loafers, emphasizing that his "Star Trek II" is so much better than the first . . . the room is aflush with a sense of achievement, of pending success . . . success even flushes the cheeks of second bananas George Takei and Nichelle Nichols, even if they had little to do with defeating Khan's wrath.

But something . . . no, someone . . . is missing from the party. Nowhere in sight is Gene Roddenberry, who created and masterminded the TV series, who produced and co-wrote the first film. That he had been listed in the credits simply as "Creative Consultant" smacked of dark, sinister forces at work. Had God forsaken His child? Or had the studio wrested power away from the Creator? It seemed an impossible thought that otherwise happy night, too sacrilegious to contemplate. The other life form missing from the party was Leonard Nimoy, or Mr. Spock. But his absence didn't seem so strange. Mr. Spock, you see, was dead.

# THE DEATH OF A HERO

*Heroes were created by the God of Adventure*
*And we the spectators were intended to cheer them to*
*   New victories.*
*Heroes are men and women sworn to excitement,*
*Citizens of a gallant kingdom.*
*Heroes are doers of deeds larger than life*
*Performing on the stages of our imagined spectacles.*
*Heroes are derring-do incarnate riding to us out of the*
*   Fog of action*
*Out of the mist of bold bravado.*
*Heroes were meant to be and we, spectators to*
*   Their noble deeds, were born*
*To dream of them as immortal, unstoppable,*
*   Incapable of feet of clay.*
*Heroes are life and its dramas exaggerated.*
*Heroes cannot be should not be must not ever be*
*Touched by the spectre of death.*
*Yet can it be that in some lost cold dark nebula of space*
*Where no hero has dared go before*
*That the fingers of death have touched one of our most*
*   Exalted heroes?*
*If it is so then the blackness of spacenight is falling darker*
*   Around us.*
*Spock is dead, his body poisoned by omega and gamma,*
*His new-dead corpse lies on Genesis, newborn planet.*
*It cannot be, it should not be, it must not ever be*
*For heroes are beings of action*
*Created by the Gods of Adventure to live . . .*
*Not to die . . .*

# CATCHING THE 'WRATH' FROM KHAN HIMSELF

*"I suppose most of us overlook the fact that even Vulcans aren't indestructible."*
– Captain Kirk in "Amok Time" (Stardate 3372.7)

Before death there must be life, and the life of the phenomenon of "Star Trek" is contrary to every rule in the book that regulates television. For what had ultimately failed on the NBC network during the 1960s in 89 episodes had suddenly shown up again on the radar during the 1970s. In 1979 "Star Trek–The Motion Picture" was greeted with criticism but criticism does not always stand in the way of popularity: there was nothing under the United Federation Heavens that could prevent the film from grossing $175 million worldwide.

In 1981 Paramount knew it was time to make another "Star Trek" feature, for fantasy and horror films were unabashedly accounting for almost 40 per cent of all box-office revenue. While the studio had turned to a member of the old guard, Robert Wise, for the first

Peer around the shoulder of "Khan" producer Harve Bennett and look for Gene Roddenberry – the creative force has to be there in the background . . . somewhere.

picture, it now turned to one of its own TV producers on the theory that he could bring his economic shortcuts to bear (a good TV producer must always find shortcuts to survive) and still produce a handsome product. The man who beamed down to take command was Harve Bennett. Turning out the TV shows "Rich Man, Poor Man," "Mod Squad" and "A Woman Called Golda" had taught him thrift and discipline. He knew the key to success with "Star Trek" was special effects and ultimately he turned to the man who had given a new state-of-the-art quality to movie trickery: George Lucas and his Marin County-based Industrial Light and Magic, a special effects house that would become world-famous.

But God-like figure Roddenberry was not to be Bennett's guiding light. Inspiration perhaps, but no more. That was an ironic fact, for Bennett knew Roddenberry very well and was an admirer of the late Gene L. Coon, who was responsible for many of the second season "Star Trek" scripts under Roddenberry's supervision. In his attitude he was reverent toward these two. "Star Trek," he believed, was one of a kind that had given inspiration to Lucas and Steven Spielberg. It was, according to Bennett, "their roots."

And just why was Roddenberry not more directly involved? "It was a decision made by Paramount that I had to honor," said Bennett, shrugging.

A member of the cast was more informative, asking not to be named. "There was too much money spent on the first film and someone had to be culpable. It was Gene. Gene loves the new picture, and his love for the series will always be. It's his baby, but let me tell you, he's very frustrated with the way he's being treated by Paramount." So, the Creator was stripped of rank and demoted to stand silently in his own Universe.

Bennett was far more comfortable talking about Ricardo Montalban. "I reran all the episodes of the series looking for ideas for a feature, and when I saw the '67 'Space Seed' I knew instantly that I wanted to have that episode's villain. Montalban conveyed a highly

intelligent but tragic man." Montalban had been fulfilling the fantasies of other people for the past six years on ABC's "Fantasy Island" as Mr. Rourke. When Montalban read the screenplay for "Wrath of Khan" by Jack B. Sowards, "I realized I was reading it with too much of Rourke in mind–after all, he's the only character I've played for five years. I needed to recapture the thoughts and mannerisms of the Khan role, so I asked Harve to send me a cassette copy of 'Space Seed.'

"I looked at it over and over, a dozen times, until I started to remember how I had played Khan. He was there before me again, the same man 17 years later with the same fingerprints but now obsessed with vengeance against Captain Kirk."

An additional key was given to Montalban in the form of a copy of Herman Melville's "Moby Dick," sent to him by director Meyer on the eve of filming. "Inside, Nicholas had inscribed something special to me: 'Welcome, Ahab . . . Lear . . . Khan.' That gave me what I needed – the obsession of Ahab

**Ricardo Montalban as Khan: The obsession of Captain Ahab, the tragedy of King Lear.**

and the tragedy of Lear. And now I could soar as an actor." Through the universe he soared . . .

Jimmy Doohan, never one to hold back any thoughts that might be critical of fellow actors or not, was willing to go on the record: "I feel empathy for Gene because I know how much pain I'd feel if the torch was ripped out of my hand. He told me he's coming to peace with himself about what's happened. And I'll tell you this: It wasn't Gene's fault about the first picture and it wasn't Wise's fault either. It was the damn executives at their committee meetings. They're the ones responsible for this tragedy."

Darkness may hide from us the reasons why Roddenberry was denied giving additional help to his child. But there is no darkness hiding the film's most memorable climax: the nuclear-poisoning death of Spock. His death was even written about in the Wall Street Journal long before the film went before the cameras.

Ask Leonard Nimoy about Spock's death and his eyes narrow to slits and his ears become pointed and he laughs suddenly, as if startled. *"Spock's death?"*

Did he have a hand in death's coming? "To talk about Spock's death is pretty grim stuff, but yes, we had a lot of conversations about it and how it should be done and what the impact would be. It seemed a nervous, dangerous thing to do. Then I became excited about the possibilities for the future, because there are possibilities. If I had to say a few last words over Spock, they would be: 'I'll see you soon.' " Nimoy made no effort to hide the fact Paramount has already discussed a third "Star Trek" movie with him. Possibilities indeed.

**Jimmy Doohan was never one to hold back a critical thought in his head and he always stood proudly in Roddenberry's corner.**

How can there be life after death? In "Wrath of Khan," Spock's sarcophagus is ejected into space and voyages to Heaven – specifically a newly-rejuvenated planet named Genesis. The Garden of Eden atmosphere suggests a biological metamorphosis might be taking place. But even if Spock is never resurrected, there are the encouraging words of Dr. McCoy, uttered on the bridge as Spock's corpse whisks through space: "As long as we remember him, he will never die."

Whether the Vulcan lives or dies, Nimoy is not restrained in his feeling for the film: "This is a movie that needed to be made to fulfill everyone's expectations. You're looking at a very, very happy actor. Because of Spock I've had tremendous challenges in stage, films, TV, writing. I have no complaints about what Spock has done for me." He has come a long distance since writing "I Am Not Spock."

William Shatner is more protective of Spock. "Who said Spock is dead? You say Spock is dead! You don't know if Spock is dead or not. It's still up in the air and people have to see the film to make their own decisions. It's been handled with great delicacy and great taste and the mystery is still there."

Shatner prefers to talk about the film itself: "It's been satisfying for me to explore the human condition within the context of 'Star Trek.' We've enlarged our base and touched the audience the way the best episodes of the series did. We've returned to the chemistry and methods that made the TV show so popular."

Nicholas Meyer, although one of the smartest Hollywood directors I have ever met, has not done a lot since his involvement with the "Star Trek" series in the 1990s. He originally wrote "Star Trek II" as "The Undiscovered Country," a Shakespearean phrase to describe the land of death, reportedly in just two weeks, after others had mucked around with the idea for years.

Ironically, the "Wrath of Khan" actor with the least to do in the film is its most active salesman away from the cameras. George Takei, who portrays Sulu the helmsman, is constantly popping up at conventions and making appearances to keep the old "Trek" values "young and alive." His pleasure with the film was uncontainable as he joked about a spin-off to be called "Captain Sulu" and told me how the characters on the bridge of the USS Enterprise "represent all people–even an alien is in a command position. 'Star Trek' proposes all things wonderful about us in contrast to hate, avarice, vice. All our hopes alive in another time and dimension."

The two members of the cast who are probably closest, and socialize the most, are Walter Koenig (Chekov) and Doohan (Scotty). They are also the most volatile in expressing a desire to work more. Whatever it is they are looking for as actors, they have not found enough of it. "I'm not content in the slightest," said Doohan. "I'll never be content. I want to act and I'm not getting the opportunity." Koenig nodded his head as if to say the same thing.

"I came as a fabled blessing," said Nicholas Meyer, who was chosen by Bennett to direct after Bennett had enjoyed his only previous directing assignment, the time-travel fantasy "Time After Time." (Before that Meyer's onc big success was his novel "The Seven Per Cent Solution," a best-selling Sherlock Holmes pastiche that was on the New York Times list for 40 weeks.)

Meyer, chomping on a cigar in producer's fashion, had few sweet things to say about Paramount management. "If I have any scars, and I do, they came from fighting with studio problems. What I call bullshit problems. Roddenberry was not involved – he was already out of the picture by the time I arrived. I wasn't a 'Star Trek' fan before I arrived but I became a convert and ended up loving all the characters."

There will no doubt be more full-length films but do not anticipate a series, forewarned Bennett.

"If we tried to bring 'Star Trek' back as a series tomorrow [on one of the major networks], it would fail because of its specialness." That specialness, he added, "appeals to the intellect and the imagination of its greatest and most supportive fans. It would attract an audience of about 10 million. Only half of what would be needed to survive the competition of 'The Dukes of Hazzard.'"

*I was ill and couldn't make the Hollywood junket for "Star Trek 3: The Search for Spock," but Leonard Nimoy was kind enough to send a telephone message to say that he was sorry I was laid up and couldn't make it. However, I was very available for the next entry in the series:*

# A WHALE OF AN ADVENTURE WITH NIMOY

**"Mr. Spock really has gone where no man has gone before."** – Dr. "Bones" McCoy in "Star Trek IV: The Voyage Home" (Stardate 1986)

### Hollywood

McCoy might have intended flippancy in his most current assessment of the strange emotionless side to Mr. Spock, but there's a serious interpretation too, one that pertains to more than just the Vulcan nature of the USS Enterprise's science officer. The "Star Trek" characters and the ideology behind the series have ascended in the past six years to take their places as major figures in 20th century mythology and pop culture. In the pantheon of science fiction, James T. Kirk, Spock, McCoy, Sulu, Chekov and Uhura have found an honored place.

Indeed, "Star Trek" has gone where no other show in television history could go – surviving for almost ten years by reruns and the "Trekkies" of fandom who kept the memory alive through feverish conventions attended by thousands. Since 1979 the series has maintained an even more heightened popularity via a combination of the ubiquitous one-hour episodes, still in syndicated reruns, and a series of big-budget Paramount movie epics, the fourth of which now bodes well for a continued longevity. It could lead one day to "Star Trek 25: The Geriatric Adventures."

"Star Trek IV: The Voyage Home," which was rewritten one final time by producer Harve Bennett and Nicholas Meyer, director of the second "Star Trek" feature, is pure "Star Trek" in the TV sense–dealing with the speculative ideas of the series as they affect the Kirk-Spock team. And it is pure "Star Wars" in the film sense, featuring the hardware, aliens and warp-drive of interstellar travel. It blends these elements into a satisfying whole, but this time without the sadistic violence and catastrophic destruction that earmarked "The Wrath of Khan" and "The Search for Spock." This is the closest thing to a family version, with the PG-rating being imposed for a few swear words that are actually amusing in their context.

It has also reached a new level of comedy ("Spock is not working on all thrusters," Dr. McCoy adds to his Spockian digs) and indulges in some whimsical historic satire that has more than a ring of truth ("judging from the pollution levels in the atmosphere, we're in the latter half of

Leonard Nimoy came home to roost as the director and mastermind behind the fourth film in the series. It would become one of his crowning achievements.

the 20<sup>th</sup> Century," time-traveling Spock observes with a straight face, while another crew member adds that ours is a "primitive and paranoid culture").

If any one person was all optimism about this fourth "Star Trek" film, it was Leonard Nimoy, who had spent two years masterminding the project—from conceiving the initial concept to portraying Spock to directing the mammoth $23 million epic. Bearded, wearing a blue turtleneck sweater and conveying an air that he was at peace with being Mr. Spock, Nimoy acknowledged the lack of violence as something he had intended from the start. "We'd just done two films with a lot of violence, with real bad bad guys, Sturm und Drang, death and dying. I'd been a party to all that but I wanted this film to be particularly different in tone. The worst thing that happens in this film: I pinch a punk rocker on the neck because he won't turn down his radio."

**The fourth "Star Trek: The Voyage Home" traveled back in time to modern-day San Francisco where a newfangled thing called a "computer" was to be seen and put to good use by Jimmy Doohan, Alex Henteloff and DeForest Kelley.**

Was he worried that some of the humorous dialogue might alienate fans? "Absolutely not. The fans are waiting for explosions of fun. Look, we had no humor in the first film and only touches in the second and third. I wanted to explore the humor within the characters and I wanted to give them a lighter tone by giving them a comedy caper to pull off. I brought 20 years of Spock to this picture and if anyone understands those fans . . . "

That "caper" involves the crew warping around the sun fast enough to return to the 20<sup>th</sup> Century in order to find two humpback whales that could save the world from destruction in the 23<sup>rd</sup> Century. "I wanted to bring time travel to this story so we could return to modern Earth and have a change of scenery—the other pictures were almost entirely shot in studios. And I wanted that place to be San Francisco because that's where the Federation is headquartered and I wanted viewers to see the roots and geography of that. But I needed a reason.

"I got to thinking perhaps there's a craft or technique of today that's been lost in the 23<sup>rd</sup> Century. Do we come back to find a medicine? But a medicine isn't very exciting, is it? Then I read a book, 'Biofeed,' which predicts that by the 1990s we will lose 10,000 species off the face of the planet, some we will never even know existed. It's called the Keystone Species Theory, in which if certain species are lost, we have an ecological ripple that affects all time to come. Like a house of cards collapsing.

"And I thought: what if a 45-ton whale, an extinct species in the 23<sup>rd</sup> Century, had to be brought back in time? And what if an alien probe played the 'song' of the whale, a mystery Earthlings will never understand. After all, there are mysteries intended to remain mysteries. Look at '2010,' which tried to answer the unanswered questions of '2001: A Space Odyssey.' That film crashed."

Nimoy continues to be amazed at the durability of "Star Trek." One of the reasons, he felt, is that "the stories have always emphasized a hopeful and positive view of our future, without resorting to pessimistic science fiction, which personally I don't care for . . . Each generation of viewers makes two discoveries: first the spaceships and the aliens and Spock's ears, and then seeing that same episode years later and realizing there was always a solid idea behind it. I think we have finally come to terms with 'Star Trek' and made a film that explores the characters, tells a strong story with wide appeal and answers all the needs of the hardcore fans."

It would be my last meeting with Leonard Nimoy.

But there had been other parts of the "Star Trek" story I had covered over the years.

# SO NOW MEET THE CAPTAIN OF THE UNIVERSE

## MAN'S ULTIMATE MISSION: FIND OTHER LIFE FORMS ... AND THE HUNK TO CARRY OUT THE SEARCH -- STARFLEET'S CAP'N KIRK

LIGHTS WINK red, green and yellow on the intricate control panel. Weird electronic noises–beeps, hums, buzzes–fill the bridge of the USS Enterprise as an electric-eye panel slides away to admit the captain, a handsome, alert young officer clad in a tight-fitting uniform of yellow velour and black space trousers. A *zzzzzz* flows from the comm board and the captain turns, his face graven with the weight of command. He speaks swiftly and confidently: *"Bridge to Security 054. Go to capacity alert decks 5 through 13. All sensors and probing scanners to become fully operational. All phaser guns to be set and locked on target. Mark and move. Kirk out."* Then to the navigator: *"Mr. Sulu, set a course for Earth Observation Post on Tarsus IV, stellar coordinates five six five, three zero five. Proceed all ahead full at Warp Factor eight."*

It is a world two hundred years into our future, depicting the kind of routine one could expect to find at the command center of a mammoth starship cruising through the Universe on a five-year search for new worlds and new forms of alien life. Call it man's ultimate mission. This "center of command" is a recurring focal point of action on "Star Trek," the most off-the-beaten-orbit offering of any TV season in memory.

Thanks to the use of a standardized set of principles basic to the realm of science fiction, life on board the 300,000-ton spacecraft has become a reality within a greater fantasy. The vessel's sophisticated weaponry and gadgetry function in a consistent, limited way and therefore have come to seem as real to its time as machine guns and rockets do to ours.

James T. Kirk, Captain, Space Service, Starfleet Command, has become a believable personality as portrayed by William Shatner. Because Shatner has worked to make him a well-fleshed individual, Kirk has emerged a firm symbol of authority who makes mind-boggling decisions with the calm efficiency and certainty of a man accustomed to moving through space at 186,000 miles per second.

Recently on a Desilu soundstage, Shatner was completing an episode set on a planet in a distant galaxy which houses the vortex of time, a gimmick to permit traveling into the past. The dialogue was cloaked in the pseudo-scientific jargon of the Enterprise–with references to memory bank tapes, body-analyzing apparatus, the teleporter room (where crew members are "energized" and "beamed" from the ship to alien places) and security alert numbers. Everything about Shatner seemed to be fast-paced, his train of thought sharp, his speech fast-flowing. He was eager to compare his opinions of certain "Star Trek" episodes with those of others, and his interest perked up noticeably when his knowledge of sci-fi was called upon.

This is the handsome, dynamic William Shatner I will always remember from those early episodes: Intense, sincere, deeply and emotionally involved with the "Star Trek" adventures that had been conceived by the show's creator Gene Roddenberry.

"This is not a device of the future," joked Shatner, pointing to a towel wrapped around one of his hands, its interior crammed with ice cubes. "We were doing a fight sequence this morning and I think I sprained it. I'll have it X-rayed later today to find out. Isn't it marvelous, the inventions man has today?"

One word describes it:
## "ENERGIZE!"

And the inventions of the Enterprise? "Yes, those are marvelous too, but you must suspend disbelief to appreciate them. For our reality is not your reality. Our reality is a turbo-lift that goes instantly to any level of the Enterprise. Our reality is the teleportation of matter. Our reality is the crossing of space at the speed of light. Besides asking for that suspension, we assume a lot of science-fiction knowledge on the part of our viewers—we consider our audience highly sophisticated in terms of what future centuries will be like. We have had no precedent to follow, so we've established our own formula as we've gone. Dare I say we made it up as we went along?

"We've been very fortunate. Despite some initially clumsy footwork, and despite the fact some writers used the inevitability of destiny instead of wits to get the spacemen out of some untenable situations, we have been renewed and will be back next season."

Interplay among the main characters "has resulted in a number of fascinating crew members, the most predominant being Mr. Spock, he with the uplifted eyebrows. Spock is my main foil. He often suggests I disown my compassion in times of duress. Despite his lack of humanity, it is with the help of his log and strength that I can solve certain dilemmas. Kirk and Spock respect each other and this allows them to function as men of action, unhampered by any petty jealousies."

As for Mr. McCoy, "he's a humanitarian always appealing to Kirk's basic instincts of decency. Thus Kirk is torn between these factors—cold logic (Spock) and humanity (McCoy)—and must take a stand somewhere in the middle."

Picture proof that we all age gracefully: Shatner as he looked when the series began in 1966 (above) and Shatner as he looked (below) when the movie series was in full warp drive.

The Canadian-born Shatner has undergone a considerable change of pace since his early Shakespearean training with the National Repertory Theater of Ottawa. He later appeared on Broadway in a number of diverse plays (including a 300-year-old Christopher Marlowe drama) and eventually had many parts in live TV shows in the 1950s, most notably in "The Defender," a court room thriller that eventually became the pilot for the E.G. Marshall series "The Defenders." Opposite Ralph Bellamy and Steve McQueen, Shatner seemed destined for greatness even then. (Look for it in DVD as "Studio One: The Defender" from Video Service.)

He had starred in one previous series, "For the People," which he felt was more "esthetic and philosophical" than entertaining, and recently was seen in Leslie Nielsen's "Incubus," the first film to be made entirely in Esperanto, the Universal language. Knowing some science-fiction writers personally (William Nolan, Harlan Ellison, Robert Bloch, Richard Matheson) Shatner feels they are a strange lot but nonetheless he admires their contributions to fantastic literature. One of his favorites (and a close friend as well) was Charles Beaumont, who recently died at the age of 38 of a rare nerve disease. In 1961 Shatner and Beaumont had traveled into the Deep South to make "The Intruder," a controversial film about racial discrimination that received a foreign film festival award in 1962.

The film was never put into general release but it was later exploited under the title "I Hate Your Guts," which was obviously a sore point with Shatner, for he became suddenly quiet for a full minute, as though reflecting on this effrontery with some inner grievance.

"Beaumont reflects what 'Star Trek' is about. Because like no previous generation, we have a chance to learn the answers to questions that sci-fi poses. We can ask 'Is there life on other worlds? Are flying saucers real?' and expect an answer in our lifetime. In a way, science-fiction tries to tell us what history is going to be like. It tells us about fiction tomorrow today as though it were yesterday.

"There's a cliche that applies perfectly here. The human race is limited only by its imagination. The same is true of 'Star Trek.'"

SHATNER was back with a kind of personal vengeance in 1988 with the release of "Star Trek V: The Final Frontier." Even during the premiere of "Star Trek IV: The Voyage Home" Shatner had told me he had already been selected to direct the next film, and the way he said it I sensed there might have been more than a touch of rivalry going on now that Nimoy had directed the third and fourth episodes, and Shatner had directed nothing. The spirit of competition has always been strong in Shatner, a man who has always allowed himself to be seen as driven and ambition when he isn't spoofing himself in TV commercials. As for directing, he had helmed 12 episodes of his cop series "T.J. Hooker" so he wasn't a complete amateur.

## SECONDARY SHIPBOARD CHARACTERS . . . BUT NOT TO BE FORGOTTEN

They were as important as the stars of "Star Trek" and they have left lasting impressions on generations of viewers. George Takei (below) will always be remembered as the helmsman Sulu; Nichelle Nichols (bottom left) was the first to prove that a communications officer of the future could look good in a miniunfirm; and Walter Koenig (bottom right) brought to the show the concept that even a Russian could work his way up to become an assistant navigator and aspiring executive officer.

He had first convinced Paramount to let him direct, and then he had cinched the deal by sending a memo to Harve Bennett: "The USS Enterprise and her crew go in search of God." Paramount had been convinced, but Trekkies weren't so sure. Rumors of all kinds began to circulate that the project was off on the wrong foot, that the script was weak, that scenes of Captain Kirk climbing El Capitan in Yosemite National Park were laughable. While the film tended to be well received

**Shot around 1991, during the making of "Star Trek VI: The Undiscovered Country," this group pose in which all the cast regulars look great represents the nearing of the end. This was the last film exclusively featuring the original characters. In 1994, with "Star Trek: Generations," the gang would make its last feature film sharing the spotlight with characters from the TV sequel "Star Trek: The Next Generation." But what a great ride they had enjoyed on the USS Enterprise.**

by fans, its box office was never as good as Paramount had hoped for–and it was judged a lesser entry in the series.

Nevertheless, listening to Shatner describe how he did it was another "Star Trek" moment. "I've always been fascinated by people who believe God talks to them and why God would choose that individual over someone else," he told me, ensconced in his Beverly Hills hotel room prior to the film's opening. "If I were an entity who crashed my UFO in a Florida swamp, I'd want to be talking to the White House, not to an ordinary individual. That's what provoked my idea of 'Star Trek Looking for God.'"

Shatner credited Nimoy with paving the way for him to direct. "Leonard, after 'Wrath of Khan,' really didn't want to do the series anymore. He'd had enough, but Paramount snagged him by letting him direct. So I decided to stick my neck out, even though I also realized I ran the risk of getting fired with my rather aggressive stance, but I was willing to take that risk."

**My favorite "Star Trek" moment was the night in 1982 I hosted a 2-hour special dedicated to "Star Trek" and the release of "The Wrath of Khan." I had interviews with all the personalities and felt great.**

Unable to get the writer of his choice, Shatner wrote 14 pages of looking for God and Harve Bennett liked it. "But then Harve decided he didn't want to produce more 'Star Trek' movies and fell by the wayside. I was devastated. I needed Harve as producer and friend. So I set out to talk him into doing it. I wanted this to be a joyous time, I told him. I felt I was too old to face the risk of having idiotic fights with a strange new producer.

"I promised Harve I'd enjoy this project more than any other. Because I wanted it to be the most rewarding moment in my career. At first he was adamant at doing no more 'Star Trek' movies . . . But finally I convinced him. Harve and I started talking about how we felt about God and the Afterlife, deep questions between friends.

"We concluded that God exists in the heart, and we struck a new rapport and sensitivity toward the idea." ■

***There is one "Star Trek" story left to tell. It is the story of the most important person ever connected to "Star Trek" because without her the show would never have existed. This woman was once considered the funniest lady in Hollywood, and even after her death she is still the funniest lady of all. I can hear her up there, laughing. So now meet . . .***

## *THE QUEEN OF THE UNIVERSE*

# SHE SINGLE-HANDEDLY SAVED 'STAR TREK' FROM CERTAIN DISINTEGRATION —THE REAL REASON WHY ALL OF YOU FANS SHOULD LOVE LUCY

The Beverly Hills home of Lucille Ball and Gary Morton at 1000 North Roxbury Drive, where one fateful night in the summer of 1975 we met Lucy and two surprise guests—and learned the truth behind "Star Trek." Below, Lucy and first husband Desi Arnaz on the day in 1957 when they bought RKO Radio Pictures and turned it into Desilu, a history-making TV factory. Hollywood and TV were changed forever.

*"Worlds may change, galaxies disintegrate, but a woman always remains a woman."*
– Captain Kirk in "The Conscience of the King" (Stardate 2818.9)

AUNTIE MAME (or Lucille Desiree Ball, whichever you prefer) strolls with theatrical decadence into the backyard of her Beverly Hills mansion, made soft and bluish by the late afternoon light and the chlorine water of a free-form rock swimming pool. She flicks ashes from her cigarette with an air of disdain, like someone flipping off the Surgeon-General, and sips a martini just handed her by a bartender stationed at a nearby makeshift bar. "Boy," she says, carefully tasting the martini, then stirring it with her olive stick, "did I need that."

Lucy has had a hard day at the studio, as they say in Hollywood, but she's not too tired to face a handful of gooey-eyed entertainment writers, gathered from a score of states in the union to hear the queen of comedy discuss two brand-new TV specials that she is co-producing for CBS-TV for the 1975-76 season with her husband of the moment, Gary Morton. (There is a husband from another glorious moment, Desi Arnaz, but he is nowhere in sight.)

A long-sleeve blouse of purple-green-red, a three-tiered necklace hanging to her waistline and dazzling ornaments on her wrists clash for one's attention, but the eye goes immediately to the most famous face in television. The face that first made history back in the early '50s with the most popular show of the time, and the face that continues to predominate the viewing habits of millions who perennially return to reruns of "I Love Lucy."

Because she has driven straight from the studio, Lucy is still wearing a black wig and heavy theatrical make-up. Remarkably, she has retained her youthful figure and still knows how to show it off; this evening the lower half is sinuously encased in tight-fitting slacks.

Sure, Lucy looks tired and there are the unavoidable traces of aging which her make-up people constantly fight against, but this is a 64-year-old who is warm and receptive and pleasantly kookie and urban and an extrovert who greets each newspaper reporter with eyes that sparkle with curiosity. She even pauses to kiss her husband, Mr. Morton, as though they have been separated for a long while. The smack resounds across the backyard. Morton, a chef's cap sagging atop his head, turns and goes back to the barbecue pit to cook burgers and hotdogs for the reporters.

A poodle named Ginger dances at Lucy's feet, constantly demanding complete attention and unwilling to settle for anything less. Lucy does her best to ignore Ginger to keep the conversation going but one can tell she wishes she could give Ginger more scratches on the top of her little head and goofy-voiced mutterings of reassurance.

This is the Lucy I remember from 1975, holding a cigarette and putting on a comedic pseudo-sophistication air–but she had her serious moments too.

Finally it's time for why the reporters have come–to discuss the new Lucille Ball TV shows which she is now filming back to back–and she plunks into a deck chair, flicking a long stem of ash into a tray labeled "Auntie Mame," a souvenir from her recent movie portrayal of the exuberant sophisticate in an updated musical version (never as good as Rosalind Russell's in the 1958 original).

Neither of these offbeat offerings, she claims, is a variety show, neither is a straight situation comedy the likes of "The Lucy Show" or "Here's Lucy," her follow-ups to "I Love Lucy."

One special, "What Now, Catherine Carter?" will co-star Art Carney. The second show will feature three vignettes co-starring Jackie Gleason. Neither, she emphasizes, is an outright comedy. "I don't want to do any more Lucy TV comedy series. I've had too many seasons of that. The people can have me that way in reruns for the next hundred years. If I'm going to do something, I want it to be different. Gary is producing these shows and refused to put them on tape. He feels too many productions on tape look like high school plays, so we're making them like motion pictures with a single camera." Morton, who's standing over the barbecue, gives Lucy a little wave, as if to thank her for getting the mention. She might have added that it was

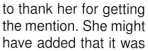

I can imagine these as the faces Lucy made when they tried to tell her how to run her studio when she was chief of Desilu.

# THE DAY THEY TOLD LUCY TO CANCEL 'STAR TREK' AND SEND IT TO HELL . . .

her first husband, Desi, who came up with the idea of using film in the early 1950s, thereby assuring the syndication of "I Love Lucy" all over the world for decades to come. And assuring enough money to allow him and Lucy to buy a film studio in 1957, called RKO Radio Pictures. Ironically, RKO had been where Lucy had worked as an ingenue contract player in the late 1930s.

After she and Desi divorced in 1960, Desi eventually sold out his interest in the studio. One morning Lucy drove through the studio gate to realize she was now the major stock holder and chief on the board of directors. She would spend the next seven years running Desilu.

I study Lucy in the diminishing light, curious about how this redhead not only had the most successful TV series of all time but had been a major Hollywood figurehead, making decisions that would in retrospect seem monumentally historic. "I never wanted to run a studio," she says in response to my query, "I hated having to do all that terrible stuff. I hated making decisions. Trying to balance budgets. Because I didn't want money to get on top of the fun of a show. I love acting and don't want to put anybody out of work. God knows I've had my ups and downs in this town. But you know what? All I ever really wanted to be was a mother and raise my children in peace. And act. Do all the funny stuff. That's what I loved. Acting. Being funny. And the kids. I loved raising those kids. Forget all that studio stuff."

Nevertheless, I remind her, it was Desilu that created "The Untouchables." It was Desilu that created "Mission: Impossible." And, I have to add, it was Desilu that created and first produced "Star Trek."

And did you know that fun-loving Lucy got caught up in the center of a firestorm in deepest space? In the center of a creative meltdown? For during the pre-production phases of "Star Trek" the studio executives were having trouble in controlling Gene Roddenberry and estimated Desilu stood to lose $65,000 on each episode, should the series find its place in the NBC line-up.

Therefore, it was recommended to Lucy one faithful day in early 1966 that she cancel both "Star Trek" and Mission: Impossible." *Dump them, Lucy, before it's too late. They're going to become the most costly productions imaginable. You're headed for the poorhouse.* If Lucy didn't cancel these shows, she was told, *the studio faced the likelihood of bankruptcy.* I envisioned Lucille Ball trapped in the center of these executives, feeling the tug-of-war between creativity and financing. Finally she shrugged and told her executives to go ahead with both series. *Go ahead with "Star Trek."*

Lucy takes a final sip of her martini and breaks the spell.

I am back to reality, in the back yard of Lucille Ball.

"Star Trek" is still, at that moment, unfulfilled history.

Nevertheless, I have to know. I have to ask. Lucy, if everyone told you not to do it, why did you do it? Why did you green light "Star Trek"?

She looks at me with a "Who cares" look. *Boy, are you dumb.* "You really wanna know?"

I nod, remembering all those interviews on the "Star Trek" set. Meeting Nimoy. Shatner. Roddenberry. The excitement of watching that first episode aired in 1966.

"It was because I'd once worked at the very studio I now owned. RKO had me under contract. Only one day I came to the

Lucille Ball with Red Skelton in her 1943 MGM comedy "Du Barry Was a Lady." The other red thing on the set, when she wasn't wearing the wig above, was her hair.

studio to find out my contract hadn't been renewed. I felt terrible. I felt awful. I cried. I thought my career was over. Of course, it wasn't, but it was the memory of the pain that I had felt that day. And now they were urging me to cancel 'Star Trek.' But I was remembering that pain. How badly I'd felt back then. So, and this really upset all the executives, I didn't have the courage to tell all those people that they were gonna be fired. Whatever the financial consequences. There was no way I could say no. And 'Star Trek' was put on the production table against all their advice and wisdom."

Yes, without Lucy there would never have been a "Star Trek."

Ginger, with yellow ribbons entwined in her hair, rolls over at Lucy's feet, seeking more attention; Lucy reaches down and scratches the upturned tummy. "And now," she says, putting down her empty martini glass, "I've got a surprise for you." She makes a sweeping motion with her arm, as though someone is about to make a grand entrance. And someone does.

Anybody can see that it's Art Carney.

Carney is fresh from the set of "Won Ton Ton: The Dog That Saved Hollywood" (a comedy that would come back to haunt all those who had made it) as he strolls toward Lucy. He shakes reporters' hands but he doesn't smile. He makes no attempt to be friendly. In fact, he looks preoccupied, as if he wished to be somewhere else. For some reason, at 56, he looks older than one might expect–perhaps it's the failing light or maybe it's the dark glasses he's wearing. He gives Lucy a kiss and asks: "Am I a good kisser or not?" He finally allows a minimal smile. He sits by the side of the swimming pool.

"I'm a better kisser," replies Lucy, informing the reporters that Art is hard of hearing and they will have to speak up. Someone asks him about the Hollywood producer he plays in "Won Ton Ton" but Lucy swings her arm like she wants to hit the reporter. "Stop asking questions about his movie and start asking questions about my TV specials. This is my home. This is my party." The way she says it, she means business. Nothing funny about this Lucy. No twinkle in her eyes as she asks for another martini. Ginger barks, as if to scold Lucy. Lucy baby-talks back to Ginger. *Coochi coochi coo. Goopsie poopsie.*

Carney sits in the gloom and doesn't say much. His preoccupation has carried him away into an unknown world that only he knows exists. He stares out across the swimming pool as if there is no one else in the back yard. Nobody asks any more questions about "Won Ton Ton."

Suddenly Lucy sweeps back her arm again and says another surprise is approaching. An "ah" leaps from the mouths of two female reporters and the male reporters all look up from their drinks. Someone drops a ballpoint pen and stops taking notes. Ginger dances with joy.

The new guest is walking up the driveway. Anyone can see that it's Jackie Gleason.

Gleason passes through pools of light as he approaches the group, looking as if he had just stepped out of a haberdashery shop. His gray suit is tailor fit, adhering to a body that must be a solid 210 pounds. The striped tie complements him perfectly; there is a handkerchief stuffed into the breast pocket and a red carnation shoved into the lapel. Gleason's face is well-tanned and the hair and mustache suavely in place. It appears he's recently lost weight but he still has that rotund look we associate with Ralph Kramden on "The Honeymooners." Or The Poor Soul or Reggy van Gleason III of the 1950s TV series. Or Minnesota Fats of his 1961 movie hit, "The Hustler."

He pauses, sizing up each individual, then he proclaims: "*Mmmmm, you're a good group.*" Gleason and Lucy kiss. Someone makes the crack that maybe Carney does it better. "Yeah," says Gleason, "Carney has a kisser all right." He whirls toward the man manning the makeshift bar. "Where's the man with the wrinkled apron? It's drinking time. Bring me a single double, triple time."

For a while Carney and Gleason talk about "The Honeymooners" days. You'd like to see Carney

The sidebar text reads: WAS THE SAME DAY LUCY TOLD THEM WHERE TO STUFF IT

leap up, shout "Hiya Ralphie!" and rush to the frig to steal a snort of millk. But he stays seated and stays sedate and distant. Not even Gleason can cheer him up. What comes out is reminiscent talk, nostalgia-hour conversation. Audrey Meadows, what ever happened to her? Ah, she's married to some millionaire now. Making a bundle off oil.

"I'm making scale," says Carney, looking at his feet. One doubts he means that.

"You made that Oscar too, Art, and you deserved it. You worked a lot of years to make that Oscar." Gleason is talking about "Harry and Tonto," a 1973 feature that brought Carney the best actor award. Oddly, Carney says nothing, gazing into nothingness.

"Hell, we like movies," continues Gleason, "because we're show-offs. Anyone who comes on being humble, that's phony. How can you command big salaries and make big demands and be humble. Hell, I was never humble a day in my life."

At the side of Lucy's swimming pool in 1975: Jackie Gleason, cocktail in hand, hovers above all others, including my wife Erica, Lucy and Art Carney. It was the kind of night that most people would never forget.

Ginger, the poodle that loves Lucy, sniffs at Gleason's highball glass. "No, bad dog," scolds Lucy. Gleason scowls. "Nothing worse than a drunken poodle. Keep that dog sober, Lucy."

Darkness falls over Beverly Hills, but not over Lucy and Jackie, who light up next to the pool in deck chairs to discuss the art of comedy. "Anybody can play dykes and gays to get a laugh," says Gleason. "Yeah," replies Lucy, "but few can tell a good solid joke."

"Our shows," says Gleason, "they had believable premises. The people were believable. Ralph Kramden's apartment was run down. You believed in those people. They weren't rich, they didn't have a Brady Bunch mansion like you have, Lucy."

"I won't go back to series TV," vows Lucy. "There's too much realism in TV today. What people need more of is escapism. Comedy. Real entertainment."

"Then you should go back and give them that," says Gleason. "Who else can give it to them like you do? I don't want to go back because I'm too damned disciplined. I stick by discipline and that makes working too demanding." Lucy's silence suggests she's thinking it over.

"Listen," says Gleason, "I'd go back if I could play Joe the Bartender. I could do that standing on my head. But I wouldn't want to do a sit-com and have to learn a new script every week. I'd hate like hell to get stuck in a rut, no matter how golden it was."

I ask Gleason where some of his catchphrases originated. The ones he always used on his Saturday night show: *"How sweet it is . . . and away we go."*

It's a question he loves to answer and bursts out immediately: "Back in my New York days, I used to take the guys out drinking to Toots Shor's, our favorite watering hole. We'd line up at the bar and belt them down. Toots always let me sign the check so when the bill came, I'd hold it up and say *'How sweet it is,'* and then pay up. Then we'd be in Toots' drinking until all hours and then someone would suggest we hit some other spot so I'd say *'And away we go!'* Meaning finish your drink, we're out of here, we're going somewhere else for another belt." Later these little expressions became naturals. Once we were doing 'Honeymooners' and I was really feeling Kramden's frustration so I blurted out *'Pow! Zoom! To the Moon!'* just like that. And that stuck too."

"Do you need another belt, Art?" asks Lucy.

"No," he says, "but I'll tell you what's wrong in the business today--"

"Demographics," interrupts Gleason. "That's what's wrong today. With show business. Everything today is based on Demographics. Statistics. Age groups. Where are there real people in statistics?"

"That's not what I was gonna say," says Carney. "What's wrong today is there isn't enough good comedy."

"I'm tired of comedy, that's it," says Lucy. Ginger barks and wants to play. Lucy doesn't.

Gleason slaps his own knee. "There's only two things I watch anymore on TV. Sports events and Sherlock Holmes."

"Gees," says Carney. "Sherlock Holmes. Yeah, Sherlock Holmes."

A reporter asks Gleason to define comedy. "If you define it, it isn't. It's something that makes you happy. Don't try to analyze it. What you need is characterization to make the comedy pay off. If you have the character, you'll find the comedy."

"Stop analyzing it," warns Carney.

"I'll never go back to TV full time," vows Lucy.

"I'd go back," says Gleason. "For the right money. It's always about money."

Carney slips off into a new reverie of silence. Gleason sips his drink. Lucy plays with Ginger. The darkness is complete now, and the discussion at an end. For just a moment, it was an event touched by the history of three popular entertainers. Now they are just three figures sitting in the semi-darkness, sipping their drinks, thinking their private thoughts.

Finally, Gleason glances up. "Hey, my glass is empty. Must've been that poodle of Lucy's. Someone find that guy with the wrinkled apron."

Everyone goes home. While Gary Morton cleans the barbecue grill, Lucy invites me and Erica inside to play backgammon, a game she loves with a passion. She spends the next hour teaching us how to play and then the evening is over. And the next day it all seems like a dream. An evening with Lucille Ball, and you know there will never be another evening in your life like it.

# FLASH-FORWARD TO 1996 . . .

Summer, 1996, seven years after the death of Lucille Ball. I am at the Universal Studios Theme Park in North Hollywood, visiting "Lucy: A Tribute," a walkthrough museum dedicated to the "I Love Lucy" series. Behind a glass-encased display, against the wall in a corner, stands Lucy's backgammon table, and suddenly that night in 1975 washes over me and I am with Lucy again. And Ginger is dancing around her feet again. And Gleason is laughing.

We are poolside, talking about how much she hated running Desilu. And I am thinking about how much has happened since that night. How "Star Trek," the show she had made possible, had exploded anew in 1979 and gone on as a franchise for motion pictures and new TV spin-offs, making billions and billions of dollars. A Universe filled with floating money.

How curious, it all seemed to me at that moment, that in 1967 Lucy sells Desilu to Paramount for $18 million. Part of the deal are the Desilu assets. Assets like "Mission: Impossible," "The Untouchables" and "Star Trek."

I think how ironic that Paramount gets the "Star Trek" franchise as part of the deal. Not even suspecting that it might become more valuable than all of Desilu and its assets put together. How many billions has the "Star Trek" franchise made for Paramount? As endless as the Universe? Did it not end up to be one of the most profitable of all time? In all of Hollywood history?

And Lucy, the funniest lady in the world, the lady who never wanted to be part of the business of Hollywood, up there right now, knowing she had made it possible, laughing her head off . . .

# LOOK AT THAT KID'S FACE GROW INTO A MATURE MAN . . .

Left to right: He started out as a high school kid in 1959; in July 1968 he made a documentary about Francis Ford Coppola making "The Rain People"; how George looked around the time Dale Pollock's "Skywalking" biography appeared; George on the set of "Labyrinth" in 1986, flushed by the success of three "Star Wars."

# NOW THE FACES LUCAS MADE FAMOUS IN 'STAR WARS'

# OTHER FACES HE MADE FAMOUS IN 'STAR WARS' . . .

Now Meet The Actors Behind Those Bizarre 'Faces' . . .
The Human Flesh-Covered Faces You Never Saw . . .
Humans Hopelessly Trapped Beneath Make-Up And Costumes . . .

# THE FACELESS RIDERS
# OF THE UNIVERSE

*It is fascinating to me David Prowse aspired to so much back in the days when the "Star Wars" films were first popular. Playing Darth Vader filled his head with visions of leading movie roles and stardom. And yet after the "Star Wars" trilogy came and went, he could not find the roles he so desperately wanted. Here is the way I wrote it on August 6, 1978:*

**"Flowing black robes trailing from the figure and a face forever masked by a functional if bizarre black metal breath screen–a Dark Lord of the Sith was an awesome, threatening shape."** – From the novelization of "Star Wars" by George Lucas.

THEY DON'T come any meaner, any crueler. He disintegrates well-populated planets before breakfast and sends his Death Star space station on merciless missions to conquer whatever galaxy he's currently warping his starships through. Egad, he'd even go so far as to threaten a Demure Damsel in Distress.

Is it any wonder then that Darth Vader is unloved (dare I use the word "despised") throughout the Universe? As the ultimate space heavy in "Star Wars" and its coming sequels, he has even dimmed the corrupt images of Dr. Mabuse, Goldfinger, Professor Moriarty and others who until now have tried to claim the Mantle of Malevolence.

Although the final soundtrack voice belongs to African-American actor James Earl Jones, the hulking presence of Vader and the elegant dastardliness of his movements, which seem to personify evil itself, can be attributed to 43-year-old British actor David Prowse.

The irony of his success is that not a single inch of his real person shows beneath the metallic mask, cape and uniform of Vader–Prowse is totally unrecognized even among crowds of devotees of the popular space adventure series. Thus he is on a one-man crusade to rectify

David Prowse – who would believe this handsome Britisher could ever be that dastardly doer of dirty deeds, Darth Vader?

Prowse demonstrates he was a heavyweight, not only as a movie villain but as a bodybuilder.

this injustice by making personal appearances all over the world, by getting his photograph in science-fiction fan magazines ("that's one way they'll get to know what I look like") and by shouting "Accept the Real Me!" whenever he passes an open window.

A native of Bristol, England, Prowse was an athletic child until 13, when suddenly a swollen knee led specialists to conclude he had tuberculosis. He spent several years in a leg iron, until doctors decided it wasn't TB after all but joints reacting unfavorably to his rapid growth. And he was growing rapidly–and tall.

To strengthen his legs, Prowse purchased a Charles Atlas course and went on to become the British Heavyweight Weight-lifting champion. He also won some bodybuilding prizes. Today he weighs 260 pounds and stands 6'7" in nonmetallic boots.

Prowse is no newcomer to acting. He's been doing big men since 1965 when he played opposite Peter Sellers in "Casino Royale." He's been seen as the monster in "The Horror of Frankenstein" (acknowledged by Prowse as "one of the all-time worst movies") and he might be remembered by American audiences in his pre-"Star Wars" days as the rogue Julian in Stanley Kubrick's "A Clockwork Orange."

"A big fella like me gets plenty of comedy mileage standing up against littler people." He refused to talk about his acting in "Frankenstein and the Monster From Hell."

Nowadays, in the wake of Vader's popularity, he has become the Green Cross Man in England – a kind of humanized version of Smokey the Bear who gives traffic safety advice to children in TV public service announcements and advertising (his face has been imprinted on 24 million margarine containers, among his other achievements).

Statistics have been compiled to show that since Prowse started warning children in Great Britain to "always stop near the kerb," accidents involving 5- to 11-year-old pedestrians have dropped by five per cent.

Passing through the Bay Area recently in ordinary nonmetallic street garb and traditional leather shoes in order to attend autograph parties and make personal appearances, Prowse and I met for a much-anticipated interview. He turned out to be a gentle man who harbored no ill-feelings against Star Wars Corporation for dubbing his voice without first telling him there was nothing in his contract to prevent this.

"It fit the character, James Earl Jones' voice, didn't it? But I do wish they had talked to me about it. It would have been the decent thing to do, wouldn't it now? I was paid a flat rate for the picture–none of us knew it was going to be *that* successful–but now I've been signed to do the next two 'Star Wars' sequels and I'll be receiving a bit of a percentage. Not much, but it could be considerable if the box office record repeats itself. We begin filming ["The Empire Strikes Back"] in Norway for an ice-pack sequence and then we're off

to Africa to simulate a tropical planet."

On one point Prowse indicated some displeasure, yet his voice lost none of its gentle evenness. "I feel very badly about all those Darth Vader personal appearances in which a hired actor wears my costume. It is a deliberate, calculated plan to preserve the anonymity of the character."

The mail from "Star Wars" fans is voluminous and Prowse claims to receive more than anyone else in the cast. "I've gotten letters from people who swear they've seen the film at least 200 times. I've seen it eight times myself, and each time I discover something new. At first Vader was hissed and booed, but now he's become a cult hero and he's cheered every time he appears on screen. I think we all recognize the fact that there's a little Darth Vader in all of us."

Look to the right of Vader and see etched in the icewall "May the Force Be With You, Darth Vader" followed by the signature of David Prowse. The autograph has faded with time proving not even "Star Wars" is forever. Or will time prove me wrong?

Prowse was first offered a choice of roles–either the part of Chewbacca ("a giant sort of teddybear") or Darth Vader. "I chose the latter because everyone remembers a villain but not always a hero. I had no idea I would be completely covered until the costume designer measured me up for the suit. I was disappointed, but I could also see that Vader was going to be a standout role."

Prowse digressed to explain Vader's background: "Years ago he fell into a flaming volcano and was terribly burned. His breathing must be regulated by a control panel on his chest–he virtually lives in an iron lung." Darth's mask, made of fiberglass, was thick and difficult to wear. At first the mask was too large and refused to turn when Prowse moved his face, so the designer padded it with rubber. That made it ridiculously hot. If Prowse did anything strenuous it would "fog up and I couldn't see where I was going."

The costume consisted of four layers: leather-pleated trousers, a bolero-type jacket, a breast jacket made of leather that tied in the back, and a heavy cloak. There was also a shoulder breastplate of fiberglass.

The mask, helmet and gauntlets, along with calf-length boots with plastic shinguards, completed the inter-galactic ensemble. To say the least, Prowse had some difficulty moving about.

Prowse found George Lucas to be a slightly-built, intent young man who often reminded him of a schoolboy. "He was completely in charge of things, no matter how difficult the production became. He didn't give us a lot of directorial advice; he left a lot of it up to us to work out. Gary Kurtz, the producer, was very dour and serious. Compared to him, George was a good humor man."

Unrecognized facially by the public or not, Prowse's career has taken a leap forward. "Until 'Star Wars' acting was only a sideline which I considered too precarious for a livelihood. I was mainly concerned with running my Fitness Center in London, serving as health consultant for Harrod's Department Store in Knightsbridge, or teaching fitness to the

crown prince of Saudi Arabia. That's all changed. Now I'm involved in a BBC-TV Shakespearean play. And a TV serial 'A Horseman Riding.' " He's also completed his autobiography [not published until 2006 as "Straight from the Force's Mouth"] replete with theories on bodybuilding and exercise programs.

Always the gentleman, Prowse shook my hand warmly as he was preparing to leave. "I want to be successful in everything I do. If I can become world renowned with Darth Vader helping me along the way, so be it. I'm a great lover of recognition. I love it because it's a sure sign of success. You know, I've had parts in 'Jabberwocky' and 'People That Time Forgot' since finishing 'Star Wars.' I want to do as many films as I can. However, I did refuse to play Richard Kiel's double in the latest James Bond film. They wanted me to do Jaw's fight for him. Jaws can do his own fighting."

# PROWSE ON DARTH VADER

*I would meet Prowse two years later, in 1980, at the world premiere of "The Empire Strikes Back" at 20th Century-Fox in Los Angeles. The interview later ran on "Creature Features." Here is an excerpt:*

**Q.: David, how would you describe The Force?**

**A.:** I think The Force is the difference between good and evil. It is the power of positive thought. If you think positively, you can make things happen.

**Q.: Describe for me the dark side of Darth Vader.**

**A.:** He is the epitome of evil. There is a subtle difference in his character between the two films. In "Star Wars" he was all black. There were no shades to him whatsoever. In "The Empire Strikes Back" there was a grayish version. But he is totally totally evil.

**Q.: Have you gotten over being upset about another's voice replacing yours?**

**A.:** As you know, I was very very mad at first. But then when you analyze the situation and study the final combination, you realize the truth. My body and James Earl Jones' voice are a marvelous combination.

*While there was no Darth Vader for David Prowse to play in the new "Star Wars" series, and he has largely vanished from the acting scene, another regular in the series whose face was never seen, Anthony Daniels, has continued to play the Threepio character as he created it for the original "Star Wars." Whether he enjoys it or not is a question I first raised when I encountered Daniels in October of 1978:*

# AND NOW MEET ANTHONY DANIELS: COMMONPLACE HUMANITY HIDDEN BENEATH THE FUSSY BEHAVIOR OF A PARANOID ROBOT

THE COLOR of gold for the exterior of the tall android C3PO (traditionally shortened to, and pronounced as, Threepio) was a prophetic choice on the part of "Star Wars" writer-director George Lucas. Threepio, a bronzed son of a complicated computer bank, with the human personification of prissy fussiness, became one of the most appealing elements of Lucas' space adventure, contributing a goofy kind of intergalactic comedy that blended ingeniously with the action and the mock derring-do.

There is no doubt that Threepio had much to do with the film's incredible financial success. The New York Times called the robot "the best thing in it." However, beneath that oily heart of gold beats another heart, a heart that is more than a bit fussy in its own way. The actor who remains largely anonymous, despite an excellent performance, is Anthony Daniels, a Britisher who came to America recently to participate in a one-shot CBS-TV offering, "The 'Star Wars' Holiday Special," directed by Steve Binder.

During his sojourn across America, 32-year-old Daniels found himself in demand everywhere including the Bay Area, where he stopped to make a few personal appearances. I caught up with him at a Jack London Square restaurant only a short while before he was scheduled to be interviewed at nearby Channel 2 by Bob Wilkins for "Creature Features."

My two kids Russ and Trista accompanied me but they were disappointed to see a commonplace human torso with ordinary arms and standard legs. And a traditional face complete with typical eyes, routine nose, mundane mouth and average hair, even though I had tried to tell the kids that the only gold they might see was the metal filling Daniels' teeth. No matter what I said, their hopes had been as zapped as an alien under Han Solo's laser gun. Once he got over his uneasiness with a stranger from the press ("I've been asked so many dumb and silly questions lately"), Daniels relaxed and became disarmingly charming, exhibiting a droll sense of

A memorable moment on Bob Wilkins' old "Creature Features" set: The day in late 1978 when my daughter Trista and son Russ visited Bob Wilkins in order to meet Anthony Daniels. But where was C3PO?

"This time we'll be destroyed for sure"

humor indigenous to the British. "The irony was that I was an actor known for my suppleness and fluidity, and and here I was, being asked to play a stiff-legged, mechanical robot. I was very nervous during the first reading of the script because there were many technical directions I didn't really understand. Then I went back a second time and began to see the enormous possibilities. So I accepted the role."

By no means, however, was the original Threepio concept anything like what finally emerged on screen. "Lucas had written Threepio to be oily and sleazy, like a used-car salesman. I saw the robot as a mad English butler-type, fussy and pedantic, always fearful he's about to be sacked, disassembled or de-programmed. Yet loveable and affectionate. And because Threepio was a robot of protocol, I felt he should have an aristocratic British accent. I daresay, wasn't protocol invented by the British?"

In preparing for the robot role, Daniels concocted a background for Threepio. "A machine is not just a machine. It has a history. Threepio was built on the planet Affa, four light years from Tatooine. On Affa there is the city of Croyden, which is known throughout the galaxy as 'The Detroit of the Stars.' It was there Threepio was assembled and programmed and given a bronze exterior, since this is a symbol of goodness."

Threepio, Daniels continued, "was plugged into the wrong power source and got a new memory bank sometime prior to the Royal Alliance. He has undergone many traumatic experiences, accounting for his fatalistic behavior and his repeated use of the phrase *'This time we'll be destroyed for sure.'* Before the period in which 'Star Wars' is set, he began by serving under Captain Antilles aboard a starship. It was then he became familiar with the compatibility factor when assigned to Artoo Deetoo."

Artoo Deetoo (R2D2) is a tripodal robot with cylindrical body – less affectionately called a "half-sized thermocapsulary dehousing assister." Artoo Deetoo is unprogrammed to speak but has an electronic system of beeps and hums understandable to all robots.

Daniels claimed that "Star Wars" has not changed his career all that much ("the British are less impressed with all this hoopla than you Americans") but, on the other hand, it's hard to overlook the special privileges it has brought him during the past year:

◻ He wore his glittering fiberglass costume to present Hollywood Oscars and British Academy film awards. A special lift was needed for his grand entrance.

◻ He imprinted his soles in the cement of Mann's [Grauman's] Chinese Theater somewhere in the vicinity of one-time pin-up movie star Betty Grable's thighs.

◘ He made a guest appearance on "The Osmonds" TV series.

◘ He hosted a royal charity show in Norway.

◘ He conducted the London Symphony Orchestra at the Royal Albert Hall. The rendering of John Williams' "Star Wars" music was so well received he went back and conducted a second time.

It had not been easy getting in and out of the 22-piece fiberglass costume which takes hours to apply starting from the feet up. (Never but never start at the head.) As for taking it off, Daniels compared it to "breaking into a combination safe. It was a Japanese puzzle of great magnitude. The fingers were of sheet steel; the neckpiece was plastic which never failed to choke me. A black hole cut in the center of the headpiece gave me constant tunnelvision. It was an excruciating form of solitary confinement."

Because it was so hard to move, Daniels would often stand motionless on the set. "People unaware that I was a live person would knock their pipes clean on me, or lean against me as if I were a mantlepiece to discuss politics, tax problems or sexual misadventures. They became most disconcerted if I happened to move a couple of inches."

Artoo, a constant companion on the set, was remotely controlled by radio, which left Daniels talking and acting to a piece of machinery. "It was rather like trying to get a cup filled out of an empty water cooler. Occasionally Artoo would go out of control and I would have to bash it on the head to keep it in line. It was extremely wearing."

Daniels is a native of Salisbury, Wiltshire, and was brought up in the countryside of Hertfordshire.

His parents tried to dissuade him from becoming an actor but he was bull-headed and playing in "Henry IV" at the age of 13. "The sword I wielded was bigger than I was," he recalled.

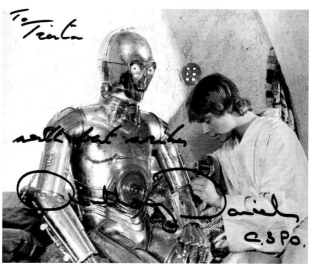

Actors often scrawl messages onto their photographs while in a hurry or eager to escape to other climes. This photo autographed by Anthony Daniels to my daughter Trista simply says "With Best Wishes." At least, I think that's what Daniels wrote . . . I shouldn't be so fussy.

Believing actors to be ruffians and vagabonds, Daniels' parents had better success persuading him to become a lawyer–but after two years of "carrying an empty briefcase" he returned to acting, learning his craft at London's Rose Burford College. Since then Daniels has played in many Shakespearean productions.

In fact, he had just played Guildenstern in "Rosencrantz and Guildenstern Are Dead" in the Young Vic Company when he was hired to play Threepio. A week later he found himself in Tunisia trying to keep sand out of his suit since one misplaced grain could bring him to a clanking halt. Crankiness, not clankiness, invariably set in.

While perhaps the rest of the world remembers Threepio with affection and humor, Daniels does not. "It's not a lot of fun playing a robot. In fact, I daresay, it was the most –and I do mean the most–unamusing experience of my life." □

# THE MOST CUDDLY OF ALL THE FACELESS ONES:
## CHEWING THE FAT WITH CHEWIE AND
## MEETING ONE OF THE TALLEST MEN ALIVE

Peter Mayhew, born in 1944, was educated in Barnes, London, and working at King's College Hospital when a newspaperman happened to ask him about his extra-giant feet (shoe size: 16). The resulting article brought Mayhew to the attention of the producers of "Sinbad and the Eye of the Tiger," so you could say it was Ray Harryhausen and Charles H. Schneer (see Page 137) who brought him to prominence. They were looking for a seven-foot-tall minotaur. Oh, why didn't you say so to begin with? Who but Mayhew could fill such "shoes."

Here's the gospel about a 200-year-old Wookie, according to George Lucas: *"Despite an almost comical quasi-monkey face, the Wookie was anything but gentle looking. He was an eight-foot-tall savage-looking creature resembling a huge grey bushbaby monkey with fierce baboon-like fangs. His large blue eyes dominated a fur-covered face and softened his otherwise awesome appearance."*

Peter Mayhew on the "Creature Features" set in 1980. Talk about a tall drink of water . . . and about the sweetest guy you would ever want to meet in all your life . . .

He was a sight to behold, for sure. Chewbacca, a role Mayhew chose because he wanted to play a hero and not Darth Vader (after being offered either part), was to become one of the most beloved characters within the "Star Wars" canon, ranking in fan popularity with C3PO and R2D2 as less-than-human favorites.

But forget all this alien characteristics stuff. At 7' 2" Peter Mayhew is a sight to see as a human. He's the third tallest Englishman in the United Kingdom.

As late as February 2006 I had a chance to speak to Mayhew at the Wondercon in San Francisco. He was then living in Dallas, Texas, and he took a few minutes from the lines of autograph-seeking fans to bring me up to date:

"I have a sense of freedom about my life. And I have this recogniton as Chewbacca that has given me the most wonderful time that otherwise might not have happened. It's great to know you've had an impact on movie-going audiences."

But it wasn't always easy – in 1973 after the coming and going of "Return of the Jedi" it seemed there was nothing else to fall back on. "So I made bedframes for 13 years. Yes, I said bedframes. It was very satisfying

but nothing compared to the glory days of the original 'Star Wars.' And then the conventions really kicked in again in earnest with the coming of the second 'Star Wars' trilogy. Chewie has been part of the connective tissue of the series and it was lovely to see everything happening all over again.

"What a galactic ride!"

*Wookie to that!*

There's nothing like Christmas. And since Santa Claus is the most beloved creature of all time, I always made certain he paid me a visit each December on "Creature Features." I hope this doesn't destroy some of your childhood beliefs, but Santa was always in the form of David Moore, a jovial and suit-ably rotund fellow worker who had once been a copy boy like me at the San Francisco Chronicle. The Christmas of '82 was especially memorable when I delivered, with Santa ho-ho-ho-hoing at my side, a special poem. I called it:

# AN ODD ODE
# TO THE ODIOUS
# AND ODOROUS ONES
# WHO ORDERED
# E.T. ORDAINED TO A SHELF

TWAS JUST BEFORE THE COMING OF THE YEAR '83
AND IN TOYSTORES THERE WAS THIS INCREDIBLE SPREE.
THE BUYING BLOOD WAS BOILING
THE CAPITALISTIC DOLLARS FLOWING
AS THE KIDS BOUGHT THE DOLL NICKNAMED E.T.
NO ONE HAD FOUND THAT MOVEMENT BORING
BECAUSE SALES WERE A-SOARING
AND SALESMEN WERE A-ROARING.
ON THEIR OWN PITARD WERE THEY A-GORING?
NOW I DON'T WANT TO SPEAK WITH SASS
I DON'T EVEN WANT TO BOTHER OR HARASS,
I PREFER TO HAVE DIGNITY AND CLASS
BUT THOSE EXPLOITATION BOYS HAD BRASS
TO TURN ONE SO LOVEABLE
INTO A STORE-SHELF SHOVEABLE.
ISN'T THAT JUST A BIT CRASS?
NOW E.T. HAS THIS THING, TELEKINESIS

AND IT JUST TORE ME ALL TO PIECES
AS THE PACKAGES WERE RIPPED
AND THE CONTENTS TIPPED
AND E.T. PIGGED OUT ON HIS REESES.
EVERYONE LOVED THAT LITTLE GNOME
EVEN A T & T BEGAN TO FOAM
WHENEVER THEY HEARD THE BELL
AND KNEW THEY COULD SELL
THAT CATCHPRASE,
"E.T., PHONE HOME."

# HOW THE MAN WHO MOVED KING KONG MOVED RAY HARRYHAUSEN TO BECOME THE NEW GIANT OF STOP-MOTION ANIMATION

**Willis O'Brien's original King Kong with the actress (Fay Wray) who would become known as "The Girl in the Hairy Paw." This monster inspired more people to become creative artists within the world of fantasy than any other single motion picture.**

He danced his puppets and marionettes with delight. And Ray Bradbury fell in love with the dancing puppets and said of the man who danced them, "The delicious monsters that moved in that man's head and out of his fingers and into eternal dreams will never be forgotten."

The man was Ray Harryhausen. One could say he was born June 29, 1920, in Los Angeles . . . but that wouldn't quite be so accurate. Harryhausen, at least the special-effects artist the world would come to know, was born in Los Angeles on the night of March 24, 1933, at Grauman's Chinese Theater, the night he saw Willis O'Brien's giant-ape fantasy adventure, "King Kong."

On that night he experienced an incident that took his breath away: He witnessed a 50-foot gorilla, the first gigantus monster of movies, storm across Skull Island, trampling on natives, fighting prehistoric beasts and scooping beautiful, screaming Fay Wray into the palm of his hot, hairy paw.

These spectacular, breathtaking sights were Harryhausen's introduction to the art of stop-motion photography, a technique first perfected by the industrious O'Brien as far back as the 1910s whereby a three-dimensional model or effigy is photographed against a realistic background a single frame at a time . . . a painful, tedious job. Played back at 24 frames per second, the inanimate armature becomes a living, breathing, fast-moving thing.

"Extravagant enthusiasm" is how Harryhausen had described his feelings from that night at the movies, and he had gone on to become a leader and innovator in the industry of special effects. So, when I met him in 1977 and then again in 1981, I knew I was confronting a most unusual artist.

One never knows how prophetic a story will be until years later. When I did my interview with Harryhausen in '81 about the release of "Clash of the Titans," there was already a feeling in the air that motion-picture special effects were undergoing a revolution. George Lucas' "Star Wars" series had set into motion a whole new set of standards, and there was this newfangled thing called "the computer" that was already being hawked as the next technological step in the alchemy of movie magic. Now we can go back and read between the lines to realize that even Harryhausen sensed he was becoming a relic of movies past, and knew that his film-making time was short. Here's how it went down that summer of '81:

# A Titan of Stop-Motion Animation in a Clash of Technological Changes of Monstrous Proportions

RAY HARRYHAUSEN may one day go the way of the dinosaur. He's definitely a part of a dying breed, a craftsman who prefers to use his own hands in bringing cinema life to miniature models through the process of stop-motion animation. He relies on neither committee nor computers.

"But," he confessed with a helpless shrug of his shoulders, "time is money in the movie business and you have to get a picture done in a reasonable length of time. With inflation it's getting harder with each picture. I'm finally seeking shortcuts. I dread to think that one day – perhaps soon – it will be impossible to seek personal expression in fantasy movies. Producers will have to rely on mass-produced expression solely for budgetary reasons."

Harryhausen's latest form of "self-expression" is in the MGM blockbuster "Clash of the Titans," in which he again uses Dynamation (or Dynarama – they are interchangeable) to breathe life into his monstrous creations. This time his stop-motion wizardry showcases a plethora of beings, entities and grotesqueries borrowed loosely from Greek Mythology. The exploits of Perseus (played by Harry Hamlin, shown below battling with Neil McCarthy's Calibos) to win the hand of the beautiful Andromeda include encounters with the two-headed wolf-dog Dioskilos, Medusa the Gorgon, Kraken the Sea Monster, three Stygian witches, the winged horse Pegasus and a comical mechanical owl, Bubo.

Harryhausen is an avuncular type, soft-spoken and temperate, moderately jovial and refusing to convey the tension or trauma that embroil him during his lengthy periods of production. To say that his movies take years out of his life would be an understatement. The important thing:

"Fantasy is a form of escapism very necessary to us all. We need some form of relief from mundane problems of everyday life. I think I work in a field onto itself. We've been making special fantasies of this nature for years and we've survived many different fads. Disaster

films, Westerns, gangster films, and we're still making fantasies. It's a place all our own."

He has worked on "Titans," for example, almost steadily for the past four years, but his mental attitude was that of a man on holiday as he leaned back to discuss the project and to answer the key question: Would "Clash of the Titans" be accepted as readily as his earlier films made in collaboration with producer Charles H. Schneer?

That, replied Harryhausen, was in the hands of the Greek gods. He might have hesitated to give a more positive answer because his first attempt to retell Greek mythology, "Jason and the Argonauts" (1963), had been met coldly by audiences. "I've always been disappointed about the reception of 'Jason' but it was really bad timing – the film came after all those Hercules pictures and audiences were tired of sword-and-sandal adventures. Despite that, mythology remains a favorite subject of mine. One of the problems, though, is its fragmentation. Rarely are there complete stories; sometimes the climax comes in the first act. I'd prefer not to tinker with myths but our writer Beverly Cross [who also had written "Jason" and "Sinbad and the Eye of the Tiger," another Harryhausen classic] used dramatic license and pulled together different elements into a screenplay that remolded the Perseus-Andromeda romance."

Ray Harryhausen proudly poses with model figures of Medusa the Gorgon and the horned Calibos, fantasy creatures that were prominently featured in "The Clash of the Titans."

Harryhausen started out by making drawings of the visual elements, which Cross then incorporated into his script. "We were faced with interpretation. How, for instance, do you depict Medusa? The classical approach is an attractive woman with snakes in her hair, but that would hardly turn anyone to stone. Gothic concepts show her in serpentine form, so I blended snake and woman. For Calibos, I created a bestial character with cloven hoof and satanic tail, who spoke only groans and grunts a la 'One Million B.C.' But we decided we needed dialogue for him so he wouldn't be dull. But you're playing God when you use dialogue in animated close-ups so we used a real actor for some scenes and a model in the action sequences."

Harryhausen and producer Schneer traveled through Turkey and Greece looking for locations "because we wanted walled cities to save on the cost of sets. You know, it's tough to find walled cities – most of them were torn down or sacked. We ended up going to Malta." Other sequences were completed in Spain, Italy and London.

Does "Clash of the Titans" represent his best work to date? "There are always problems of wanting to do some things over. We weren't in a position to reshoot and reshoot until it was perfect. We had so many scenes that represent 3-D animation. Ultimately we sought shortcuts. You mustn't create a Frankenstein Monster that goes on for years and years just for animation alone. There's an expensive and an inexpensive way. Sometimes, moving the camera three or four feet up or down can make a difference between a week or two days to animate a scene. I get so involved I can't see my work as others might see it. All I can remember are the difficulties behind the camera. Sometimes the completion of a film

# NOTHING TO SCHNEER AT: HARRYHAUSEN'S PRODUCTION PARTNER OFFERS A FANTASY TONIC WITH JINN

*In 1977 Charles H. Schneer, Ray Harryhausen's partner in cinema, passed through San Francisco with Ray promoting "Sinbad and the Eye of the Tiger." We talked:*

CHARLES H. SCHNEER was in his suite at the Hyatt on Union Square, surrounded by three of the "stars" of the new film he and Ray Harryhausen had just finished. The jinn, a skeletal figure of flesh without skin, was the shortest of the three, but no less menacing than his associates. Towering above this legendary "ghoul" of Arabian Nights fantasy were the Troglodyte, a prehistoric man with a horn growing from his furry scalp, and a bronzed Minator, a kind of overdeveloped, bull-headed metal man. These rubber latex, multi-jointed creatures were the prototypes for the mythical monsters in "Sinbad and the Eye of the Tiger."

Since 1954 Schneer, 57, has worked exclusively with Harryhausen to produce a string of special effects fantasies that have found box-office success all over the world. "We're always having to top ourselves," he said. "Each film requires something more sensational than the last. We seem to be on a Sinbad kick that won't die. It takes us considerable time to develop a story for it

A rare photo: While Bob Wilkins conducts a filmed interviewed with Harryhausen and Schneer in the lobby of a San Francisco screening room, my son Russ appears in the background to be fast asleep as I await my turn to talk to these ultimate masters of sci-fi/fantasy special effects.

demands its own unique plot and the monsters must blend. We don't make a regional picture. We make a world picture. Through marketing research we've discovered that our fantasy audiences are worldwide, from all kinds of social and cultural backgrounds. We attract the hardcore movie-going audience of 15-27 years. Because Sinbad wears a turban we're big in India. And we have enormous appeal in Hong Kong, Taiwan, Singapore, Japan, the Philippines. The world seems to love a good fantasy.

"All our pictures take years because of the complicated special effects. I consider myself rare because few producers nowadays want to tie themselves up that long on one picture. But I believe in what Ray is doing, and I'd rather make one really unique film than five ordinary ones."

For one sequence only 60 feet long, "we had to combine several pieces of film. A high-speed miniature was shot in Malta; a scene of the Minator in England; two actors in Malta against a blue screen; a sky background, a pyramid setting. It took us four months before it all came together. And it runs all of 40 seconds.

"I've seen Ray take an entire day with his stop-motion process to achieve only 13 exposed frames of film. He refuses to work with gigantic staffs of animators, preferring to sketch all the production boards himself, and oftentimes laying out entire sequences scene by scene for the director. It's the difference between a painting by a Master and a painting by committee."

Schneer, who started out producing low-budget films at Columbia Studios in 1948, acknowledged that the Sinbad film had cost at least $7 million and the budgets continue to climb. "Whatever our next picture we want it to have the same kind of magic in our earlier pictures. We're in this to make money, sure. But we keep to a standard. We insist on the G rating and we want people to leave the theater feeling like they are children again."  □

is anticlimactic—years of work dismissed with a critic's pen."

With so many new fantasy and sci-fi features being made, and continuing technical advances in film stock and equipment, does he feel he is in competition with other producers? "I wouldn't use the word competition. I like to think I work in a specialized area with a specialized fantasy. We go into the past. Yes, we're aware of technical advances but I think it's wrong to decide to do something visually spectacular at the expense of the story. We considered a space adventure, 'Sinbad Goes to Mars,' but then decided our fantasy wasn't compatible with realistic space action. You will not see scimitars in the far reaches of space–we cancelled it."

Harryhausen's fascination with animated creatures began when he was 13. "It was opening night of 'King Kong' at Grauman's Chinese Theater in Hollywood and it had all the glamorous showmanship they used to put into gala openings. They had a bust of Kong in the courtyard, surrounded by pink flamingoes pecking away at the sand at his feet. That screening had an instant effect on me. That night I gave up my desires to be an actor and knew I wanted to be an animator. I started producing my own film, 'Evolution,' but it was a bit too ambitious . . . the history of the world since prehistoric times. But what I did finish I showed to George Pal at Paramount and he hired me to work on Puppetoon cartoons."

It was during this period that Harryhausen met Willis O'Brien, the man who had moved King Kong. They worked on a project, "War Eagles," but it was never produced. After World War II, Harryhausen made his first impression on the world of fantasy films by assisting O'Brien on "Mighty Joe Young," a project that took three years and won O'Brien an Oscar for special effects. While O'Brien entered the 1950s to animate a handful of lesser films and see his best ideas aborted or cancelled by changing studio bosses, Harryhausen struck out on a more successful trail and was destined to surpass his mentor-teacher in a few short years.

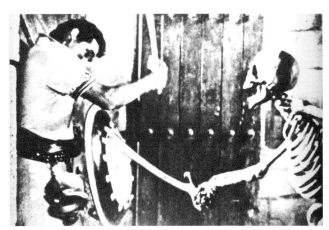

**The Greatest Skeleton in Harryhausen's Closet: When Kerwin Mathews picked at the bones of his opponents in "Jason and the Argonauts"**

Harryhausen's first solo effort in 1953, "The Beast From 20,000 Fathoms," which he claims was made for just $250,000, was crude but displayed a deftness for stop motion that became more polished by the time of "It Came From Beneath the Sea" (1954) which was the first film he did working with Schneer. (Harryhausen has always claimed the giant killer octopus of that film had only six tentacles instead of eight to save money – "but hell, who was counting arms," he added.) "Earth vs the Flying Saucers" (1956) and "20 Million Miles to Earth" (1957) were the last of his modern-day visions of monsters attacking mankind. The tone and style of the Harryhausen films would change drastically with the release of "The Seventh Voyage of Sinbad" in 1958, being the first of his Arabian Nights adventures. Meanwhile, Willis O'Brien had found it harder and harder to get projects off the animation board and finally died in 1962 – but not before seeing such Harryhausen triumphs as "The Three Worlds of Gulliver" (1960) and "Mysterious Island" (1961).

To make his next picture, "Jason and the Argonauts," Harryhausen and Schneer moved permanently to London, where facilities for processing traveling matte shots and other special effects were greatly improved and exotic foreign locations were closer at hand. They made "First Men in the Moon" (1964), "Valley of Gwangi" (1969) and "The Golden

Voyage of Sinbad" (1973). Now, ironically, Rank Laboratory has closed its special-effects processing department and most of the traveling mattes must be shipped to Hollywood for final processing. But Harryhausen and Schneer have no intentions of leaving London.

As for their next film, 1977's "Sinbad and the Eye of the Tiger," "it was a love affair from the start. Sinbad, you see, is the personification of adventure. The Arabian Nights live again. The heroics of Sinbad open the door to so many new creatures and mythological apparitions." And so would they return to that theme again in 1979's "The Golden Voyage of Sinbad."

The team spends three to four years on each project. "Schneer, like me, has great sympathy for fantasy. We have many disagreements but if two people think exactly alike, one of them is unnecessary. We battle out many things and reach many compromises, all in the name of the film."

A Harryhausen-Schneer film I remember fondly: "Mysterious Island." It was one of the first films I was asked to review for the San Francisco Chronicle just before Christmas of 1961. It was an assignment of pure joy.

Harryhausen vows he will not abandon movie fantasy. "The main idea behind our pictures is to pick subjects that cannot be normally photographed. I remember seeing those Arabian Nights movies with Maria Montez, Jon Hall and Sabu, but the producers always left the fantasy elements out. The only film to deal breathtakingly with fantasy was Alexander Korda's 'Thief of Baghdad.' I vowed when I saw that classic that I'd devote my life to putting illusions on the screen."

*And stick to his vow he did. And for that all sci-fi/fantasy fans should be grateful.*

"Frankly," he continued, "I don't like to talk much about how I do my films because I fear the audience will lose interest. It's like a magician showing you what's hidden up his sleeve. The trend nowadays is to tell all. I know the fans love that because often they're trying to do animation themselves. I suppose I should bend with the wind but I don't."

The dinosaur is an endangered species indeed.

*"Clash of the Titans" would be Harryhausen's last picture. He retired gracefully from the screen a year or so later, realizing that there would soon be a boom in computerized graphics. The day of Dynamation was over. But Harryhausen movies live on.*

### AND NOW PREPARE TO MEET THE MOST INSPIRING FANTASY WRITER WHO EVER LIVED . . . THE MAN WHO CREATED "THE MARTIAN CHRONICLES" . . . THE MAN WHO HELPED SHAPE MY ATTITUDE ABOUT LIFE . . . THE ONE AND ONLY . . .
# RAY BRADBURY

nderstanding life has always fascinated me, but only after I was introduced to the problem by the wondrous writings of Ray Bradbury. Youth? Who young thinks about youth? When young, you are forever you and you do not ponder about anything beyond young. Old is forever never.

Thank God for Ray Bradbury. I discovered his books and stories about the time I was coming out of my adolescence and was wondering what the word "teen" meant. As I began to read "The Martian Chronicles" and "The Illustrated Man" I sensed something magical about the words. There was a newly felt emotion behind them. The images and feelings he painted were so simple, and yet so profound. Even after all that Mr. Bradbury has given me, I still wonder about much of this place we call This Island Earth and I ponder age and how the passing of days changes how we feel – and look. And how we behave. He is right: Life is an ongoing, changing thing that can be wondrous one moment, and not so wondrous the next. If ever I had a mentor throughout my youth, it was this remarkable man, this Ray Bradbury.

But as I established myself professionally, I knew had to seek him out if I never sought out another person my whole life. I had to meet the man who had done so much for me without ever knowing me. Ultimately I had to share with him how I felt. And allow him to know who I was. And how he had helped to shape whatever it was that I was becoming.

*"Life to all of us is an endless coil of rope, playing through our hands every moment of every hour of the day. The long line of the rope goes back to the time we were born and extends out ahead to the time of our death. In between lies the Eternal Now. The flickering moments when each of us must play the rope as best we can. Without burning our fingers, snarling the coils, or breaking the line."* – **Ray Bradbury**

SOMETHING
SPECIAL
THIS
WAY
COMES
WITH
AN
UNDYING
SENSE
OF
WONDER

I N THE SUMMER of 1968, the Los Angeles weather is hot enough to raise Fahrenheit to 451, the temperature at which paper catches fire and burns. It is late afternoon and in a cramped sixth-floor office overlooking Wilshire Boulevard, Ray Bradbury sits at his manual typewriter. If there is an electronic machine on which to type, it is a dream locked away in his imagination. He has just typed: "The soldiers turn their heads." He is on page 162 of a screenplay he calls "And the Rock Cried Out," a Bradburyian projection of what could happen one day if the Caucasian became subservient to the black man. He is writing it on speculation and hopes it will become the latest in an explosion of fantasy and science-fiction creativity that has catapulted Bradbury to a height few others in his genres have achieved.

As he mutters to himself and revises his tale of topsy-turvy intolerance, he sits surrounded by the mementos of his success. Behind him hangs a painting used on the cover of his 1962 childhood fantasy novel "Something Wicked This Way Comes." The surrounding walls are patchworks of sketches, photographs and plaques. Bradbury is even wearing a token of his own good fortune. He is clad in a summer suit of pure white which, in the world of Ray Bradbury, would be described as The Wonderful Ice Cream Suit – also the title of a play that three years earlier had promoted him into fresh eminence as a playwright.

A t 48 Bradbury remains a handsome man who has lost none of his vernal charm and ebullience that fans have been describing and enjoying for 30 years or more. As usual, he is gracious as a host, inviting me into his specialized and visually exciting office without hesitation, and yet at the same time volatile and voluble on the subjects related to his fields of endeavor.

Many feel those fields – science fiction and fantasy – have been imbued with entirely new strength by Bradbury. As Kingsley Amis put it: "He is the Louis Armstrong of science-fiction. He is the one practitioner well-known by name to those who know nothing about it." Ray Russell carried the same thought further: "Bradbury has achieved mainstream eminence and has elevated science-fiction."

It was Bradbury, early in his career, who sold a vampire story to Mademoiselle magazine, a psychological fantasy to Harper's – markets hitherto unapproachable by writers of his kind. Bradbury's poetic style gave new dimensions to witches, Martians, carnivals, spaceships, freaks, skeletons, mummies and things that floated in bottles. His themes extended beyond the usual horizons into a new territory of the bizarre and the frightening that brought newfound salience to fantasy fiction. As Isaac Asimov put it, "Ray does not write science fiction. He is a writer of social fiction."

The late Anthony Boucher once wrote: "Bradbury is the best writer in science fiction, rather than the best writer of science fiction. I won't quarrel with those who insist he's never written a word of s-f in his life." Even Time magazine voiced recognition: "Bradbury's elf of fantasy is obviously only one element in a larger talent that includes passion, irony and wisdom."

So it has gone for Bradbury, a writer admired (and sometimes condemned for lack of scientific concept) by critics and fans alike, his stories forever the center of focus when science fiction is discussed. William F. Nolan, one of Bradbury's greatest admirers, once described him as "a prose poet in the age of space, a man possessed by the beauty of the written word." I remind Bradbury that his work has often been compared to poetry and he taps a folder on his desk labeled "R. B. Poems."

"Although I've only sold five poems in my life, I guess the great thing over the years was discovering I was a poet. A lot of people, at least, began telling me I was. I guess that's the best way to become a poet–to do it without knowing. Because if you get self-conscious it doesn't work. The best way to be any kind of writer is to live and to write and to get the job done every day and have a wonderful time with it. And don't look back and don't look too far ahead."

In the beginning, he tells me, "my sense of fantasy and magic was always immense. Since I was a child. And I've always been afraid of the dark. But the reason for writing science fiction is to insure that the future I describe will not happen. You don't write about it because you want it to happen."

Bradbury calls himself "a child of many forms." He expresses great love for movies (he still remembers seeing his first film, a Lon Chaney horror epic, at three) and for the stage. In more recent years he has selected the play form, not because of any variations in ideas but because "it is a direct way of saying a thing where you have a direct reaction from an audience that's really there. When you write a book it sometimes takes years to learn what people really think."

It is not surprising that many of his fantasies and horror stories have been adapted to the comic book page. When William Gaines at E.C. comics began to "borrow" Bradbury plot twists for the science-fiction comics "Weird Science" and "Weird Fantasy," Bradbury contacted the company and asked for compensation. Not only was he paid real money but Gaines began putting Bradbury's name on the covers of his comic books whenever a story was adapted. Bradbury has always been an admirer of comic art since discovering the Flash Gordon and Buck Rogers comic strips and says he will never turn his back on those things which gave birth to his urge to create.

His themes have emerged as thoughtful and invigorating – sensitive to both beauty and ugliness, ridden with disturbing insights into the eccentricities of the human race, and conveying a melancholy that tends to linger long after the read. While "The Martian Chronicles" (a series of short stories he wove into a novel after the fact) depicted the worst of man in the environment of a world better than his own, "Fahrenheit 451" examined a future wherein men endured and kept alive those values which other men would destroy.

"Dandelion Wine" was a nostalgic collection based on his upbringing in Waukegan, Ill. And "Dark Carnival" (one of the rarest of Bradbury editions where collectors are concerned) was an assortment of macabre tales the likes of which Bradbury has not written since 1948.

Even though he has sold hundreds of short stories, written and produced plays through his Pandemonium Playhouse and written films ("Moby Dick," "It Came

From Outer Space"), Bradbury still faces rejection. "A week doesn't pass I don't receive rejection slips. So I haven't got it made. I doubt I'll ever reach that. You see, I shift gears. Each story I write is a new thing that suddenly hits me. It's not a conscious effort to be different. It's just that any wild thing that comes into my head, I write it. No, it writes me. I sit at the typewriter and it rushes out on paper and suddenly it's finished."

In the past, Bradbury has admitted he drew heavily on his childhood experiences for stories of fantasy mixed with magic. And what has he drawn on in later years? "I think my sense of the miraculous remains pretty constant. I'm still pretty bewildered by the universe we live in. Too many people are mistaken in their attitudes toward life. They allow their critical facilities to so overwhelm them, they can't even enjoy the fact of living. But you can't allow the inequities, the vices or the destruction of other people to destroy your own sense of the miraculous."

I ask Bradbury if he is aware of any writing weaknesses. "I don't think you can analyze and correct weaknesses. All you can do is have hindsight and keep writing and reading and hope you learn more about people, places and atmosphere. The greatest thing, though, is developing a style totally suitable . . . totally yourself. Style isn't worthwhile unless it's absolute truth. They're synonymous. If you tell the truth you automatically have a style. What you're trying to do is bring out all your truths at various levels. Your fear of the dark, your dread of violence, your hostility of one thing, your love of another."

Is he willing to reveal the ultimate secret of good writing? His voice begins to throb with sincerity as he replies: "Yes, there is a secret: It has to come fast. If you go slow on anything it's automatically bad. If you're slow you intellectualize and destroy and pontificate and become self-conscious and create reasons for what you're doing. This is a danger in this country–we're getting so intellectual and super intellectual and fake intellectual we're destroying our creative talent. Destroying all the intuitive things . . . they are the real truths."

Bradbury believes all the great creative things have happened on a subliminal level. "There are no intellectual writers who've been any damn good. I do not believe in the intellectual writer. A lot of my ideas, I find when I'm printed, are intellectually accepted. But they weren't consciously intended. The fight will always be between creative persons and intellectuals. For the intellectual, per se, is not a creative person. He can't be – it's totally impossible. You cannot think your way through to a solution. The intellect is the destroyer of the intuitive and the creative process. It tries to guide things, it tries to be pompous and to be popular and to be loved. To hell with all that. You write because you have to write."

Bradbury rarely rewrites a story, though he does retype it several times, changing individual words or phrases. He seldom injects new thoughts into what is already on paper. "First you nail down the big truth. But if you start fussing with those little truths while you're still writing the story you'll never finish it. You'll be messing with grammar and single words and adjectives. Who cares? Not important, not important. The whole story finished is important. Get it down, get it down. Get a skin around it. There are two great arts, you see. One is learning to let go and do the story. The second is learning how to cut it. And knowing when to stop before castration. You have to write every day and learn both processes.

"But the more you write the better your work will be. There's a direct relationship between quantity and quality. It's a flat rule – there's just no way to contradict it."

When I leave his office and walk out onto Wilshire Boulevard, the Fahrenheit temperature has dropped a little. So has the blazing sun, which is beginning to sink in the western sky. I sigh relief.

There will be no book burnings today.

BRADBURY'S SENSE OF THE MIRACULOUS REMAINS ALERT BUT HE'S STILL BEWILDERED BY OUR UNIVERSE

R ay would weave himself in and out of my own career in the years to come. In 1983 he and his wife Maggie came to San Francisco to promote "Something Wicked This Way Comes," a Walt Disney production of his 1962 autobiographical novel. One evening we went to dinner at a restaurant near the Fairmont Hotel, where it was apparent from the start that Mrs. Bradbury was feeling some deep-rooted anger toward the Disney company.

She never revealed what it was but it was a moment I haven't forgotten. For she further demonstrated her feelings by picking up the wine menu and shoving it under Ray's nose, telling him to order a particular bottle of champagne.

Ray looked dubiously at her. "But honey," he said, "that bottle costs a hundred dollars." Her look back at him: So what? Order it. She didn't have to say the words.

Ray obeyed Maggie and ordered the champagne.

As the dinner and our interview wound to a close, Maggie shoved the menu under Ray's nose again.

And looked him squarely in the face.

And pointed to the champagne list, to the same item.

Without hesitation, Ray ordered the second bottle of $100 champagne.

Maggie made it a point to remind us that Disney was picking up the tab.

# 'We're All Disney's Children'

I n the morning of his life, growing up in the golden rays of youth in Waukegan, Ill., 12-year-old Ray Bradbury stood in a crowd and watched as Mr. Electriko, a defrocked Presbyterian minister, strapped himself into an electric chair and sucked in his breath.

*And then someone threw the switch.*

Yellow arcs sizzled the air. Startled, Bradbury jerked as though a bolt had struck from Heaven. Or Hell. Mr. Electriko's torso tensed and tingled. A thousand particles of air seemed to spark around the vibrating man and his eyes radiated with new-surging current. When the display was over, Mr. Electriko leaped to his feet still solidly alive and touched young Bradbury. The boy glowed anew. "Live forever," advised Mr. Electriko.

In the mind of Bradbury, Mr. Electriko never died after that summer of 1933. "We became friends and talked these great philosophies, and finally he had to disappear from my life. When he didn't come back with the carnival the next year I was destroyed. My heart was beating like a lover's. It's not often when you're 12 that you have heroes who are so beautiful and great and conquer the world. I missed that contact, and that's why Mr. Electriko has returned so often in my stories, first as the Illustrated Man."

E lectriko was recast and bathed in shades of the supernatural as Mr. Dark, the villain in "Something Wicked This Way Comes." The novel, about two boys growing up in a small Midwestern town and their encounter with a traveling carnival of oddities, was now a Disney feature movie. "We love our villains, don't we?" queried Bradbury. "Mr. Dark is a delicious villain. He's stuffed with all of the malevolence of the witch in Snow White. So evil you feel wonderfully occupied."

Mr. Dark, an evil spielmeister who preys on human weakness by promising oldsters their youth back or youngsters the advantage of adulthood if only they will ride his calliope,  is played by Jonathan Pryce. And what a calliope. For each full turn in forward gear, the merry-go-round will age you one year. Two revolutions, two years. And if someone forgets to stop the whirling time machine, it keeps going until you are beyond your death; going backward it will skin years off your oldness and you can step off blossomed again by youth. The years you've lost or gained are the years reclaimed by Mr. Dark and his freaks to assure their immortality.

As the above indicates, Bradbury's scenes are metaphors as often as they are real images, and he writes of colors and smells and sensations with a sensitivity like no other "prose-poet" before or since. Hence, Bradbury is never easy to translate to the screen. And hence, most adaptations are doomed to failure. Director Jack Smight couldn't pull it off in "The Screaming Woman" (TV 1972) or in "The Illustrated Man" (theatrical 1969) and Michael Anderson had problems with the 1979 TV miniseries "The Martian Chronicles."

When Bradbury decided in 1981 to let Disney produce his most personal novel, he wanted Jack Clayton to direct. He got Jack Clayton. Bradbury also told Disney he wanted Jason Robards to play the father, a character based on Bradbury's own father. He got Robards without argument. Bradbury wanted the British director because of their 30-year association. The two first met when Clayton was John Huston's associate on "Moby Dick," which Bradbury was writing at the time. That relationship might have been strained during the making of "Something Wicked" because Clayton had to order Bradbury to cut his 240-page screenplay in half. "But our friendship wasn't afflicted. Each day at 4 p.m. we'd meet over brandy and talk. He told me, 'Search for the image that'll take the place of a paragraph or page.' It turned into a joyful game of search. It became a challenge. And then it was 200 pages and then 150 and then 130 and then the final 120. Thank God for Jack. He made me work like I've never worked before, and I still kept the essence of my book. I still recaptured the madness of adoring life and youth. I was in touch with my childhood again."

Then Clayton had to look coldly at the first rough cut and decided more footage was needed. Some authors might have rolled over and screamed, but Bradbury agreed – and Disney agreed to the additional money for the reshoot. More special effects were added, but not to the point they overshadowed the story, according to Bradbury.

"If this film depended on special effects alone to succeed," Bradbury said, "it wouldn't deserve to succeed. We hold back our effects for key moments, for just the right touches. The story must come first, always. Don't misunderstand me. I love special-effects movies. They're wonderful. George Lucas went back to the essential child in all of us that loves the toys we play with, and he gave us characters who act out our dreams. Time for the Wizard of Oz, Tarzan and John Carter of Mars. All good primeval, mythical stuff. I love Lucas because he has enough guts to stay young and warn the intellectuals to stay out of it. He wants to play in the sandbox, and I hope he and Steven Spielberg go on forever."

Describing the new movie as "a plum cake full of nuts and raisins, all love, sweat and agony," he still felt that "Something Wicked" was his best novel. "For one thing it mirrors the joys of youth. But there is another reason. I didn't know it until two years after I'd written the book, but one night when I was prowling around the house, I suddenly realized that the librarian in my book was my father. I had put him in the proper place. Not in a graveyard somewhere forever, not forgotten somewhere in the past, but in the middle of my book. I was so pleased this son had honored his father in that way." One would assume the two boys in the story, Jim and Will, are Bradbury's alter egos. "Yes, but when I was writing I didn't know I was writing two halves of myself. You must never think when you write. Thinking is dangerous. You get self-conscious, you begin to posture for politicians and aesthetic friends. You must perform only for the inner self."

Bradbury says he has seen what happens to those who don't listen. "Some of my best friends are screenwriters and they are the unhappiest people I know. They're making ten times the money but they're aging fast. Never take a job based solely on money. Only if it's something you can assimilate and enjoy. I was offered the chance to write 'Anatomy of a Murder' and 'Man With the Golden Arm' but I turned them down. They were alien to me. They were antagonistic, distasteful. Who needs it? Life is too short. If more people listened to their stomachs instead of their heads. Your head will rationalize you right into a job you shouldn't take. Listen now or you'll have to buy a psychiatrist later in life to cure you.

"This principal applies to everything in life. It's advice I'm giving to you free. Going to bed with the wrong person, having the wrong business partner, trying to write something you shouldn't write or making films you shouldn't make. The magic time is lying in bed at midnight and listening to *you*. And you look at the wall and you say, 'What am I doing here?' And you'd better head for the door if you're miserable because you've got only one life and you're never coming back, never."

For Bradbury to speak highly of Disney sounds like hype – but Bradbury has loved the man Walt Disney for decades. Disney once allowed Bradbury into his archives and told him to take whatever he wanted. As a result, Bradbury saw every Disney cartoon and took 20 animation cels which he still has today. "We're all Disney's children," he said. "We all care about grand fun, yes? I've always wanted to see my heroes on the screen, because I wanted to believe in them and their dangers. I wanted to be chased down a hill by a giant boulder. It's not a great Jungian-Freudian thing to be chased. It's simple exhilaration."

Bradbury remains intrigued by the awesomeness of humanity and space and less with science and its applications. "To be first," he enthused, "that's what writing is all about. To blow off the first firecracker on the Fourth of July and to stand on the lawn at midnight and light the tissue paper of your fire balloon and watch the warm air go into it like a multi-colored angel. You let go of the bright angel and it floats away into the sky and it's all of the holidays that you ever know, floating away forever, and you weep, you weep, because you know beauty, you know time and you know death. Everything is in that fire balloon. The joy of living, breathing and fear of dying, which is in that fading beauty of the night sky. That's what you must put into your writing."

# THE LAST MEETING

It is the last time I see Ray Bradbury. It is 1985 and I am walking down Powell Street on a warm San Francisco morning, approaching the block that has Union Square to the left and the St. Francis Hotel to the right. As I approach the entranceway to the hotel, I see a lone figure leaning against the gray wall, as if waiting for something. As I walk closer, I suddenly feel as if I know the figure. There's something about the way he stands, the way he turns his head to look in my direction. He reacts as if he has recognized something. As I walk closer, the figure smiles and gestures. The figure has aged since last I saw him. The hair is whiter. There are wrinkles I have never seen before. But the enthusiasm, the joy, all the things that are Bradbury are there as he extends his hand to welcome me. The thing that I had wanted most has been fulfilled. Ray Bradbury knows who I am, and the importance he has meant in my life. And some magical thing has brought us together at this moment, the Eternal Now.

*"The rope of life hisses through our fingers. We reach, it's gone. The beauty of any particular flower, song, poem or person lies awesome in the fact that roses must fade, songs die with the breath, poems burn in the fire, golden lads and girls all must, as chimney sweepers, come to dust."* – **RAY BRADBURY**

## WRITERS' BLOCH: A DARKLY MACABRE MAN WHO WAS PSYCHO-LOGICAL AND HE MADE YOU WANT TO LAUGH . . . YOURSELF TO DEATH

I would meet Robert Bloch many times before his death in 1994 from throat cancer, and I would come to know him as an unforgettable character. He was eternally ready to assault me with his wry, always-macabre and dark sense of humor. The final macabre joke of his life is that the cigarettes he constantly smoked may have finally been the nails in his coffin, finishing him off too soon at 77.

But even on the eve of death, Bob had the ability to face it with that same sense of humor by writing an article for Omni magazine about what it was like to prepare for one's own demise. Bob's tragedy was our laughter, even at the end when he was facing the Norman Bates we all must confront when it is time for "The End."

Of course, my fondest memories of Bob relate to "Lost in Time and Space With Lefty Feep," a collection of short stories that I published in 1987, with his complete cooperation and blessing. These tales, originally published in the 1940s in the Fantastic Adventures pulp

Kenn Davis' wonderful cover for "Lost in Time and Space With Lefty Feep," published in 1987.

A Kenn Davis sketch of Lefty Feep.

magazines, were about a race track tout who was constantly sliding off into bizarre and comedic fantasy worlds. They totally reflected a side to Bob that many were not aware of: That he was a master of word play, and loved puns and any other twist on the English language that might provide a chuckle, a laugh or a guffaw. Many of the photographs displayed here were taken by me at his home in the Hollywood Hills, where he lived with his lovely wife Elly. The great thing about Bob: His wit was always at the forefront of our conversations, and it inevitably wove itself into our many interviews together. The first took place in October 1968:

# Trapped in the Inner Sanctum of the Master of Macabre —Purely for Laughs

*"Mary Crane started to scream, and then the [shower] curtains parted further and a hand appeared, holding a butcher knife. It was the knife that, a moment later, cut off her scream. And her head."* – **One of the more quaint passages from Robert Bloch's "Psycho"**

NEXORABLY, it is "Psycho" and the shower scene that one returns to in the study of Robert Bloch. And that is where I found myself, in the study of Robert Bloch. The one in his home in the Hollywood Hills. Seated behind his typewriter, Bloch was dressed in black turtleneck and slacks. As he smoked St. Mortiz cigarettes in a long holder, he conveyed an air of cordial aplomb, responding to preliminary small talk with typical punnish and punnish-able punch-lines.

He lovingly fondled an old German desk set, explaining it had been given to him by fans who feel his soul must crave such things; the blotter was shaped into a skull and skeleton. The letter opener resembled a decomposing corpse. A woodcarving of a Rheshasa, a Hindu demon, depicted a grotesque monster devouring little children.

On a wall of the study was a Count Dracula Award and a Hugo for his short story "That Hell-Bound Train." A portion of bookcase housed all the crumbling pulp magazines in which his earliest works appeared (Strange Stories, Fantastic Adventures, Thrilling Mystery, Weird Tales), as well as assorted hardcover and paperback editions of his books (foreign included).

He was working on "The House That Dripped With Blood," to be a Hammer anthology film of several Bloch stories. He wasn't too happy with the way the Britons cut up his last one ("Torture Garden") but perhaps this one would turn out better. (It would contain some of his best short stories: "Sweets to the Sweets," "Waxworks," "The Cloak" and "Method for Murder.")

"Why wasn't "Torture Garden" better?" I asked. "Few directors, British or otherwise, truly understand the medium. They confuse excitement with gore and they don't know how to build to a series of climaxes. They emphasize the wrong things, they know nothing about tempo. Buster Keaton was big on the necessity of exact timing, and many of his silent pictures exemplify what I mean, though in a comedic, not horrific, sense."

Bloch has often commented on the fact that writing for TV never comes off successfully for the writer ("too many fingers in the pie"). So why then were his scripts for "Thriller" (the hit series hosted by Boris Karloff) so successful? He betrayed the advance warnings of a smile.

"That show was a different proposition. Almost always my first draft script would be used exactly as I wrote it. The director didn't change the angles or the dialogue." The smile breaks out broadly. "It was photographed as it was conceived and it came off on the little screen."

For Bloch, "Psycho" would appear to be his all-time best. His voice, however, dripped with vitriol. "It was considered too far out, too shocking, too daring for its time. Fortunately, director Alfred Hitchcock maintained control and refused to let anyone tamper with it or water it down. As almost everyone in Hollywood wanted to. When I saw the picture, the lights went up and Janet Leigh turned to me and said, 'When that knife went into me, I could feel it.' I was especially pleased because there was my book on the screen. Something that seldom happens today–or any day."

Any horror film worth its screams, Bloch felt, should be made (as "Psycho" was made) in black and white. "Many so-called horror and psychological suspense films have been ruined by color because color has emotional overtones which sometimes overshadow the essential starkness of black and white. When you get warm flesh tones you lose something. Then there is the temptation to substitute shock color for true horror. You turn a man green or pour on the catsup. It becomes lurid, unreal, comic strippish, disgusting in most cases. I remember Bill Castle did just that in 'The Tingler.'"

Bloch, his wonderful sense of humor forever at work, posed for this photograph in the backyard of his Hollywood Hills home, standing next to the swimming pool. The edition of "Fantastic Adventures" he held was from his personal library and contained one of his short stories.

When writing films of this type, what is he striving hardest to put across? "I've always approached writing with the idea to entertain. I've never had any notion about doing anything more than that. If I interject a personal comment, it is still a form of entertainment rather than an artistic endeavor.

"My prime duty is to satisfy the demands of an audience. If you were to call me an entertaining writer, I would consider that the highest compliment. Am I a bad writer? Sometimes. Many of my books would qualify for a bookburning. But are they dull? Never!"

Bloch is especially proud of a 12-minute segment of "Straitjacket," which he says William Castle (see Page 187) filmed exactly as he had written. "I think it proves my point. For the tension built unbearably, then a lull came. The audience sighed – and wham. The shocker, which really worked. Again, it only worked because it was done as it was conceived."

This predilection for abnormal psychology – from where did it come? "It's not a love. Nobody has yet discovered this, although I've dealt with it in 50 or more stories, but I'm totally unsympathetic to the Freudian point of view. In almost every instance the psychiatrist's attitudes are exposed or downgraded. In last analysis, I'm writing morality pieces. My villains don't triumph – they don't really enjoy their frustrations or perversions, their savagery. I'm square in my attitude toward people like Norman Bates.

"The grotesqueries are merely illustrative, they are not written with admiration, but written only to entertain."

Which exactly describes "Psycho."

"Who did you say your psychiatrist was, John?"

Having Robert Bloch on "Creature Features" to discuss the history of "Psycho" in detail was one of the most memorable moments of holding down the job – if you want to call such a pleasurable task work.

Ever ready to cooperate, as long as he could bring his personal macabre touch to the occasion, Robert Bloch agreed to pose for these photos in front of his special "Psycho" shelf, an international representation in every language imaginable. All I had to do was ask Bob to hold one of the foreign editions – and he did the rest.

*"She screamed when she saw the old woman lying there, the gaunt gray-haired old woman whose brown, wrinkled face grinned up at her in an obscene greeting."* – **Another subtle passage from Robert Bloch's "Psycho"**

Then there was the night in October 1982 when Robert Bloch showed up on the set of "Creature Features" to have a grand time, again by demonstrating his macabre wit. I opened the show with a bit of diabolical doggerel:

"A writer was beginning to flower
Attaining to a higher power
When he went to great pain
To put poor Marion Crane
Into the Bates' Motel shower."

# An Intellectual Interview About "Psycho" – With Emphasis on Graphic Shock, Bloodletting and the Unpleasantness of Plugged Up Shower Stall Drains

*Stanley:* Mr. Bloch, you have avoided writing a sequel to "Psycho" for 20 years. Why have you decided to bring him out of the insane-asylum closet at this time with your sequel "Psycho II" [Warner Books, September, 1982]?

**Bloch:** I think the time is ripe to bring Norman back into a world that is even crazier than he is today. I wanted to see what happened if he got loose from the asylum and found out they were making a movie about him in Hollywood. I couldn't resist that. Had to give the readers the chance to decide for themselves if Norman is crazier today than the people in the media, movies, events.

*Stanley:* One of your critics once alleged that in spite of all the horror movies and stories you've written, you really have the heart of a small child? Is that correct?

**Bloch:** Well, I wanted to show you that my heart was in the right place. *(Unveiling an object on a table next to him – a heart floating in a huge glass container filled with a thick transparent fluid).* It's a good thing I wasn't stopped by a traffic cop on the way to the studio. I might have been placed under cardiac arrest.

*Stanley:* [After chuckling for several seconds] *Alfred Hitchcock first adapted your novel "Psycho" in 1960 and its shower sequence stunned the movie-going audiences of America. And now Universal is preparing a sequel, but it is not based on "Psycho II," the novel you've just had published. Would you please explain what the hell is going on?*

**Bloch:** In 1959, at the time the movie rights were sold, I was living in the small town of Weyauwega, Wisconsin. Weyauwega, by the way, is an Indian name for sanitary washroom. My agent sold 'Psycho' blind. I signed the contract, not realizing I had signed away all the sequel rights. I could write a novel but a studio could make their own movie.

The new movie will have nothing to do with my novel.

*Stanley: Did you look upon writing the sequel as a form of revenge on Hollywood for what had happened when your agent blew the contract deal?*

**Bloch:** Not at all. I just felt it was time to comment on the violence of our era and in some way make a statement. I don't think Universal and I are really at odds. In fact, before I left L.A. to make my trip up here, Universal was kind enough to give me a travel kit with a bottle of extra-strength Tylenol.

*Stanley: There are those who will read your book of violence, and it has many violent scenes, and they will say Bloch is using violence to make a statement about violence. How do you react?*

**Bloch:** Violently. I feel that if you're going to deal with that subject you have to present it. But not quite as graphically, or as pornographically, as some of today's filmmakers do. I tend to take a dim view of splatter films in which there is nothing but violence. No characterization, no semblance of a plot line that holds up or has any interior logic.

*Stanley: Reflective on society as a whole or just the film industry?*

**Bloch:** I'm afraid there is a reflection, a dim reflection, that violence in all forms is the solution to every problem. But it isn't, of course. When I write I never present my sociopath as being a happy character or fulfilled character or likeable character. They don't come to a good end and I don't think anyone would desire to emulate their activity. Actually it's in the realistic film where somebody performs an act of vengeance and gets away with it that a role model is created. Very bad for young people who would think this is the way out.

*Stanley: You remarked earlier that we've had a bloodbath but the tub is now full. Where can horror films go from here?*

**Bloch:** I think they will go back to strong solid storylines. There has been something sadly lacking in horror films in the last ten years. Have you ever thought, running the films you do, with the exception of British films, that the movies of the last 20 years have created no new stars? No Lon Chaneys, no Boris Karloffs, no Peter Lorres. No, the emphasis today is all on special effects. In me they induce nausea rather than genuine terror.

*Stanley: How did your writing career begin?*

**Bloch:** I sold a cannibalism story at the tender age of 18 to Weird Tales magazine. I also wrote psychological suspense tales. I was very active in fandom. I was admired for my personal qualities. I was earning a penny a word for my pulp-magazine stories.

*Stanley: Has it gotten any easier?*

**Bloch:** Not particularly. Inasmuch as I don't know how a story is going to turn out. I type

with my eyes closed. It makes for personal problems. Shortly after writing "Psycho" I met a woman and we've now been married for 18 years and because of "Psycho" she refused to have a bridal shower.

**Stanley:** *Are you trying to water down some of your comments?*

**Bloch:** Perhaps I am tapping into my subconscious.

**Stanley:** *Some of your stuff does have a whimsical quality.*

**Bloch:** It's a subconscious and instinctive thing, writing. I know it frightens me and I try to convey that fear to other people but in such a way that won't repel or disgust. I believe leaving a good deal to the imagination is a worthwhile way of going about it.

**Stanley:** *I've found one consistency: Your stories are entertaining.*

**Bloch:** I consider myself primarily to be an entertainer. Storytelling began around the campfires in the prehistoric days. I was one of the few people to be present at that time.

**Stanley:** *Why do we keep reading horror stories?*

**Bloch:** We all have a need for reassurance. The worse reality becomes, the more we retreat to fantasy. For in fantasy we can control our fears. We can switch channels, we can leave the theater, we can close the book. We can shut the door to the shower room. In real life that happy privilege is denied.

**Stanley:** *Tell us about the origins of "Psycho."*

**Bloch:** Remember I was living in that small town in Wisconsin? Well, in another small town 40 miles away, a fella named Ed Gein had committed several atrocious murders. He had been a resident of the town all his life. Everyone knew him. He used to babysit for the neighbors' children. During deer season he would give gifts of liver to his neighbors. It wasn't until later that it was discovered he never hunted deer. And I wondered how was it possible, in a small town where everyone knows everyone else's business, for such a man to perpetrate such crimes without discovery? I realized there was a story there. Without knowing all the details I invented a plot. I decided it was easier for a killer to conceal his crimes if the murderer didn't know he had done them. Thus was born Norman Bates. Years later when I studied Gein, I found out I had come very close to Gein's actual character. And for years after that realization I refused to look at myself in the mirror.

**Stanley:** *I've been told that you don't go to explicitly violent films.*

**Bloch:** Quite correct. I much prefer comedy. Which of course is the other side of the coin of horror. Both depend on the grotesque and the unexpected for their effect.

**Stanley:** *You started out writing in the H.P. Lovecraft style but then after his death, you drifted into the couch area of psychological terror.*

**Bloch:** I'd written hundreds of stories of supernatural fantasy and I was exhausted by that vein. All the blood ran out of it so I decided I had to find a new zeal. And I decided that the greatest horrors are not those of the supernatural but those that work in the dark recesses of the human mind.

**Stanley:** *Since leaving Milwaukee, where you worked full time for an ad agency, and settling in Hollywood around 1960, you've constantly fluctuated between books, episodic TV and movies. Striking when trends were hot, always finding new markets for your skills as a macabre storyteller. One of your better working associations was with William Castle.* [See Page 187]

**Bloch:** He was pleasant, indeed, he allowed me to do what I wanted to do. He would sneak in some grotesque effects that I didn't know about and was squeamish about. Certain segments of "The Night Stalker" stand out. On the other hand, no writer is ever 100 per cent satisfied with what's up on the screen. We all have our own concepts. It's commonplace for a producer to try and place his values on top of the writer's.

**Stanley:** *What would an ideal film contain without being totally explicit?*

**Bloch:** Something that would terrify an audience by virtue of placing it into a normal situation: *"Oh my goodness, this could happen to me!"* Such as the shower sequence in "Psycho." How many people each year stop at a motel and have a shower? And the proprietor sneaks a peek through a peephole in the wall? In this milieu, something horrifying could occur. The best horror stories are not hundreds of thousands of words. Some of the finest have been very very short. Edgar Allan Poe, H. P. Lovecraft. It should only take as long as necessary to achieve the required effect.

I cannot help but wonder if that damn cigarette perpetually clutched in Bob's hand did not ultimately lead to his death. He was even clutching it when he guest starred on the show. Now I wish I had ripped it away from him.

**Stanley:** *Is our society too permissive?*

**Bloch:** Yes, and responsible for us accepting violence as the solution to every problem. Of course, accepting violence is never the answer.

**Stanley:** *Will we one day read "Psycho III"?*

**Bloch:** Maybe, but right now I'm trying to get over doing this "Creature Features" program. I'm more comfortable doing my talking on a typewriter. You see, in order to come here tonight I made considerable sacrifice. Before coming I cut up a corpse. But fortunately for me I saved a stiff upper lip.

*There once was a fella named Bloch,*
*To whose books fandom did flock.*
*They all said right-o each time they read "Psycho,"*
*That yarn has a helluva shock.*

# Going Psycho on a Stairway to Doom

In the fall of 1983 I was invited to meet and interview Anthony Perkins prior to the opening of "Psycho II," in which Perkins brought back to life the Norman Bates character he had first introduced in 1960 in Alfred Hitchcock's classic adaptation of Robert Bloch's novel, "Psycho." During our meeting (described on the next page) I asked him to read a "wild line" (a term describing a bit of voice work designed to be dubbed into a film later), which he gladly did without asking questions. Later I dubbed that line into a segment I had done just prior to our meeting. I had been permitted to stage a stand-up introduction while perched on the front steps of the Bates mansion on the Universal Studios back lot. Here is how all the pieces fit together and how audiences saw the final piece:

**EXT. PSYCHO MANSION - FULL SHOT - DAY - A FIGURE**

*"Creature Features" host JOHN STANLEY, handsome and debonair, and clad in black slacks and a bright red dress coat and tie, is standing with the eerie house framed behind him. Appearing more than just slightly agitated and nervous, he speaks into a handheld microphone.*

**STANLEY:** The gothic mansion behind me is known around these parts as the old Bates place. It's located off the old highway that used to take you into Fairvale . . . until they put the freeway in and then nobody came out here much, especially at night.

Down over there, that's the old Bates Motel. It's been boarded up for 22 years or so now. Over there . . . beyond that knoll, Greenlawn Cemetery, where several generations of the Bates family are buried. Norman Bates used to live in that house–until they carried him away in a straitjacket and put him safely away in Atascadero State Hospital. His mother used to sit up by that window when she was still alive and she'd sit there, and she'd watch, and she'd wait, and she'd watch. Never did figure out what she was waiting for.

I guess you heard about that business 22 years ago, about what happened to that girl Marion Crane down at the motel and that snoopy private investigator Arbogast, who came nosing around here and . . . well, we all know what happened to him at the foot of the stairs, don't we. Fairvale being a small town, there's been a lot of talk, a lot of rumors, inuendos – but I wouldn't put too much stock in all that talk about the number of knife wounds they found in Marion Crane's body. Or what that doctor, that psychiatrist found down in the fruit cellar. Well, it's a funny thing. Fairvale is a small town and a while back there were a lotta rumors going around . . . *they were going to let Norman Bates out of Atascadero.* Now I'll admit the courts are pretty lenient these days but . . .

*Norman Bates loose on the streets of Fairvale? Maybe living in this house again?* Why, that's enough to give a grown man . . .

**ANOTHER ANGLE - TIGHTER ON STANLEY**

*Suddenly a butcher's knife is pressed against his throat, the identity of the assailant OFFCAMERA. Stanley turns slightly and recognizes who it is.*

**NORMAN BATES' VOICE** (Very pleasant): Hello, Mr. Stanley.

**STANLEY** (more than mildly agitated): *Norman, is that you?*

**NORMAN BATES' VOICE** *(as the knife pushes a little harder)*: Welcome to the Bates place. We're very pleased you've come. We'd love to have you up to the house for dinner . . .

*You see, mother is receiving visitors again.*

# FADE OUT

# MEET NORMAN BATES – IN THE FLESH!

WHEN I met Anthony Perkins I had a commonplace, ordinary butcher knife and I asked him if he would please hold the knife during our interview. Perhaps he would feel more comfortable with this ordinary kitchen tool in his hand. He could relax with it by cleaning his fingernails or cutting a sandwich in half while we chatted casually about beheadings, multiple stab wounds in a single body and other Fairview-related phenomena. However, Perkins rejected the idea immediately.

**Stanley:** *Then you don't like the idea.*

**Perkins:** Such a kitchen tool would be improper in the hands of the man who played Norman Bates. I reject the idea because it seems gimmicky to me, or gratuitous. It might have been appropriate for some pictures I've done or may do yet, but what attracted me to "Psycho II" and what makes it dignified and honorable is that it doesn't have those qualities.

**Stanley:** *Has it ever bothered you to portray the most infamous killer in all of cinema?*

**Perkins:** It used to bother me a lot. But I got over it.

**Stanley:** *Sometimes I get the impression that you're having fun playing Norman Bates.*

**Perkins:** Hmmmm. (Lengthy pause) It certainly wasn't meant to be for Tony Perkins to be having fun, because everybody took the idea of Norman Bates very seriously [once I had played him]. There's no camp humor in the film. I think Norman . . . one of the qualities he doesn't have is a sense of humor. His life has been too tragic and sad.

**Stanley:** *How has Norman changed over 22 years?*

**Perkins:** He's sadder than before. In "Psycho" he spent most of his time repairing damage done by his mother. Covering her traces. He was motivated by love and affection for her. In "Psycho II" he's sadder because he realizes he has potential for anti-social behavior. When we are robbed or denied our spontaneity, and Norman is denied those very things, that makes him a little melancholy. I liked the way the musical score [by Jerry Goldsmith, spinning off from Bernard Herrmann's score in the 1960 original] focuses more on that melancholia and wistful emotion rather than the [outright] scary music from "Psycho I."

**Stanley:** *What is the most challenging thing about playing Norman? You seem to get under his skin.*

**Perkins:** To get all the facets in. When an actor signs on to do horror or gothic films, and I'm no exception,  it's convenient to emphasize the qualities of the role that are the most prominent and to forget the subtleties. But I wouldn't have felt right about performing him a second time with lack of subtlety. He's too interesting a character. I wanted resonance but without being a carbon copy. I refer to Norman as "The Hamlet of Horror Roles."

**Stanley:** *Did the role of Norman typecast you after the great popularity of "Psycho"?*

**Perkins:** You have to know who you are not to get typecast. Then there is nothing to overcome. You have to wait it out and not accept such a thing as typecasting. It's important never to allow it to invade your own personality.

**Stanley:** *How do you feel about the violence and the special effects in "Psycho II"?*

**Perkins:** They're discreet and subtle when you compare them to those in less reserved horror movies. We're very very low key. One of the murders was filmed over and over again from different angles just to get the one that was just right. The director didn't want to make the audience feel it was being roughed up in anyway.

HOWEVER YOU SLICE IT, YOU HAVE TO ADMIT PERKINS IS ONE OF HOLLYWOOD'S MOST VERSATILE ACTORS, WHO GIVES NORMAN BATES AN UNDYING SHARP EDGE. OKAY, CAMERAMAN. THAT'S IT. NOW YOU CAN

# CUT!

NOW THAT YOU UNDERSTAND THE KEY TO NORMAN BATES' SUCCESS, PREPARE TO MEET AN ACTOR OF A THOUSAND FACES . . . HE COULD SPOOF HIS OWN ABOMINABLE CHARACTERS OR HE COULD MAKE YOU CRINGE WITH HIS BEINGS OF PURE EVIL . . . AND WHEN YOU GASPED AND REALIZED THE DIABOLICAL NATURE OF HIS BEING, YOU CRINGED KNOWING YOU WERE PAYING TRIBUTE TO

# THE PRICE OF FEAR

I n his youthful days as a handsome, debonair leading man at 20th Century-Fox, Vincent Price portrayed sinister characters in such films as "The Invisible Man Returns," "Tower of London," "Green Hell," the classic film noir "Laura" and the 1946 "Shock." But he was also an art connoisseur who soon turned collector, and he was a chef and gourmet who would write many books on the preparation of good food. But the preparation to playing evil, unforgettable movie characters would be far more important to him in the years to come. And there would also come a time when he hated being associated with horror movies and its icons, and unfortunately for me it happened right when I needed Vincent Price the most. Come with me now to a time when he still flourished as an actor and intellectual in so many different ways, but wanted nothing to do with people like . . . me.

# Don't You Dare Call Vincent Price a Star of Horror Pictures, You Cad

T HE FIRST TIME I met Vincent Price in the summer of 1979 he wanted to deny his heritage of horror. And he would have nothing to do with appearing on "Creature Features." That, he said, "is the very thing I am trying to stay away from." And stay away from Channel 2 he did.

Call him an art collector and connoisseur, call him a raconteur, call him a gourmet and call him an author. But please, do not call him a horror-film star. Part of the problem: I wanted to talk genre movies, he wanted to talk Shakespeare and music, since he was appearing with the San Francisco Symphony to read selections from the Bard's works. The needs of popular entertainment were in direct conflict with a level of intelligentsia to which Price aspired that summer, and I could say or do nothing to change his mind about the TV venue. When we did finally sit down together for a Chronicle interview, I wanted to talk horror films. He would have little to do with such a blood-drenched, gore-infested, gut-wrenching, lowbrow conversation.

"First, these things I have done aren't really horror pictures," he told me empathically, as one trying to tell an historian that the facts have been incorrectly recorded.

I loved the way Vincent Price clenched his fingers together in such a way you could almost hear him cracking the knuckles. The gleam in his eye, the hint of a diabolical plan on his lips. This is how he must have looked when he refused my request to appear on TV. Ah, a man of taste, after all.

"They're adventure thrillers. The world 'horror' should refer only to dope-taking and car crashes and other real-life tragedies. Secondly, out of all my films only about 20 have been of a horrific nature, usually gothic in structure, and therefore are only a minor part of my life." (I marveled that Price had allowed the word "horrific" to fly from between his lips.)

W hy is it that there are so many performers who deny what they do best? Why don't they accept the way the public perceives them and enjoy the notoriety? Did not Julia Adams finally acknowledge the fact that wearing a virginal-white bathing suit in "The Creature From the Black Lagoon" was the defining moment of her career and not portraying the wife on "The Jimmy Stewart Show"?

Does it not teach us to enjoy something for what it is worth at the moment it is worthy? Tomorrow it might be worth nothing. Or we might be too dead to enjoy it. Thank you, Janet Leigh, for your book on the effect making "Psycho" had on the rest of your career.

"I do not rest on my laurels," Price further told me. "I keep my career alive by moving among all the entertainment media. If one business is slow, another will be fast. Movement of the body and a challenge to the mind are stimuli for a full, happy life."

But sir, I reiterated, is it not "House of Wax" and "The Tingler" and "The House of Usher" for which you will be forever remembered? Is it not "The House on Haunted Hill" and "The Fly" that will be engraved on your tombstone? He shook his head. "They are but *minor* stops along a long pathway, my boy."

Not *minor* to the millions of fans who had enjoyed his films on TV and in revival series. Price could try to deny that "House of Wax" in 1953 revitalized an otherwise ordinary film-acting career and set him on a new path to cinematic heights he would have otherwise never achieved, but it wasn't working with me.

The movies that followed "House of Wax" were to give him an honored, lasting place in the Macabre Hall of Fame. "The Mad Magician" (like "House of Wax," made in 3-D) was followed by "The Fly," "The Return of the Fly" and "House on Haunted

I will forever remember "House of Wax" as my introduction in 1953 to the three-dimensional process and to Vincent Price. This was the film that really launched his career as a horror icon and convinced me that I wanted to see as many horror films as I could before the day of reckoning. Alas, Price had little need for me.

Hill." The latter was a rewarding collaboration with the suspense master William Castle (see Page 187), followed by a second Castle classic, "The Tingler," which displayed Price at his ultimate best when it came to hysterical behavior.

If the word "despicable" emerged from his mouth, I did not allow it to stop me. He was a red herring in "The Bat," a genuine herring in Roger Corman's "House of Usher," the first of many excellent Edgar Allan Poe adaptations produced by American-International. After 1960 Price's "despicable" career was on the upgrade, headed for a new horror-splattered plateau.

The chemistry was so successful between Price, director Corman and screenwriter Richard Matheson that several more Poe tales were adapted. Although Poe might not have recognized some of the plots, they all furthered Price's career: "The Pit and the Pendulum," "Tales of Terror," "The Raven," "Masque of the Red Death" and "The Tomb of Ligeia."

*Excuse me, Mr. Price, but the list runs on endlessly, does it not, sir? Ahem . . .*

There were non-Poe adaptations as well: "Master of the World" (borrowed from two Jules Verne fantasy-adventures), "The Last Man on Earth" (a fair treatment of Matheson's classic vampire novel "I Am Legend"), "Confessions of an Opium Eater" (never released theatrically, to the

The most grotesque, and memorable, of Price's horror roles was the leading character in 1970's "The Abominable Dr. Phibes." (The scene above would live a second time in 1972's "Dr. Phibes Rises Again.") But even when he wasn't in horrific make-up he was certain to be surrounded by others who were, such as in "Monster Club" (1982) depicted below.

dismay of fans), "The Haunted Palace" (an H. P. Lovecraft tale), "Comedy of Terrors," (a spoof on horror cliches–see photo left) and "Twice-Told Tales" (Nathaniel Hawthorne for the screen).

Of the genre, Price said, realizing I would not take no for an answer, "These pictures, they do go on forever because they can't become dated. They're like fairy tales. Fantasy has been one of our greatest literary exports for years."

Following "Cry of the Banshee" and "The Oblong Box," Price was to play his finest hideous-monster role – that of the maddened, thoroughly depraved Dr. Phibes, a deformed physician who inflicts the Curses of the Pharaohs on those responsible for the death of his beloved wife. The film was "The Abominable Dr. Phibes," of course, and it was released in 1971. Face devoid of flesh . . . a speaking tube thrust through his throat . . . the portrayal was so unforgettably grotesque it was crying to be repeated–and it was in "Dr. Phibes Rises Again." (below right.) Since then, Price admitted, he has made only two horror items: the excellent "Theater of Blood" (1972) and the less excellent "Madhouse" (1974), a muddled mess of a movie thoroughly squandering his talents and no fitting swan song.

A better group of horror stars there never was: Basil Rathbone towers over (left to right) Boris Karloff, Peter Lorre and the indomitable Vincent Price for this portrait snapped during production of "Comedy of Terrors" in 1963. Below, Lorre and Price trying to make points.

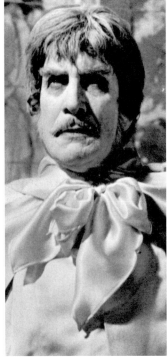

Please, Mr. Price, are you returning to the genre? "My boy, despite the enthusiasm in your voice, I have no such intention. For the past four years I have concentrated mainly on theater work. I've always done theater–that's where I started. I thrive on live performance and the immediate response of an audience."

I could not help but think that no matter how many Shakespearean readings he gave, or how many erudite art lectures he delivered, he would forever be Dr. Phibes, the resurrector of the dead, and the insane Henry Jarrod of "House of Wax" as his plaster false-face fell away to reveal the burnt hideousness that was charred underneath.

Mr. Price quickly ended the conversation, no doubt hoping he would never meet me again. But alas, that was not to be. The Son of Creature Features would rise again to meet Dr. Phibes, and this time it would not be so abominable.

# OKAY, FANS, NOW IT'S NON-ABOMINABLE TO CALL VINCENT PRICE A HORROR STAR

This stately pose exemplifies the erudite attitude Vincent Price brought to his role as the host on PBS' "Mystery" series.

And when we did meet in the spring of 1985, the Gothic still clung to Price like blood-sucking leeches. But by then he had given up the fight and had become comfortable with his "dubious profession" as horror actor. The Prince of Smirk was still there in the face and the gestures and the style. And he had returned to the fold by hosting the PBS version of the British "Mystery!" series: each week's opening was reminiscent of the opening of one of his Roger Corman-produced Poe films as the camera approached the window of an old gothic structure called Gorey Mansion, named after its designer Edward Gorey. Inside a library resplendent with Victorian decor and ambience was Price waiting to introduce an Agatha Christie whodunit or a Judge Rumpole courtroom drama.

Something else clinging to Price was the thing with whom he had fallen in love while making "Theater of Blood" in 1972: Australian-born actress Coral Browne, a long-time star of the West End stage where she had flourished in a number of comedies. In "Theater of Blood" his role as ham actor Edward Lionhart had allowed him to dispatch Ms Browne's character (a newspaper critic) to a sudden and permanent grave. But in real life they had found magnetic attraction and an undying love. And matrimony. And now they sat in a San Francisco TV station clinging to each other.

Although they had been married since 1974, they acted like silly school children who had just discovered they were smitten with each other. They held hands, addressed each other as "darling" or "dear" and otherwise behaved like infatuated teenagers. And because Price was having a happy moment, and had wisely given up his pretensions of pursuing art and not genre movies, I discovered in him a boyish quality, as one on the verge of bursting into laughter for some macabre joke he is about to play on all those legions of fans. There was a decided twinkle in his rich voice and he admitted to me that he loved to be scared as much as the next

At last! Myself and Vincent Price – the only photographic proof we had ever been together. Just off camera, waiting to hold his hand again, was his actress wife Coral Browne. My God, were those two in deep love with each other, showing the passion of teenagers.

Coral Browne was to be the last lady in the life of Vincent Price – and he couldn't have been happier in her company on the day we met.

person, and that the silliest things still frightened him. Being interviewed by Barbara Walters, for example. An "utter terror." Or just a good loud shrilly "Boo" cutting through the air one breathes. That always worked on Vincent Price, horror icon or not. Or a hand out of nowhere, suddenly falling on your shoulder. The quivering joys of life. Fear into laughter.

But, he said, "I shudder to think about contemporary horror films that are totally lacking in humor . . . there's nothing you want to give a good healthy scream at, you're too busy dodging the chainsaw or the electric drill. People used to say, 'You scared me, you scared me,' and be delighted to say it. It was fun to be terrorized then. But now, people come out of movies feeling afraid and disturbed. In our day it was the ridiculous. We were indulging in hokum suspense. Everyone was supposed to have fun."

As they relaxed in the Green Room of the TV station, Price carried a British air about him, a characteristic that the St. Louis-born Price has picked up after living in London for so many years with Browne. Price was decked out in a black tuxedo coat and a bow tie with huge blue dots. He held Coral's hand the whole time we talked. She kept looking into his eyes as one who is hopelessly trapped in the spiderweb of love.

(Call me a sentimental fool, even though I am supposed to be an expert on the horrible things in life, but I am sure they realized they were in the twilight of their lives, and perhaps that is why I felt such a strong bond passing between this star-struck twosome. Coral, whose film "Dreamchild" was playing in San Francisco that very week, would not make another movie, falling into the clutches of breast cancer soon after our meeting. She would die in 1991 at the age of 78 with Price at her bedside. He would die two years later of lung cancer at the age of 82. It does pay to enjoy the moment while you can, and these two were enjoying that moment. May we all be so lucky when twilight descends upon us.)

Only three months away from his 74th birthday, Price gave me the impression of a man who continued to strive within a professional whirlwind, moving from lecture to acting job to TV hosting to personal appearances to fixing gourmet meals, and barely having time to absorb the details of day-to-day life around him.

Clutching Carol's hand ever tighter, he said he hoped to cap his horror career with a Gothic tale for children, "a spectacular Gothic, because I love working for young people. This would be the ultimate horror film, the legend of Bluebeard, but told as a really terrifying story. It's never been done the way I've visualized it." Alas, this Bluebeard who wandered the chambers of Price's imagination would never come to exist on celluloid.

Price, after serving 60 years in the theater off and on, and Browne, after serving 50 years on the British stage, expressed no interest in going back. "I don't like to be away from Vincent for very long," she said. (Was she thinking that time was growing short?)

Price nodded. "Yes, my dear, you get to a certain age and absence is . . . " Was Price on the same wavelength? Browne cut in: "We've done it all and had it all and we want to be together. I want to be with Vincent. That's all I care about any more."

Price was eager to talk about his current TV role, hoping I would plug his introductions to the "Mystery!" series. The very reason he had sojourned to San Francisco. "Oh, he loves mysteries," said Coral, "but I can't take them." She looked away as if seeing evil nearby.

Yes, yes, said Price, "I love P. D. James, Josephine Tey and Agatha Christie. Those who have thoughts in their heads love a mystery. You let them do it for you, the murdering I mean. You just follow along as if you did it and say 'Yes yes yes.' It's marvelous to follow the convolutions of crime and murder. What a vicarious experience it is. If they're good writers, I can't put the books down. I love them. I travel a lot on airplanes, which I hate, and mysteries're the surest and best way to forget you're on an airplane."

And he laughed, the same laugh he's laughed as an executioner wielding an axe or as an evil scientist or as a mad king or as a downright psychotic madman.

I felt comfortable because I knew that the King of Leer was back from the dead–alive and living again in the body of the master of terror and horror, Vincent Price.

*(Postscript: In 2006 20th Century-Fox released Price's "Shock" on a high-quality DVD for the first time. I am happy to report I provided the running commentary for the 1946 feature.)*

Photo By John Stanley

AND
NOW
MEET
THE
PRODUCER-
DIRECTOR
WHO
HELPED
TO MAKE
VINCENT
PRICE A
HORROR
FILM
ICON
–THE
ONE AND
ONLY
ROGER
CORMAN

Corman Photos by John Stanley

# AN A-CLASS B-MOVIE MERCHANT WHO CHANGED THE MEANING OF Z-BUDGET

H E IS considered the master of independent film production in Hollywood and he doesn't miss a movie trick. Roger Corman has never been accused of going out of his way to make art films, but he has been called the King of B producers, and justifiably so. The "B" doesn't bother him as long as you mean "budget" and not "baloney."

Shock and schlock might have been his battle cry. He has been prolific like no other producer-director in history, and he's thrived admirably in a business known for its high casualty rates.

His history as a director suggests boundless energy and chutzpah, backed by an impatience to get each film made as quickly as possible for as little money as possible. At 23 he was working as a story analyst at 20th Century-Fox by day. By night he was writing a screenplay "Highway Dragnet," which he sold for $4,000. Borrowing another $8,000 from associates, Corman cut his producing teeth with "The Monster From the Ocean Floor," produced in six days in 1954 for just $12,000. He followed that up with "The Fast and the Furious," which led to a meeting with Samuel Z. Arkoff and James Nicholson, fledglings to the movie business who wanted to become distributors. Meeting with Corman would lead to the formation of American-International Pictures, a vastly successful enterprise in Hollywood for two decades.

AIP, as it become better known, quickly developed a reputation for inexpensive exploitation pictures with Corman serving as one of the company's guiding influences. He shot films faster than any other film-maker before or since, he created new genres, revitalized old genres and gave rise to the careers of "young hopefuls" Francis Ford Coppola, Martin Scorsese, Peter Bogdanovich and Jack Nicholson. John L. Wasserman, one of my late colleagues at the San Francisco Chronicle, once said of Corman: "He could teach Barnum about getting people through the tent."

H e single-handedly created the drug cycle of films with "The Trip" (1967), his gangster efforts were spearheaded by such efforts as "Machine-Gun Kelly" (1958) and "Bloody Mama" (1970), he gave birth to the Edgar Allan Poe series with "House of Usher" (1960) and carried it on with "Pit and the Pendulum" (1961) through "Masque of the Red Death" (1964). Science-fiction he exploited with "Attack of the Crab Monsters" (1957), among so many others.

He worked like a man with a death wish to produce scores of movies. His reputation was that of a madman who completed films in six or eight days, often for as little as $50,000. His timing was perfect – theaters needed minor pictures at a time when the major studios had stopped producing them.

Corman became weary of the treadmill he was on in the late 1960s – after all, he had directed nearly 50 films in just 15 years – and decided he'd take a rest from producing and distributing his own pictures.

Some rest. He ended up taxing his strengths even more with the formation of New World Pictures, which

in the 1970s became one of the biggest, and most successful, of independent companies. New World produced its own pictures and also "picked up" independent films for distribution. Some were domestic quickies or exploitation flicks, others were distinguished European art films such as Fellini's "Amacord." In 1978 he established his own New World studio in a rundown section of Venice so he could produce "Battle Beyond the Stars." The new facility now allowed him to make bigger pictures with "a little more" financing. He also created his own special effects division at the Venice studio.

Early in 1981 Corman paid a visit to the "Creature Features" set for the following exchange:

**Stanley:** *"Planet of Horrors"* [eventually released as "Galaxy of Terror" in 1981] *is one of your new films. Does it bear some resemblance to "Alien"? Was it inspired by "Alien"?*

**Corman:** Not necessarily. "Alien" is in the tradition of the sci-fi/horror film, which I did a number of in the 1960s: "War of the Satellites," "Battle Beyond the Sun." Of course, "Alien" is the biggest. Probably the best of that type – until "Planet of Horrors." However, the genres keep going.

**Stanley:** *How different is "Planet of Horrors" from "Alien"?*

**Corman:** We tried to make it work on a full-out shocker basis. *Shock the audience,* but at the same time we wanted to have an intellectual subtext. I don't mean to get pretentious about it, but the premise is, somewhere on [an alien] planet is something that has the ability to go into the unconscious mind of every member of a spaceship that comes to this planet. And that something uncovers the unconscious fears of those persons, and forces them to carry out their worst fears. So each person essentially sees a different kind of planet and experiences a tailor-made fear that fits the personality, the psyche.

**Stanley:** *Speaking of fear, what is your basic philosophy about scaring an audience?*

**Corman:** I Try to re-create the childhood fears of the little boy or girl or the baby. I feel I have to break through the senses of the conscious mind and attack the unconscious.

**Stanley:** You're running your own studio now in Venice. What are the advantages?

**Corman**: If I had been at a regular studio paying rent, I would have had to compress the time I needed to shoot the special effects scenes. What I like to call the shock shots. On "Planet of Horrors," because I was in my own studio, I could spend more time shooting and go back as many times as I needed. One wild scene showing a girl's fears and her encounter with a phallic-shaped monster was problematic. I told the director [Bruce D. Clark] that if he didn't get an R-rating, he had failed in his assignment. So we reshot the scene. X is X but I had to tell [Clark] he had really gone too far. We had to go back three times to the MPAA [the movie-code organization in Hollywood] and barely got it reduced to an R-rated scene.

**Stanley:** *I have always felt you tried to mix exploitation with story quality. True?*

**Corman:** Yes, that has always been a conscious policy at New World. With most films we do try to work on two levels. Always the commercial exploitation level but underneath that there must be another level – theme, statement, message, something important to the audience. Always what I call the subtextural level.

**Stanley:** *I read you're doing special effects for films not your own?*

**Corman:** Absolutely. We did [work on] John Carpenter's "Escape From New York," for a Star Bar commercial we created a [candy bar] flying through outer space, and we are scheduled to do work for John Carpenter's new film "The Thing." I like to be part of everything that's happening in movies.  ◘

**Something Strange Is Happening Out There Among the UFOs, Alien Abductees, Psychics, Mystics, Hypnotists, Split Personalities, ESP Jocks And Ghostbusting Ecto-Destroyers – Not to Mention Demonic Forces! It Must Be . . . It Is . . . A Neverland Daring Us to Enter Its True-Life Zone . . .**

# THE UNSEEN WORLD BEYOND THE PALE

*I always loved it when I was able to take one step beyond into another world, escaping the mundanities of everyday life. When I crossed over the threshold into the realm of the unexplained. Rod Serling called it "The Twilight Zone." Leslie Stevens called it "The Outer Limits." I've always preferred to call it "The Unseen World." This is that inexplicable place of "urban legends" that deals with things much discussed but never proven in a court of law. No smoking guns, no irrefutable confessions on the witness stand. No President of the United States standing on the steps of the White House embracing an alien creature with three-foot tentacles. (Would anyone believe it even if the President did it? Wouldn't the opposition party call it CGI?)*

*"The Unseen World" is where you find the legends of the human race: ghosts and other spectral images, parapsychology, extrasensory perception, hypnotism, split personalities, UFO sightings, reported alien abductions, little-green-men-from-Mars appearances, reincarnation, Ouiji Board analyses, levitation, walking-on-burning-coals and all those other puzzling "can-it-really-be-true?" mysteries of our universe.*

*Here's a story for you. One day my wife Erica, my 15-year-old daughter Trista and I were standing in the kitchen, next to the sink on which rested an empty mundane-looking Coca-Cola can. Suddenly the can moved all by itself–moved several inches before it stopped. I pointed this out excitedly and the others saw the can moving too. We all stood there open-mouthed, speechless. After a pause, the can suddenly moved again–back to where it had started from. A parapsychologist might guess it was caused by Trista, for adolescents and teen-agers are often held responsible for such poltergeist-like activity. But don't ask me to produce the evidence. And the can wasn't talking.*

*Part of the fascination with "The Unseen World" are the stories that others have told me, and I in turn have reported how they had taken that one step beyond, vicariously reliving the "unsolved mystery" experience with them.*

*Let's start with **Harvey Bernhard,** the producer of "The Omen" and the things he claimed he had experienced while producing that 1976 horror classic. It started a whole cycle of son-of-Satan movies. Was Harvey just trying to give me a good story, to ensure bigger audiences? After all, the film made so much money for Harvey that he went on to make sequels ("Damien: Omen II" in 1978, "Omen III: The Final Conflict" in 1981 and "Omen IV: The Awakening" in 1991) and none of the life-threatening experiences he described to me seemed to hold him back. Or was every word he told me completely true, the utter gospel?*

*So here is the first of many steps beyond. Make of these slices-of-unlife what you will . . .*

# Roman Omens That Came to Haunt Producer Harvey Bernhard

**Harvey Bernhard**

For everything positive there is something negative. For every thing good, there is some thing evil. If there is a Christ, it stands to reason there is an anti-Christ. The Book of Revelation makes the prophesy that

*When the Jews return to Zion*
*And a comet rips the sky*
*And the Holy Roman Empire rises*
*Then you and I must die.*
*From the eternal sea he rises*
*Creating armies on either shore*
*Turning man against his brothers*
*Till man exists no more.*

Theologians have interpreted this as a warning of Armageddon, the ultimate confrontation between good and evil; screenwriter David Seltzer has carried the idea further to suggest that the "he" of the prophesy is the anti-Christ, the son of Satan, who will one day rise up through the world of politics, ultimately destroying mankind.

All this was dramatically depicted in "The Omen," the current horror thriller that has become one of 1976's biggest box-office hits. It was made on location in Rome, London and Jerusalem and stars Gregory Peck, Lee Remick and David Warner. It is clearly a commercial film filled with graphic murders with a bone-chilling plot about a U.S. Ambassador to Rome who adopts a newborn baby only to discover that when the child is five it has strange tendencies and supernatural abilities. Each death seemingly caused by the child is brought about through an ironic set of circumstances, and the death is a horrible one.

Although I met Harvey Bernhard in 1976, it wasn't until years later that he paid me a "Creature Features" visit to discuss his latest, "The Beast Within." Sitting with him on the set, I had no premonitions or omens but I thought it unusual he wore dark glasses – was he warding off something I had no way of seeing?

While such a violence-driven plot has outraged some, it has proven to be thought-provoking to others. Harvey Bernhard, who spent 11 months abroad to produce "The Omen," showed up recently to sell his popular motion picture and passed along some hair-raising stories – or should I call them *yarns*.

When he saw my mouth falling open, Bernhard insisted emphatically they were as true as the existence of the Bible itself. For the record, I now pass them along to you readers.

"I'm not a religious man," Bernhard began,

"but there was some greater power at work . . . something that definitely didn't want us to make this picture. I felt it. Gregory Peck and director Richard Donner sensed it. Before I started the film a group of friends including Pat Boone and Dean Jones warned me I was in danger and would need watching over; they said they'd pray for us. Inwardly I thought nothing of this . . . until strange things started to occur."

The first thing that happened, claimed Bernhard, happened when Peck was flying to Rome and a bolt of lightning struck his airliner. Since a bolt of lightning is instrumental in causing one of the hideous deaths in "The Omen," one could call it a mere coincidence. And Bernhard shrugged it off.

But it was the second bolt of lightning that began to bother the movie producer. Brought a little sweat to his brow, perhaps? "You bet. It happened when writer David Seltzer was flying to Rome. A bolt of lightning struck his plane, too. He glanced over and saw one of the stewardesses down on her hands and knees in the aisle praying that they wouldn't crash." Okay, I had to agree with Bernhard, so coincidence was stretched just a little thin.

But a third bolt of lightning? Now I was on the edge of my chair. "Yes, it happened in Rome. I was staying at the Hotel Flora Grande. It was about 3 a.m. when I was awakened by a tremendous explosion. The entire sky seemed to light up. I've witnessed some A-bomb blasts in Nevada and I thought the end had come. Thirty feet away, a bolt of lightning had struck Hadrian's Gate, set in the wall of Rome."

One of the eeriest publicity pictures for a motion picture: British-born Harvey Stephens playing Damien Thorn in "The Omen." He went on frightening people as a London stock market figure and then became a property developer–hopefully not where cemeteries are located.

From that moment on, Bernhard told me, "I wore an Ethiopian cross" which he had picked up while making "The Adventure of the Jade Sea" [a project never finished?] in 1969 with William Holden. Maybe it was a good thing Bernhard did that, in view of what happened next.

It was the first morning of production, according to Bernhard. He was driving to the set when another car shot in front of his, totalling out his front end. Nobody was hurt, but everyone was "well shaken up." On another evening Bernhard was driving Donner to his Rome hotel. Donner started to get out when a car, its headlights turned off, shot out of the darkness and flung the passenger door completely off its hinges. Donner escaped injury, possibly death, only by jumping back into the car at the last second.

Part of "The Omen" is set in London's Safari Park, and one sequence features angry baboons leaping onto Lee Remick's car in an effort to attack her seemingly innocent son. The day after the scene was filmed, the head baboon trainer was attacked by a tiger; his skull was crushed and he died instantly.

Peck was accustomed to eating each night at Scott's Oyster Bar in the heart of Mayfair, London. Peck had no sooner left one night when a terrorist bomb exploded, killing two people. Then, continued Bernhard, as if the end would never be in sight, there was the incident of the Hawker-Sidley aircraft which was used in a flying sequence in "The Omen." The very next day it was chartered to Japanese tourists and the plane crashed on take-off, killing all the passengers on board.

"You can believe what you want," Bernhard told me. "Myself, I do believe in evil. And I believe that if the Devil or his son was among us today, you wouldn't see hooves, red glowing eyes or forks or tails. They would be unobtrusive. You would never know when these evil forces were about. Armageddon could come about from something other than atomic bombs or all-out warfare. Perhaps it will come about through our weaknesses and blindness as a people. If it ever happens, I hope we don't lose the final battle."

*The most bizarre "step beyond" was the night in 1982 when Erica and I had dinner with Ed and Lorraine Warren, who were self-proclaimed "Demonologists." They had served as technical advisers on "Amityville II: The Possession," which dealt with murders that had taken place inside the Amityville house before the story that had first unfolded in "The Amityville Horror." Just another interview for another prequel horror film about to open at Bay Area theaters, right? Slightly wrong. Instead, I came back with the makings of a creepy ghost tale. To this day I have to wonder: Did the ghost-chasing Warrens inadvertently bring something horrible with them that night that hovered in the doorway, something from a misty land of horror that scared the hell out of my beautiful Erica?*

## THE HAUNTED SAN FRANCISCO WINE CELLAR WHERE THE DROPS DRIPPED FROM . . . HELL?

Today I'm going to tell you a ghost story. It begins after the fall of darkness in the wine cellar at Orsi's Restaurant in [San Francisco's] Financial District. As the hour grows late, strange things will happen. Don't nod off.

The reason for the dinner is to meet Ed and Lorraine Warren. She's meticulously dressed and groomed, very attractive, instantly charming. He's a portly, avuncular type, immediately cracking jokes and having fun. Both are 55. They seem so ordinary during the first few minutes and only mundane things are discussed so that at first I'm feeling journalistic disappointment.

Nothing mundane, however, about their professional pursuit, and that's why I wanted to meet them. They are demonologists, specialists in researching the phenomena surrounding inhuman spirits, which are frequently referred to in layman's terms as demons and devils. Imps if they happen to be very young. Although the Warrens refuse to conduct seances, considering them "far too dangerous," they say they understand the religion

Ed and Lorraine Warren, the sweetest couple of Demonologists this side of . . .

of driving evil spirits from the human body. As Ed points out, every religion on Earth has its own variation of exorcism.

Granted, they are on the road pitching "Amityville II: The Possession," but this will be no ordinary sales pitch. But first the sales pitch: The new movie is a prequel to the first "Amityville" movie, depicting an earlier supernatural event at the three-story, six-bedroom Dutch Colony-style house at 112 Ocean Avenue in Amityville on Long Island. The film depicts how, in 1974, 23-year-old Ronald DeFeo Jr. shot to death all the members of his family: his father Ronald, his mother Louise, his sisters Dawn and Allison, and his brothers Mark and Johnson. DeFeo claimed he had heard voices urging him to commit the murders and that a "shadow ghost" was beside him as he pulled the trigger.

As the interview begins, my lovely wife Erica starts to get restless and keeps peering over her shoulder toward the cellar door. Across the table from us sits a representative from Orion Pictures. He keeps looking overhead. Erica and the rep are feeling uneasy, for good reasons, but for the moment they are keeping those reasons to themselves.

Meanwhile, the Warrens get down to a serious discussion of demonology, to which they have devoted their professional lives. The unusual "talents" they have are not alike, but working as a team they complement each other. Lorraine claims to be a clairvoyant and light-trance medium who can "pick up vibrations, thought waves and impressions." Ed can't do any of that. His specialty is the ability to see apparitions and his forte is in-depth field research. Are you following this carefully?

"A parapsychologist and psychic researcher," says Ed, "are people who think scientifically when they go into a haunted house or confront people seemingly possessed. On the other hand, a demonologist looks for something preternatural or supernatural. Lorraine and I have also studied ghosts and apparitions but our main interest is looking for the non-human spirit. Demons, lieutenants and captains have terrifying powers, but the devils, the generals, they are frightening beyond belief."

Ed is convinced he saw the Devil in 1980 during the exorcism rites for 11-year-old David Glatzel in Brookfield, Conn. "The room grew cold and a dark form materialized. Normally, in a case like this, features of the entity are not discernible, but I saw a face that kaleidoscopically changed from human to inhuman to satanic to animalistic to snake-like to lizard-like . . . I never want to see anything like that again." The controversial Glatzel case was documented by a writer named Gerald Brittle, who also wrote "The Demonologist" (Prentiss Hall, 1980), the life story of the Warrens.

Ed continues on his thematic path: "A ghost is traditionally a human spirit trapped on the earthly plain, which manifests itself in its original form. A demon has far greater powers. When we see a thousand-pound refrigerator levitating, or spontaneous fires, or slashes and other physical wounds being inflicted on the possessed person, we know we're dealing with diabolical demons."

To ask where these demons come from is to open the Pandora's Box to all the questions about Heaven and Hell, good vs. evil, God vs. the Devil – what Ed calls "The

Fallen Angel Syndrome." The Warrens claim to be devout Roman Catholics and can discuss the Biblical implications of demonology at great length. To support their beliefs they carry the weapons of their trade. Ed always comes equipped with a wooden cross and container of holy water. In Lorraine's possession at all times is a photograph of the Cauchin mystic monk, Padre Pio, and scapulars–small sacramental cloths designed to be worn around the neck.

Jack Manger takes a flying leap, supernaturally speaking, in "Amityville II: The Possession," the film that had brought me together with the Warrens. I too would climb to the ceiling the night we met in a wine cellar.

But her greatest weapon against the evil she often faces, she says, is her faith. "Many times I've wanted to run away, I was so frightened. But it's this trust in God that enables me to stand my ground. I feel guarded in what I do. I'm doing what God wanted."

The Warrens first got involved in the Amityville haunting in 1976, a few weeks after the Lutz family (whose story was documented in Jay Anson's 1977 best-selling book "The Amityville Horror") had fled the house after living there for only 28 days, leaving all its earthly possessions behind and refusing to go back. Lutz, who would be played by James Brolin in the film version, refused even to meet the Warrens at the house to give them the front door key–they met four blocks away, a "safe distance" from the accursed residence.

First, Lorraine's story of her first night in the house. I ask her to walk me through it – not literally of course. "I started up the stairway to the second-floor landing. I carried with me a relic blessed by Pedro Pio. I felt a pressure like a waterfall against my chest. I held the relic up and asked for Pio's and God's help. Then I was able to continue on to the third floor. I went into the room where Missy [one of the Lutzes' daughters] had slept. I closed my eyes, and horrible images came into my mind, images that Missy had experienced when she was haunted by one of the children who had been shot in that room. Without knowing it, Kathy Lutz had allowed her daughter to sleep in the same bed where Jodie had been murdered."

Then, Lorraine continues, "I went into the master bedroom. I knew instantly two people had been killed in that room. How in God's name, I asked myself, had the Lutzes been able to sleep in this horrible place? Suddenly I felt the presence of Robert DeFeo Jr. It was an overpowering feeling of someone committing murder. I definitely felt his evil presence. Questions in my mind: why hadn't the first shots awakened the others in the house? They were all found dead on their stomachs, as if fast asleep. Why hadn't neighbors heard shots? He hadn't used a silencer. This cursed bedroom, it was the worst place of all. Two people had died there. The mother had been shot twice. Twice!"

Returning to the front room, Lorraine was asked to communicate with any spirits in the house. As she did so, "an investigator from Duke University passed out. A cameraman from Channel 5 News in New York complained of heart palpitations and had to sit on the floor. Mary Pascarella, a prominent psychic researcher from New Haven, became ill and had to be taken out of the house." She concluded: "I am never going back. Never, never, never. Going into that house has plagued me for years."

Now listen to Ed's story: "I'll never forget that first time in the Lutz home," he recalls. "I was standing in the cellar when I felt a tremendous pressure pushing me down on the floor.

floor. The only way I can describe it is to compare it to the onrushing water in a stream. There was a suffocating feeling. I couldn't breathe. It felt as though hundreds of pinpoints of electricity were hitting my body."

Lorraine tells what happened that night, after they returned home: "Ed was in his study. It was about 3:10 a.m. when suddenly the door flew open and a black whirlwind entered the room. It came within two feet of Ed. He always keeps a crucifix in his desk so he grabbed it and held it up. The dark cloud retreated upstairs to my bedroom. In the name of Jesus Christ I commanded it to leave. Ed found me clutching a book to my chest and our dogs cowering in a corner, the hair on their backs raised. Something was warning us to stay away from Amityville."

The Warrens intrepidly continued their investigation nevertheless. Their conclusion: the house was definitely inhabited by demons. "Lorraine and I," says Ed, "are convinced the house at 112 Ocean Avenue in Amityville, Long Island, was invaded by demons a long time ago when a man named John Ketchum practiced black magic rituals there. Before that it was an Indian burial grounds, where the dying were brought. There had been a great deal of trauma and suffering in that accursed place."

The Amityville House as created for the film series, taking on a sinister "facial" look with windows for eyes and a deck fence for a mouth.

Lorraine cut in: "For a demon to come to the earthly plane, a door has to be left open. Sometimes it's through a Ouija Board, which is a dangerous, dangerous thing. Other times people practice satanic masses, witchcraft or black rituals. Once the inhuman spirit has been 'invited in,' as it were, we see infestations. This is psychic cold, when temperatures drop 35 or 40 degrees. There are footsteps, heavy breathing, apparitions, moving furniture, strange phone calls. Sometimes these things are blamed on a poltergeist, a mischievous ghost. (I was reminded of that moving Coca-Cola can.)

"Infestation is the beginning stage of the haunting. It progresses to oppression, when an individual undergoes personality changes. He or she seems to be motivated by outside influences. Behavior patterns shift. Possession is the final stage. The person speaks obscenities, often in strange tongues; levitates; takes on bestial facial features; attacks others violently; suffers wounds from an unseen source. The only way to rid the body of the demon is to perform an exorcism."

Now that I have told you the supernatural story of the Warrens, let me tell you my tale of the supernatural. Early in the interview Erica becomes so nervous I finally ask her what's wrong. She tells me there is "something evil" standing in the doorway. Something watching all of us. She's so frightened that she clutches my arm, her fingernails digging into my flesh. I actually excuse myself from the table and step out into the corridor, but neither sense nor see anything out of the ordinary.

Erica, removing her sharp nails from my arm, calms down when "the something" is gone.

The publicist from Orion Pictures keeps looking above his head. I am looking at him when suddenly I see a large drop of water splatter on the table in front of him. Ed sees it and shrugs it off as coming from the water pipes that crisscross the wine cellar's ceiling. I can see the pipes in the semidarkness above.

Yeah, I say, those pipes must be leaky.

I can tell by the look on the face of the Orion guy that he isn't buying that because a moment later another large drop splashes in front of him. He jerks away, repulsed.

So unnerved by this plunging second drop, the Hollywood publicist scoots his chair back and walks to the other end of the table, taking another seat.

"I'm not sitting in that chair again," he says, his voice shaking. He means it. And stays where he is.

Ed dismisses the drop redundantly as coming from a leaky pipe. Finally I cannot contain my curiosity any longer and I climb up on the rep's now-empty chair and search the area overhead, running my hand along all the pipes I can reach. There is no sign or feel of moisture anywhere. "Hey," I say, "these pipes are completely dry."

Leaving that wine cellar comes none too soon.

Erica Stanley, my lady companion who sensed something horrible was in the doorway of the wine cellar when we met the Warrens.

*In later years Ed Warren fell ill and collapsed in their home in Monroe, Conn., where the two had established the Occult Museum and the Psychic Society of New England. Bedridden and unable to speak, Ed no longer pursued ghosts, but I would have one more encounter with Lorraine Warren for the opening of a remake of "The Amityville Horror" in April of 2005. She retold me parts of her experience in the Amityville home, but then brought me up to date about a more recent event. Here it is in her own words:*

# The Curse of the 'Lord's Valley' in the 'Promised Land'

"Ed and I had finished dealing with Amityville and had tried to put it behind us, yet I always sensed something from that house was following us. Something dangerous. Ed was uneasy about it, too. Well, it was a beautiful day and we were driving in a brand-new car on Interstate 84 [Connecticut].

We passed one exit sign marked 'Promised Land' and Ed made a joke about it. He had left a religious medallion, his Miraculous Medal of the Blessed Mother, at home so I slipped a [religious] chain around his neck. When we came to another turnoff marked 'Lord's Valley,' the car suddenly went out of control. Inexplicably out of control. Ed was always such an excellent driver. But he couldn't control that steering wheel. We crashed through a guardrail and plunged down a 40-foot embankment. I prayed aloud to God because I could see an outcropping of rocks below, and I knew if we hit those rocks, the car would explode and burst into flames."

Miraculously, she continued, "the car rolled to a stop on its side, avoiding the rocks. We were both alive and unharmed." According to Lorraine, Ed turned to her utterly shaken and said, *"Even the Amityville Horror couldn't get us."*

*I* will forever remember him as the man who first gave validity to what I have called "The Unseen World." After all, if a television show claims its stories are based on reported cases, there has to be something substantial going on, and you have to believe in the message carrier. Or so I thought as a late-blooming young adult. I had first seen his "One Step Beyond" series which he had narrated, hosted and directed from 1959-61 and it had been my initiation into weird things that continue to fascinate me to this day. He often documented cases with the actual participants featured on camera, and he had presented an unforgettable two-part history of Dutch psychic Peter Hurkos (played by Albert Salmi). As on-camera narrator, a sincerity in what he was presenting came across strongly, and I knew that he believed in what he was saying.

It was therefore a special moment to meet John Newland in the summer of 1978 and discuss so many inexplicable things: the spectral images of the dead and other phases of parapsychology, and other anecdotal events that have taken on urban-legend proportions. Newland always claimed the stories were based on reported if not completely substantiated events. Newland was hawking his followup series, "The Next Step Beyond."

# A Step Into the Bizarre World of the Inexplicable With a Man Who Understood Mysticism

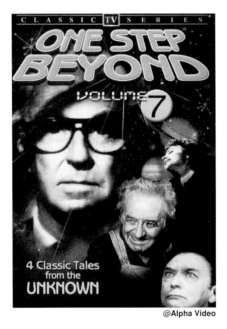

@Alpha Video

The face of John Newland, actor, producer and director of feature films and episodic TV, now graces the Alpha Video DVD boxes of his beloved, still-admired "strange but true" series "One Step Beyond," which ran on the ABC network from 1959-61. When he revived the series in 1978 as "The Next Step Beyond," it would mark the end of his long and prolific career in Hollywood as an actor and as a creative producing force. He died in 2000 at the age of 82.

JOHN NEWLAND looked scholarly at 59 years of age, a shock of white hair offset by large academic-like eyeglasses through which he stared at me professorially. While he had directed countless episodes of television (with a preference for "Police Woman" and "Wonder Woman," among so many others) and had also directed the horror-oriented telemovies "Don't Be Afraid of the Dark," "Crawlspace" and "The Legend of Hillbilly Johnny," he had still managed to maintain one basic identity for 19 years as host-narrator-director of "One Step Beyond" – allegedly true stories of psychic phenomena that were still being syndicated all these years later. "One Step Beyond" – with its three seasons of half-hour episodes – had maintained a spirit that would not die.

It was a time when exorcism, UFOs, ghosts, and Amityville hauntings were at a feverish pitch in America, so Newland had decided to dust off the old format and return with "The Next Step Beyond." "My involvement with all this paranormal business," he told me, "has become personal over the years and there's no doubt in my mind that something strange is happening out there."

Our interview, in a bar lounge at the St. Francis Hotel, was interrupted by the appearance of a total stranger, a young woman who had recognized Newland from across the room. She apologized for

interrupting, then told Newland she had to share a strange experience with him: she had heard ghostly footsteps in her attic. And whatever was up there was protective and benevolent.

Newland, with the knowledge of a parapsychologist, questioned her at some length, probing with astute questions and expressing no incredulity when he further learned that objects in the woman's home were disappearing and reappearing in places where presumably they had not been placed by human hands.

"The credibility for psychic phenomena is now at an all-time high," he said, once the young woman had scurried away. "There's a need nowadays for mysticism, especially among the young who're cult or 'ology' oriented. This has evolved out of a definite

TRUE STORIES OF THE MYSTERIOUS AND UNEXPLAINED.

disrespect for bureaucracy and religion and the Establishment and other things that don't always provide suitable answers to these questions." This new awareness, he continued, "has created a demand for more programming about the world of the bizarre. The college students who were so fascinated with the original 'One Step Beyond' are now the new probing audience." Demographics for the new show had revealed that there was an 18-26 age group keenly fascinated in ghosts and other supernatural manifestations.

"I think we're bolder and braver this time out and we're tackling some pretty mind-boggling themes that the network had shied away from 20 years ago." Each story, according to Newland, "has to be fully documented by other sources before we even begin to consider it. And then the facts and sources are double-checked by our staff of researchers." Unsubstantiated personal experiences are automatically disqualified.

I asked Newland if he had any answers to the mysteries he explored. "I don't believe in chance. We make our own fates and disasters. I do believe in the Jungian theory of oneness–that there is an omnipresent, omniscient force, a warehouse of knowledge if you will, that we can tune to consciously or unconsciously with the cellular portion of our brain. I've only had one personal experience of any consequence.

"In the early '60s I was in Mexico making an episode of 'One Step Beyond' about so-called sacred mushrooms, from which LSD is distilled. At that time LSD was still in its very early experimental stages and had yet to be discovered as a mind-expanding drug by the youth cult that would ultimately become a major part of the psychedelic movement of the '60s, the love generation of hippies.

"While we were filming a tribal witch doctor, in an isolated jungle village, he drank a potion of mushroom juice and made a number of startling predictions about members of the production team, all of which later came true. A few weeks after that incident, in a Palo Alto [California] laboratory with a movie camera turning, I drank down a blend of mushroom juice. Suddenly I felt very odd. A strange warmth came over me. I felt brave, I felt pioneering. I felt big and loud." His eyes were covered with thick adhesive tape and his hands were placed on a lead shield, behind which was a book. In weird geometric terms, he described images from the book which he saw mentally.

Newland claimed that "I saw two white columns making an enormous amount of noise. This turned out to be a picture of Yosemite Falls. Then I saw two heads, one bigger than the other, both benign. This was a picture of the Virgin Mary and her child. These odd phrases blurted out of me and to this day I can't explain why. I could see those images even with my eyes so tightly bound. I spent seven days recuperating from the hangover and I was disturbed by the experience for weeks afterward.

"I'm very aware there're believers and nonbelievers. Personally, I'm a believer and accept with glee any involvement. If I'd been afraid, as some people are, I would've never entered such a realm of possibilities – or impossibilities, whichever way you look at it."

# A Real Ghost Story

*I have saved the most haunting of my haunted stories for last – for this is one episodic adventure I lived firsthand. It was a two-part experience that started with me attending a seance . . . here is the story describing the first step that occurred in November 1978:*

"IN SEARCH OF . . . ," the syndicated Alan Landsburg series that travels the world to examine weird mysteries in a pseudo-documentary style, and which is narrated by another traveler into unusual universes, Leonard Nimoy, recently went in search of a haunted house in the Oakland Hills. Landsburg's producer, Howard Lipstone, asked me if I wanted to go in search of a story about ghosts, and attend a seance. The house in question, he said, "has quite a reputation. It's scared the pants off a lot of people."

I predicted to Lipstone I would materialize shortly after dark on the night in question, but well before the witching hour. The Bavarian-style mansion turned out to be one of the oldest in Oakland, part of a 49-acre land grant dating back to 1854. It sat below street level, at the foot of a steep slope, but because it was double-story, the top floor was flush with the street. In total darkness, and wondering if I might be slightly crazed, I descended from the street down a flight of sharply angled cement steps.

I felt immediately uncomfortable. The old, two-story chalet, flanked by majestic eucalyptus and redwood trees, looked strange and mildly foreboding. But I told myself, so do a lot of older houses which have no ghostly reputation. I chalked it up to surplus imagination caused by seeing too many horror movies. I was sane after all.

Inside the house's dining room, the "In Search of . . . " camera team had already set up – one 16 mm camera to record the pending seance from a wide angle, a second video unit nearby to record a window believed to be "hot," i.e. haunted.

The interior was orderly and well kept, though most of the furniture was turn-of-the-century or older. A darkness clung to the corridor outside the room and I decided to stay out of that corridor as much as I could.

The seance was being readied at the table in the dining room – rumored to be the most haunted area of the house. A man and woman had reportedly been seen outside one window; a sea captain with Nordic beard and mustache had been spotted outside another.

At the head of the table sat Sylvia Browne, a well-known psychic in the Bay Area. For this show they were calling her a transmedium from Campbell, CA. With her were Frank R. Nocerino, a parapsychologist and psychic investigator from Pinole, a small community to the north; writer-researcher-investigative reporter Antoinette May, and the husband and wife who owned the house, John and Brenda Slaughter. (Of this group I knew only May, who wrote the horoscope for the Chronicle's Sunday Datebook under the name Minerva.)

Chronicle Photograph by Vince Maggiora

Ordinary photo of a man standing in front of his home, right? Wrong. Extraordinary photo of John Slaughter standing in front of the most haunted house in Oakland, CA, at least according to the urban legends and his own reported experiences. I went there for a seance and later for a "Creature Features" report and I'm not planning to go back.

The Slaughters asked that I keep the location of the house secret so curious ghost-chasers wouldn't be coming around to peer through their windows. "I already have enough people at the windows," Slaughter said. "And they're all dead."

Before the seance began I talked to Nocerino, who turned out to have a friendly, jovial side – not what I had expected from a seasoned psychic researcher (he had held the job since the 1940s.) Nocerino's investigation of the Slaughter House had extended over a two-year period and he had at least 500 "spirit" photographs with him that night – shots of walls, rooms, ceilings. He had set his camera on a timer to take snapshots at regular intervals, and left it there for long periods. Some of the photos he showed me had strange distortions and wavy lines on them. These were "hits." Unexplainable forces of energy recorded on film. In one photo I saw two floating objects next to a dining-room window. Slaughter informed me they were human heads. Perhaps it was the power of suggestion but when I looked again I thought I did see two heads–male and female.

Slaughter, a 39-year-old former San Francisco advertising executive turned marketing consultant, had lived in the house on and off for 15 years and had come to accept its oddities. "You adjust yourself," he told me. "You expect the inexplicable. Sometimes I'll feel excessive energy in a room, so I won't walk into it. Lights go off and on mysteriously, windows open and close when we've double-weighted them down. There are no easy answers so after a while you stop looking for easy answers."

There were, he continued, "four major hot spots: the dining room windows, the L-Shaped Room upstairs, the garden hillside and the hallway. Sometimes the manifestations are so oppressive I have to leave the house. Or the grounds will reek with malevolence and I'll have to go back inside. One time I was standing on the porch when something knocked the cigarette out of my hand and it rolled along a bannister for 30 feet. We've counted 27 different entities in the house or on the grounds. Four seances have already verified that number. What will this fifth seance yield? Stick around and find out."

At first there was none of the heaviness I've always seen associated with seances in movies. Nocerino cracked some ghostly jokes and everyone at the table laughed or chatted away as if a Sunday dinner was about to be served. Finally Nocerino said, "Once we touch hands, don't break the contact for anything." Everyone got down to the serious business of raising the dead. The film and tape units rolled.

Dal, the husband of transmedium Sylvia Browne, placed his hands on her forehead. She tensed, snapped her head and groaned, then leaned back normally. Speaking slowly, Browne described the air as "highly charged . . . two brothers are here, near the window . . . one is dark and curly-haired . . . I get a name: Adrian. Someone . . . Katy. Strong presence here." In detail she described a clash of egos and a beautiful woman over whom two brothers were jealous. "One brother is killing the other with a long-handled knife. The loft room upstairs . . . heavily pressing . . . a hotbed of whirling energy . . . fourth step on the stairs has energy."

**Psychic Sylvia Browne**

Browne suddenly returned to normal and the seance was officially over. I turned and spoke to Antoinette May, who had been seated next to Brown. "I'm not a psychic," she said, "I'm a researcher and observer. But I did feel a tension and a temperature change. I turned cold. And I saw a flash of white light at the window. At least I think I did." Nocerino overheard us and leaned in: "I saw as many as five flashes of white light coming from that window." Antoinette fell silent as she studied him.

Nearby, Slaughter was smoking a cigarette and looked relaxed, seemingly not bothered by the unusual proceedings. "Hey," he said, beckoning to me. "How'd you like to explore the L-Shaped Room?" He made it sound like a jaunt. It turned out to be a tiny sewing loft at the top of the stairs off the kitchen.

The room had a decidedly oppressive, musty atmosphere. I noticed the wooden window ledge looked like a practice board for a team of woodpeckers. "We keep trying to nail that window shut," Slaughter explained, shrugging. "But every time we return to this room, the window's open."

Could he shed any light on this mysterious house? "I'll try," he said. "In 1947 a reclusive couple lived here. The woman disappeared and was never seen again. Neighbors suspected foul play, but nothing was ever proven. According to mediums who've conducted seances here, the woman was strangled in this sewing room. Her body is buried somewhere in the house—we think in the wall behind the fireplace. Why is the window always open? The spirit, or energy force, of that woman is eternally being strangled and she's seeking air. So I'm told."

Psychics have also told Slaughter there is a body buried in the basement, victim of a hatchet madman. Another person was allegedly murdered in the kitchen and dissected into small pieces. "Originally," he explained, "this house was a hunting lodge, with nothing for miles around. It could be that poachers were shot and killed and buried on the grounds by the gamekeeper. They're also legends of an Indian massacre in this area in 1867. Bad stuff has gone down around here."

Antoinette May: A good friend, a fellow Chronicle writer (as Minerva, the Horoscope Lady of Mystery), author of the novel "Pilate's Wife" and haunted house investigative reporter who probed the mysteries of the Slaughter Mansion the night I was there.

Meanwhile, let me tell you about Antoinette May, the horoscope expert and psychic investigative lady who was also at the seance table that night. "Sylvia and I are very much rivals, we're cat and dog [fighters] when it comes to investigations." Nevertheless, they had tolerated each other's presence that night, and if anyone had impressed May it was Nocerino (or Nick). "I was very intrigued by Nocerino's photographs. There were some of an overstuffed tufted chair where the back was pyramid-shaped. Nick took photos when nobody was in the chair and yet there was a bolt of lightning coming out of it, and two strange dots on the photos that I thought made it very dramatic."

She also told me that while they were seated at the seance table, a flame had shot upward out of a candle that flew about "three feet into the air." Overall, she concluded, "I felt very uncomfortable. I felt the Slaughter House had bad vibes. It was, to say the least, not a good feeling to be there."

(Toni, as her friends call her, went on to write "Haunted Houses of California: A Ghostly Guide to Haunted Houses and Wandering Spirits" [Wide World Publishing, 1993] but told me in preparing this update that she had not included the Slaughter House in her coverage. "I was asked by John Slaughter not to do so, and I honored that request.")

During my four-hour visit to the house I had seen nothing to support the theory of ghosts. But the seeming sincerity and candid of Slaughter and Nocerino had convinced me that something strange was happening here. For which there didn't seem to be any easy answers.

When it came time to leave, I felt an uneasiness as I ascended the stairs back to the street. I felt as though something, or somebody, was at a large window, glaring at me.

When I reached the sidewalk I was glad to be on my way.

But I would be going back to the house, whether I liked it or not.

A few months later I began hosting "Creature Features" and thought that a film report about the Slaughter House would make an impressive impact on my audience, so I returned to the house on Jan. 12, 1979. Accompanying me was my wife Erica, who acted as an assistant producer. (She would demonstrate unusual powers that day.)

My cameraman Ron Willis (see Page 198) filmed me in 16mm in several rooms of the house and we also did an interview with John Slaughter. Nothing unexpected happened although I noticed that the family dog, a small terrier, had a crazed look in its eyes – a kind of look I had not seen in a dog before.

San Francisco Chronicle photographer Vince Maggiora's photo reveals unexplained splotches of light that to this day have never been explained. They can be seen above the window at bottom left, and again just below the roofline to the right of the peak of the roof, drifting downward to a larger splotch to the right of the windows. Vince called me at home that night, he was so puzzled by what he saw. "I checked all the other photos I took and could find nothing else wrong."

Erica later told me the dog looked her into the eyes and she received a message: *Get out of this house before it's too late!* She was gravely affected by this but chose not to tell me about the incident until we had left the house. (Over the years Erica, a provocative woman in many ways, has undergone unusual ESP experiences such as this one.)

That Friday night she went to bed and slept constantly *for the next two days.* This was not customary behavior and I am still puzzled about how the visit to the Slaughter House had such an adverse effect on her. What strange moments she has lived . . .

There is one final postscript to this story: On the day we photographed the report, a Chronicle photographer named Vince Maggiora, one of the paper's finest, showed up to take pictures for my scheduled story about the "In Search of . . . " seance.

He called me at home that Friday night to say that one photo he had taken of the exterior of the Slaughter House had turned out with a nebulous whirl in two different places on his negative. He had examined the negative carefully and felt there had been nothing wrong with it. All the other pictures on the same roll of film had turned out fine.

The following Monday I conferred with Vince and examined the photo that had puzzled him. *The two troublesome foggy swirls looked exactly like some of the weird stuff I had seen on Nocerino's photos.* I was flabbergasted, but still had no solution.

Vince's photo ran in the Chronicle with my story and it was the talk of the paper for a while. We had certainly come back with more than we had bargained for.

But nobody ever came forward with an explanation.

I doubt that anyone ever will.

What about you?

Maybe you know the answer.

# THE WICKED WICKER MAN AND THE HAMMER-HEAD ACTOR WHO GAVE BRITAIN GREAT HORROR MOVIES – INCLUDING THAT PRINCE OF DARKNESS, DRACULA

*A Meeting with Christopher Lee in 1977:*

The Man With the Golden Gun points his weapon at an empty bottle of Cabernet Sauvignon, squeezes off an imaginary shot and unscrews the barrel. It now becomes a leak-proof Waterman fountain pen. He detaches the trigger housing and it now serves as a cuff link of Victorian design. He next disengages the firing mechanism which, in the palm of his hand, is a functional Colibri cigarette lighter. And the pistol grip, once flipped over, turns into a cigarette case.

The Man With the Golden Gun lays the four pieces in front of him, looks utterly defenseless, shrugs and remarks: "See, I'm totally unarmed."

He might have added, "disarming." It's part of the Christopher Lee charm. Seated at a banquet table at the Stanford Court, he has flown to San Francisco to display the custom-made, gold-plated pistol which he wields, and frequently fires, as the unique hit man Scaramanga in the latest of the James Bond films, "The Man With the Golden Gun."

Scaramanga is an international killer with a third mammary gland (an oddity the film doesn't milk too much) who hires out for $1 million per hit. He always works alone and prefers cat-and-mouse games with his intended victims. Scaramanga is a departure for Lee from his usual villainous roles in low-budget genre films.

Certainly Scaramanga is the classiest villain Lee has played, although he is quicker to pick up on his personal opinion that the Bond nemesis is "by far the most interesting of my villains, for he's a loner who relies on his own wits to destroy his greatest adversary, James Bond." (In those days Bond would have been Roger Moore.)

Fans all over the world would disagree Scaramanga is his ultimate villain. They would argue and debate. They would go so far as to bite Lee in the neck to prove that his greatest role was that of Count Dracula in those Hammer horror epics from England. Dracula is a part Lee now eschews in favor of "bigger and better things."

The sacrophagi in Lee's career are at least in the process of turning, a fact made all the more ironic by something he once said to a chronicler of horror films: "There's more violence, sadism and obscene beastliness in three minutes of a Bond film than in 20 Hammer pictures combined."

But that, of course, was before he made any Bond films. Now he's into the A category he has sought, and found elusive, for so long. He thinks "The Wicker Man" is his best horror film, although its box office returns have been meager based on poor distribution.

He is fond of his Rochefort, the one-eye dastard in "The Three Musketeers" (the 1974 version directed by Richard Lester) and in its sequel, "The Four Musketeers." New doors are opening, and just as quickly he is closing others behind him. Well, not all the doors.

"Of course," he comments in his impeccably polished British manner, "I'm not averse to playing in other horror films, if I felt they were in the proper vein. I'm dying to do Bram Stoker's 'Dracula' but only as it was originally written. If a producer with the money and guts offered me the role, I wouldn't hesitate. But the costuming, the sets, the characterization – all would have to conform to the standard set down by Stoker."

To trace Lee's growth one must go back to 1947, when he made his first minor thriller "Corridor of Mirrors" (a beginning he acknowledges as "dreadful"). Newly discharged from the Royal Air Force, tall, lean, gaunt, eager, he was suited for action and adventure pictures, although his height of 6'4" curtailed any leading-man aspirations.

"Doing little pictures" – that's how it went until 1956, when Hammer decided his gaunt features were spawning ground for a new Frankenstein Monster. Mercifully (for the make-up job wasn't all that good), it was the only time Lee would have to play the Monster, but the exposure attracted him to Hammer directors Anthony Hinds and Terence Fisher, who were lurking in the vicinity like figurative body snatchers, digging for the remains of a yet-unearthed Count Dracula. Lee was their "pay dirt."

"The Horror of Dracula" (released in the U.S. in 1958) did it for Lee – the picture made money all over the world. Audiences and Hammer demanded Lee for more cloak-and-swagger dramas, but he steadfastly refused for the next few years, hoping he would find more "beneficial" roles. It didn't happen. He shambled as the Mummy, sneered and leered as Fu Manchu, blinked an evil eye as Rasputin (occasionally he was the good guy – as in "Hound of the Baskervilles" in 1959), but never in the A pictures he so desperately sought.

So, with "Dracula, Prince of Darkness" (1967) he returned to the crypt and continued to portray the Transylvanian count, racking up seven Dracula epics for Hammer. But after "Dracula Is Dead and Well and Living in London" (1974) he refused to bite the creamy throat of Veronica Carlson or admire with lusty, flaming-red eyes the heaving breasts of Ingrid Pitt. "The films were deteriorating," he recalls with distaste. "I wanted more production quality, better scripts, but Hammer didn't want to spend more money. They've

always been in the business to entertain, not ascend to new cinematic heights. Why bother, they would argue, when we know the films will gross well whatever the budget?" So died Dracula, while Lee began to live his new career for the first time.

Now, with 125 feature films behind him, Christopher Lee is pointing the Golden Gun and saying things United Artists expects of him. Yet, as he has done in so many of his films, he has risen above the situation. Lee remains superior to his material. Forever the gentleman, dignified, reserved, yet demonstrating a warm spirit that returns to haunt you later – a sunlit form of haunting that is in cheerful contrast to the forces of darkness he has so often personified, imitated or invoked.

*That was in 1977. Here's what happened in 1979:*

# THE DAY CHRISTOPHER LEE DRAINED MY BLOOD – ALMOST!
## OR
# WHY DID I BLANCH WHITE WHEN DRAC WALKED IN?

I've already told you on Pages 75-76 the story about Christopher Lee and why he almost walked out of the studio, which would have left me guest-less at a time when I thought he was going to be my showcased, much-admired star. And how he paused to watch my filmed interview with Ray Bradbury. And afterward decided, *"Well, I guess if it's good enough for Ray Bradbury it's good enough for Christopher Lee."* And stayed to fulfill his obligation. It would have been a fate worse than having your blood drained out of your body by a vampire. And then finding out the vampire wasn't even staying to drink it. Or being enwrapped in thousands of yards of gauze like an Egyptian mummy, and left to be blanched and withered by the blazing sun. Lee and I did three interview segments. Here are the highlights of our "bloody good" conversation:

Christopher Lee, lost beneath the muck of a monstrosity he murkily played in Hammer's 1959 thriller "The Mummy."

**Stanley:** *How do you feel about the direction horror and sci-fi films have taken in recent years?*

**Lee:** Irrespective of whether they are good or bad, and of course I haven't seen them all, I feel that the main difference today is that they spend vast sums of money on these pictures which gives them greater production values. These pictures rely on special photographic effects and bigger sets–all of which comes down to money. Whereas when I made pictures, which was a very long time ago, things depended more on the

performances of the actors and actresses. So [this overpowering effect] can have an impact on the outcome of these pictures.

*Stanley: Sometimes we see you in films that aren't top grade, such as "The End of the World" and "Starships Invasion."*

**Lee:** Yes, well, I've been in quite a few of those.

*Stanley: Do you take these lesser roles just to keep yourself working? Is that your philosophy?*

**Lee:** Not entirely. I took 'Starships' because it seemed to be a good idea and Robert Vaughn had agreed to do it. You always go into a film with the best of intentions and the highest of hopes. Unfortunately, and this happens too often, the picture didn't end up to be as good as one had hoped. That's something beyond an actor's control. As for 'End of the World,' I had been informed categorically that Arthur Kennedy, Jose Ferrer and Richard Basehart had all agreed to be in the film and based on that, I agreed to do it. When I arrived on the set I discovered I had been lied to, their involvement was completely untrue. I did the picture but of course I regretted it.

"Take Mr. Stanley to the Dungeon . . . Where He Will Await My Pleasure"

Fu Manchu was a role that brought out the best of Christopher Lee's dastardliness in at least five Hammer horror thrillers. Look at those lips . . . study those eyes . . . here and above.

*Stanley: Have you any goals yet to achieve as an actor?*

**Lee:** Lots. Some of them I don't know of yet, because the stories and parts haven't been written, or offered to me. But the goal of every actor is to go on to one good picture after another. I am always hoping that magical part or magical picture is waiting for me. I just finished my 141th movie, and although I'm not likely to make another 141, I do hope to keep making interesting pictures with worthwhile parts. That's all that matters.

*Stanley: What are some of your favorite films [in which you have appeared]?*

**Lee:** As far as Hammer is concerned, "Scream of Fear," "Devil's Bride" and "Rasputin." The others . . . I would say Billy Wilder's "The Private Life of Sherlock Holmes," "The Three Musketeers" and "The Four Musketeers," and now I would add Steven Spielberg's "1941."

*Stanley: What about "The Wicker Man"? You didn't mention it. Although made a long time ago, in 1972, it finally came out on a limited basis. In the past you've spoken of it profoundly. What exactly is going on?*

**Lee:** Audience reaction was everything we had hoped for. I've said many times, nobody has ever seen a film quite like it. I will always maintain that. I still think it's the best part I ever played. A remarkable and extraordinary movie. Since 1972 this film has been dogged

by ill-fortune. Mainly based on personality conflicts, politics, all sorts of things. Nothing to do with the quality of the picture. Someone even succeeded in losing the film. Three hundred cans of out-takes disappeared and ended up under a freeway. But we can't recut the picture because so much of the original material doesn't exist.

**Stanley:** *What about the films you like least?*

**Lee:** The list is rather large. It might take some time. (Laughs) No, I'm not going to say the titles. Because nobody sets out to make a bad movie. If I was to say this or that was terrible, that the direction or acting was terrible, that wouldn't be fair. We all get involved with films because we hope they will be successful. To think otherwise would be madness.

# HE TRIED TO SCARE THE PANTS OFF AMERICA, THIS LIVING CASTLE OF HORROR

*(I would first meet William Castle in his Universal digs in the summer of 1964. I had grown up watching his gimmick-filled horror pictures so it was a decidedly memorable event.)*

Gimmick-meister Bill Castle.

THE SEXUAL dreams of teenagers–that was on the mind of William Castle as he reposed in a green leather chair in his bungalow office at Universal, taking a deep, contemplative pull on his ever-present cigar. As billowing smoke formed over his head, the dean of horror-movies-with-a-gimmick mused, "First, let me make it clear that we all have sexual dreams." A wry smile curved around the lips of the white-haired producer-director and his eyes sparkled for a moment. Then: "But with younger people their sexual dreams offer a release from the violent age in which we live, and all of its accompanying frustrations. These nocturnal nightmares subconsciously dictate teenager's taste in films; what is on the screen helps satisfy suppressed desires."

Was Castle putting me on? I wondered. All this serious stuff about sex, when I had dropped into the bungalow to find out about his next gimmicky motion picture. But wasn't sex the best gimmick of them all?

Castle pushed his glasses onto the top of his head, a habitual Castle practice, and went on: "I don't mind telling you, I have my share of dreams, just like everyone else. In fact, I dream most of my movie plots, or at least the basic idea for them. I keep a small night lamp at my bedside [with pad and pencil] and I jot down notes when I awaken."

Castle blew cigar smoke at the ceiling – and I wondered if he wasn't blowing just a little smoke my way too. But there was conviction in his voice. Sincerity. If Castle was a con man, he was the most charming con man I had ever met. His elaboration continued: "I keep having a recurring nightmare: I'm always winding up in Europe without a passport.

Now find something sexy about that, young fella."

As Castle leaned back in his chair, he explained that all this "current dream kick stuff" is allied to his current film project, "The Night Walker," which he had recently finished shooting at the studio. For Castle, everything about a movie had to be thematic. Including a conversation with a newspaperman, because he started telling me that "I'm taking a survey of sexual dreams of film-goers 10 to 80 all over the United States." His list of questions was going to include "Do you ever dream of murder or violence?" and "Do you ever dream of love-making?" There was the sex again. With Castle, it was never far away.

Barbara Stanwyck and Robert Taylor in Castle's 1954 film "The Night Walker."

What exactly, I had to ask, was "The Night Walker" about? I could tell by his expression that he was glad I had asked. "Yes, 'The Night Walker,' it's a study of sexual dreams. Barbara Stanwyck, she plays a woman who repeatedly dreams about a hideously deformed man. But is she really dreaming? Or is it actually happening? Is she living through some horrible experience? And that is the basis for Robert Bloch's screenplay: the line between dream and reality. And wait until you see the surprise ending. Wow!" Castle was never shy about providing his own hyperbole.

"I had to safeguard that surprise ending," he added. "When we were filming I put a sign on the studio door: 'Sorry, No Visitors. Too Scary Inside.'"

Stanwyck's costar, he told me, was Robert Taylor – but not because they had once been married and wanted to get together again. "Taylor is gravy to nab the oldsters. I already have the teens snagged with the horror theme. But why not appeal to the more mature set? Hell, you make twice as much money that way."

The 50-year-old director explained that until the late 1950s he had been a contract director at Columbia Studios, turning out such genre pictures as "Cave of Outlaws,"

"Serpent of the Nile," "The Americano" and "Duel on the Mississippi." One night he and his wife went to see a French thriller, "Diabolique," directed by Henri-Georges Couzot and starring Simone Signoret.

They became impressed with a huge crowd outside the theater made up mostly of "teenagers in leather jackets." Why had they come to an art house to see this particular French thriller? Apparently, he decided, after seeing the film's use of cinematic horror, "to sate the morbidity in their youthful systems."

Deciding to become "a shrewder operator than I had been," Castle gave up his then thriving TV ventures "Men of Annapolis" and "Meet McGraw" to produce and direct his own thrillers with slanted appeal to those teenagers in the leather jackets and their girlfriends.

His newfound "ghoulish attention" went to a mystery novel, "The Marble Forest," and he had it adapted into an $80,000 flick called "Macabre," released in 1958. He had never sprinkled his earlier works with "gimmicks" but he came up with the idea to have Lloyds of London insure those who went to see the film for $1000 apiece, should anything happen to them during the screening of the film. "I thought it would be good for publicity, something to stir up extra interest in the film. I had no idea it was just the first of many gimmicks."

Here's how "Macabre" worked: "We gave out $1,000 insurance polices at the door. All you had to do to collect was die of fright watching my picture. What's so hard about that? Nobody did, of course, but one guy went to see the picture five times, each time hoping to die of fright so his destitute family could collect."

Since "Macabre," Castle admitted he had been having a devilish ball with his "contrivances." Of course, they were designed more for publicity than actuality, so only a handful of viewers ever got to see any of the gimmicks actually carried out.

For "The House on Haunted Hill" (1959) a skeleton slid across the top of the audience on a wire. For 1959's "The Tingler" (see opposite page for silhouette of Castle and Monster) seats were wired to quiver – a gimmick called "Percepto." For "Thirteen Ghosts" (1960) a pair of colored glasses enabled a viewer to see (or not see) supernatural beings – a thing called "Illusiono"; and for "Homicidal" (1961) a 60-second "fright break" was provided so "terrified viewers" who wanted to leave the theater and reclaim their entry fee could. All of these ghostly novelties had put Castle into the category of money-maker.

The only time he had gone astray was with "Zotz!" (1962), a film he wished he had never touched. "I made it a la Disney and it was bad for my horror-driven reputation," he lamented.

"I received 5,000 angry letters because the picture wasn't a bit scary. I've learned my lesson since then: It's only when I shock that I do business."

Whatever one might think about Castle's huckster-like attitudes, I couldn't help but feel that his unflagging enthusiasm for his movies was sincere and enthralling. His eyes flashed with (fiendish?) delight as he discussed his future projects in horror with me.

"One of my pleasures," he told me, "is flying all over the world to promote my pictures. There're some theater managers who won't book my films unless I promise to make a personal appeance. I've even worked as an usher to seat my own fans." And presumably carried popcorn, candy and soft drinks to their seats to impress them.

The critics had slammed his last picture, "Straitjacket," for which there had been no gimmick per se, unless the tag line "Just keep saying to yourself: It's only a movie . . . it's only a movie . . . it's only . . . " could be called a gimmick. "But I don't let those kind of things bother me. Sure, I'd prefer good reviews, but only foreign films are affected at the box office by criticism. After all, I'm still making money, right?"

Nobody has ever argued that point.

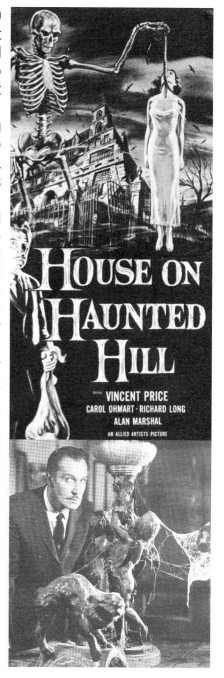

Castle continued to make money with "I Saw What You Did" (1965), "Let's Kill Uncle" (1966), "The Busy Body" (1967), "The Spirit Is Willing" (1967) and "Project X" (1968). He finally decided to carry his love for horror films to an all-time high with "Rosemary's Baby," by first buying the rights to the Ira Levin novel before it was published. He sold the project to Paramount but the studio refused to accept him as director for fear his reputation for making low-budget horror movies would destroy the project's reputation. So he stepped down and hired Roman Polanski to direct. The film became an international hit starring Mia Farrow and brought Castle a kind of prestige he had never known before.

I had such fond memories of meeting Castle that when I learned he had died on May 31, 1977, at the too-early-age of 63, I wrote up a special obituary:

# The P.T. Barnum Who Tingled Us With Gimmicky Horror Films

One of the more famous stills from a Bill Castle film: That's Joan Crawford wielding a murderous axe in "Strait-Jacket."

I shall always remember William Castle, who died recently of a heart attack at the age of 63, as a delightful Hollywood huckster. He never uttered a word about his films without tipping you off that his tongue was firmly lodged in his cheek – usually by phrasing his stories in a highblown way, or smiling wryly or knocking the ashes from his ubiquitous cigar with the flourish of a Damon Runyon racetrack tout.

The handful of times we met at his bungalow at Universal in the 1960s, he would swivel flamboyantly in his green leather chair, engulfing everything in a billowing cloud of cigar smoke.

Running idle fingers through his snow-white hair, he would wax lyrically about his latest horror film as if it had been deemed one of the seven wonders of the modern world.

Reporters like me never failed to record his verbal gems for prosperity, even if they had nothing much to do with the films. It was colorful copy and Castle knew exactly what he was dishing out. He had told me "The Night Walker" was about sexual dreams when in fact it had nothing whatsoever to do with the psychology of dreams and was merely a vehicle in which Barbara Stanwyck could go hysterial and hold Robert Taylor in her arms. He had told me "Homicidal" came to him in a dream and had deep-rooted personal symbolism, when in fact it was a blatant and obvious rip-off of Alfred Hitchcock's "Psycho."

Castle was a charming charlatan, refreshing to find among the pompous and the bombastic of Hollywood. The memory of the man will long outlive the memory of most of his movies, which, with the exception of "Rosemary's Baby," were largely marginal.

He was born April 24, 1914, in New York City as William Schloss Jr. (schloss is "castle" in German). His early love for the Great White Way of Broadway began when he saw Bela Lugosi in a stage version of "Dracula" and he had the presumption to rush backstage that night to suggest other ways Lugosi might portray Bram Stoker's vampire character.

By the age of 25 brashness and audacity had developed into major parts of his chutzpah personalty and he had worked in many stage productions. One day he coerced Orson Welles into leasing him a theater, and then connived a producer into believing he had the rights to a play, when in reality no such play existed. So he wrote one over a weekend, "Not for Children." The subsequent production was a success and his career as a producer was questionably underway. Not long after that bit of connivery, Castle left for Hollywood, having been summoned by another con artist, Harry Cohn of Columbia.

The film career that resulted can be broken down into four phases. The first was as a director of countless low-budget potboilers, action pictures, pirate movies and Westerns – for a while it seemed he would go on grinding out similar grade-B fodder for the rest of his career. He did "The Whistler" and "Crime Doctor" series for Columbia, as well.

His career took a major turn the night he saw the French chiller "Diabolique." The lines of young people outside the theater piqued his curiosity: Could it be horror films were big grossers? Independently he produced "Macabre," a cheapjack thriller with a surprise ending but little else. It probably would have made no inroads except for the fact Castle tricked it up by carrying an insurance policy by Lloyds of London that would pay $1,000 to anyone who died of fright while watching. Nobody died, nor did the film. It was a smash.

The Castle trend was established. For his next pictures he would spend little money on scripting, producing or casting, saving the big bucks for the gimmick, which was largely spent on marketing, since the gimmicks were impractical to maintain for more than a few times just for show. It was an ingenious way of doctoring the deficiencies of his film-making and still capturing the deep-felt appreciation of his fans.

Castle created gimmicks he described as "Emergo" and "Percepto." The critics called it all "Stinko" but the teenagers loved it and plunked out the bucks. Castle flew all over the world to meet his fans. This graveyard-grass-roots approach built fan clubs and undying adulation that would later pay off in films that had no gimmicks. During Castle's period of great success, no one (least of all the studios) cared much that the films were generally poorly produced. The exceptions would be "The House on Haunted Hill" and "The Tingler," which live on today as low-budget cult classics.

Castle was a fast-shooting director who seldom took time to develop subtleties or rewrite scripts even when they cried out for revision. He was a P. T. Barnum who always kept his finger on the pulse of the ticket-buying public.

The third phase of his career consisted of only one picture. It was "Rosemary's Baby" (1968) and it attained new heights of suspense and horror for a Castle picture, since he had had the good sense to hire Roman Polanski to direct it. The worldwide success of the film, based on Ira Levin's popular novel, brought Castle a new prestigious image.

The fourth and final phase of his career is somewhat sad. He tried to live up to the fame of "Rosemary's Baby" but the films he chose were horribly inferior. "Shanks," though an unusual attempt to bring French mime Marcel Marceau to the screen, was a total failure. Even his attempt at another horror film, "Bug," met with scathing reviews and was in obvious need of a gimmick. And there were periods of ill health, beginning in the late 1960s with a kidney stone attack that came in the wake of much hate mail over the satanic themes in "Rosemary's Baby."

The impish gleam in Castle's eyes finally died out on May 31 at the University of California Medical Center, where he had been taken following a heart attack at his Beverly

Hills home. He was working at the MGM Studios at the time on a film to be entitled "200 Lakeview Drive."

Castle leaves behind a fascinating autobiography, "Step Right Up!... I'm Gonna Scare the Pants Off America" (G. P. Putman's Sons, 1976). In addition to "Rosemary's Baby" there are all those gimmick films which will continue to entertain those who are looking for something not to be taken too seriously. And perhaps "tingle" the spine a little?

As he would have probably put it, "Life is but a gimmick, sweetheart."

# The George Romero Story:
## Night of the Living Career That Died –And Was Resurrected to Bleed Again

George A. Romero, surrounded by his "fans" during the production of "Day of the Dead."

THE career of George A. Romero has been a combination of "living" and "dead." The Pittsburgh director made a consideration reputation for himself in the late '60s as a master of the macabre with "Night of the Living Dead," a low budget ($150,000) horror/science-fiction film with an army of walking undead flesh eaters that almost overnight became a cult classic.

Produced over a period of weekend-only shooting sprees, "Night" was made in and around Evanstown, Pa. It emerged from the cutting room as a black-and-white surrealistic horror tale in which a spore from outer space infects corpses and turns them into shambling, flesh-seeking zombies. In about a ten-year exhibition period, the film had earned $11 million and the praise of fans as well as critics – including Rex Reed, Jean-Luc Godard and Jean-Pierre Gorin (the latter two called the film "revolutionary").

That's the "living" part.

Now comes the "dead" part.

After the success of his zombie movie, Romero couldn't give blood away to the nearest Red Cross plasma center. His next two movies, "There's Always Vanilla" (a 1971 light-hearted romantic comedy he made in Pittsburgh with a cast of unknown locals) and "Jack's Wife" (an odd 1972 study of suburbia witchcraft, eventually to be released on video as "Season of the Witch"), saw hardly any U.S. distribution.

Critics felt that perhaps Romero had jumped too quickly from the exploitation market–which he obviously understood all too well–into "significant" film-making that the rest of the viewing world could live without. In 1973 Romero should have returned to the "living," but didn't. For his next film "The Crazies," finally released in 1975 as a horror item (aka: "Code Name: Trixie") that featured a different kind of army of walking corpses, fell into the clutches of a weak, impoverished distributor and was shelved after a poor New

York debut. Romero had attempted to duplicate "The Night of the Living Dead" by creating another "virus" (this one manmade by the military) that gets into the drinking water of the town of Evans City, Pa., and turns anyone who drinks it into a stark-raving maniac who soon afterward dies.

It was more a frightening comment on martial law (the army comes in to restore order and the townspeople resist) than another cult classic. It demonstrated Romero's sense of quick pacing and unusual story-telling but it just wasn't "Night of the Living Dead." (Will anything ever be? Some successes can never be duplicated.)

It was in 1978 that Romero's career returned to the "living" – a success he could contribute to his film "Martin," the character study of an 18-year-old who fears he is an 84-year-old vampire. This time the blood banks were thriving again, even if the film was not traditional vampire horror. For the youth of the film is incapable of entrancing his victims and must resort to razor blades (not incisors) to spill the blood from his pretty female victims. Garlic wreaths, crosses and other Christian imagery don't bother him at all.

Portions of "Martin" were so graphic as to be unsettling and the film possessed a raw, primitive power despite flaws in dramatic structuring and a shootout between cops and robbers that didn't belong in the picture.

Following these "living" and "dead" periods in his career, Romero would enjoy, in 1978, total "resurrection."

His return to international prominence had occurred with the European release of "Dawn of the Dead," the second in his intended "Night of the Living Dead" trilogy. The film had opened in Spain and Italy with a $9 million gross.

Romero had begun shooting in 1977 at the Monroeville Shopping Center near Pittsburgh for just $1 million. And in 1979 the acclaimed horror-gore feature was opening in major cities all across America. "This isn't a sequel per se, since all the characters are new," explained Romero, when I caught up with him at his office in New York via telephone. "But it does deal with a similar phenomenon [spores from space invade bodies of the dead and bring them back to life

George A. Romero, circa 1993, around the time he was making "The Dark Half."

as bone-chewing cannibals]." Romero defined himself as a "pop film-maker working in the traditional sense," and seriously questioned whether his work belonged in the same genre with "Eraserhead" and "The Rocky Horror Picture Show," works that were then part of a "midnight movie" craze sweeping across America.

I asked Romero about "Martin" and why such an unusual theme: "I wanted to depict a young man who was a psychotic," he answered, "and not someone wrapped up in gothic symbolism. In my vision, Martin is the innocent of the film. He has a problem he desperately wants to talk about, but others perceive that problem in their own ways and fail to help him find his way back to sanity."

Romero's use of black-and-white flashbacks in "Martin" resembles footage from old Mexican horror films – an effect he purposely intended. "I wanted Martin's memories to be ambiguous – are they fantasies in gothic gauze or honest recollections of murders from a previous era?"

Because the movie code had loosened up so much since 1967, Romero was able to make "Dawn of the Dawn" far more violent and bloodthirsty than "Night of the Living Dead." Four helicopter travelers are forced to take refuge in a shopping center, which just happens to be crawling with those zombies. The only way to stop one of these walking nightmares is to blow its brains out, so the main characters are armed to the teeth with the latest in automatic weaponry, and are constantly blasting open heads and spattering the walls with blood. Even though there is little characterization and few of the gothic qualities of "Night of the Living Dead," the sequel became a box-office smash in America too.

No doubt about it. "Night of the Living Dead" brought Romero uncommon respect as a creator of low-budget movies. "The film," he explained, "made most of its money back in its initial release through Walter Reade, but it had an afterlife that attracted the critics and turned it into a phenomenon. To have people recognize that and put me in a category with other film-making greats was a very gratifying experience. Yet I've always been paranoid about being typecast as a horror director. I knew I had an affinity for the genre but I didn't want to spend the rest of my life trapped there."

Did he indeed feel trapped at this very moment? "By no means. I'm glad I made 'Dawn of the Dead' because I think it's going to lead to bigger and better movies."

(Romero's penchant for horror goes back to Richard Matheson's vampire novel, "I Am Legend," which was the most influential inspiration for "Night of the Living Dead.")

Besides his feature-film career, Romero had kept busy producing syndicated TV series and documentaries with partner Richard Rubinstein out of offices in Pittsburgh and New York. (That included 1974's "O.J. Simpson: Juice on the Loose.")

"Our focus has not been the development of George Romero but rather corporate survival in order to stay afloat and remain outside the Hollywood mainstream. I haven't been selling myself to the studios because I don't want to go into any deals without adequate clout. I don't want to work on a $20 million project built of straw and dreamed up by others. I'd much rather spend a million on something I want to make."

Of all phases of film-making, Romero enjoyed editing the most. "It's what I'm all about. It's what I do best. I don't study film a great deal. I improvise at the Moviola and try to find texture and expressiveness. I never cut in my head while I'm shooting. I'd much rather seek a tempo that will excite or calm down an audience. You can accomplish more through editing than anything else."

One final "living" note he told me about that day. "The Crazies" was being turned over to another distributor for showing in eight foreign countries and television. The film, Romero felt, "was my best in terms of shattering time and space through editing. It's the one film I've done that emerged on celluloid exactly as I conceived it in my head. And that is something that all film makers try to attain."

PREPARE TO MEET THE DAUGHTER OF HORROR . . . BUT DON'T EXPECT A MONSTROUS OFFSPRING . . . THIS WOMAN IS SWEET AND GENTLE, SHE WOULDN'T HARM A HAIR ON YOUR HEAD . . . WELL, I DON'T THINK SHE WOULD . . . WHY WOULD SHE?
. . . JUST BECAUSE SHE'S A KARLOFF?

# As Surely As Her Father's Name Was... Boris Karloff

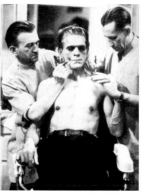

**Sara Karloff signing photographs at the Balboa Theater in San Francisco. She might be an offshoot of the Frankenstein Monster, but she's one of the sweetest ladies I've ever known.**

SARA KARLOFF is the Daughter of the Frankenstein Monster. That is as certain as knowing that Mary Wollstonecraft Shelley's "Frankenstein" will never die. Since 1993, with the DNA of Boris Karloff surging through her veins, she has run Karloff Enterprises "to preserve, protect and share my father's memories." Among her achievements: getting more than 17,000 signatures to help create a set of horror-star stamps produced by the U.S. Postal Service in 1997 that included her father, Bela Lugosi, Lon Chaney and Chaney Jr. Her purpose is to "resurrect" from the dead her most beloved icon, so that new generations can appreciate the contributions made by her father when he frightened the movie-going world from 1931-69.

When she makes personal appearances, Sara, now in her late 60s, introduces rare color home movies. Taken by her mother Dorothy (nee: Stine), who was married to Karloff from 1928-46, they include footage of Sara's christening as well as Karloff clowning on the set while being turned into the Frankenstein Monster by make-up man Jack Pierce. Sara also has excerpts from TV appearances Karloff made with Carol Burnett and Dinah Shore. There is also a "Peppermint Twist" segment from a "Shindig" show cut around 1965.

If nothing else Karloff was versatile – capable of playing mad doctors and evil scientists as well as sympathetic characters. Success didn't reach him until he was 43, after decades of working in Canadian theater and making silent films in

Escort Mr. Stanley to My Dungeon . . .

**Karloff as the insidious Fu Manchu.**

Sara Karloff with John Stanley

Photos by Laura Irvine

Hollywood in now-forgotten low-budget film productions.

"The nicest thing about being my father's daughter," Sara said recently, from her summer home in Lake Tahoe, where she rollicks with husband Bill Sparkman, "is that my father was a man about whom nothing negative was written or said. Cynthia Lindsay, my godmother, was doing a book about him and everyone remembered him so fondly they prefaced their stories with 'Dear Boris.' That became the book's title. Being respected was his personal legacy. The films are his professional legacy. I love meeting his fans and those who knew him and hearing stories about him; they know far more about him professionally than I ever will. What I bring to the party is what I know personally."

An ironic fact: Sara Karloff was born on Feb. 2, 1938, the same day of her father's 51st birthday. And on that day he was at Universal making "Son of Frankenstein." "Sara Jane Karloff" appears on her birth certificate but her father had never legally taken the surname, having used it only as a stage name (he was born in 1887 as William Henry Pratt in London, England.)

Karloff with Sara's mother, nee Dorothy Stine, to whom he was married from 1928 to 1946. Here they are with Silver, a Bedlington terrier, as they cruise to London where Karloff will make "The Ghoul" (1933).

Sara was raised in Los Angeles' Coldwater Canyon but has few memories of her father making movies during the early years. And she knew nothing about their horrific nature. "My father was very modest and never brought his work home with him. He didn't talk about his movies. So as a child I was out of synch with his career."

*Sara's Morality Story #1:* "I wanted a rabbit more than anything in the world. So my father made a deal with me. *I had to take care of the rabbit.* Feed it. So I picked one out. On the way home my father said he would have picked a different rabbit – one he had seen with a floppy ear. 'That rabbit,' he said, 'needs more love than the others.' I felt regret for my decision but I also got the message: Don't judge a book by its cover."

*Sara's Morality Story #2:* "I took the rabbit home but failed to care for it. One day it wasn't there. I ran to my father. 'Where's my rabbit?' I cried. He told me, *'You didn't keep your part of the bargain with me. So I gave it back.'* My father had a tender heart when you made a deal with him. But if you didn't keep your promise . . . you lost something precious in the bargain."

Sara has clear memories of her father never being in the best of health. "He suffered from osteoarthritis, not just

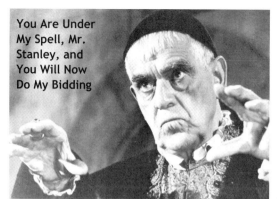

You Are Under My Spell, Mr. Stanley, and You Will Now Do My Bidding

Karloff in "The Raven" (1963), one of many good films produced by Roger Corman that allowed Karloff to soar as an actor.

Boris Karloff with his daughter Sara.

in the back but in the legs, the price for hauling Colin Clive [who played Dr. Henry Frankenstein in the 1931 version] up the back lot hill at Universal. He was also bowlegged and it got worse year by year. You could roll barrels between his legs."

Sara's parents divorced when she was seven and her mother remarried – to a San Francisco attorney. "I lived in a house on Lake Street just a block away from the Presidio [a one-time U.S. Army base that has since been closed] wall." It was the late 1940s and "young girls didn't go rushing off to see horror movies."

It was while she was attending Colorado College at 19 that she finally saw "Frankenstein" on TV for the first time. There were other famous titles she would see on VHS – but she has yet to find the rarer titles. To this day she remains a fan of the more subtle horror film of yesteryear, having no place in her life for the current blood-and-guts approach. "If my father was alive today, he would consider such films disgusting and unnecessary, an insult to the intelligence of the viewer."

There was more to her father's career than movies, explained Sara. "He could turn his boogeyman image around and spoof himself. He was always able to embrace each new medium [Broadway, radio, television, LP record albums) that came his way."

Toward the end of Karloff's life, Sara saw less of him because he was living in England. "We would visit when he came to work in America but he was always in declining health."

In addition to his other problems, doctors had diagnosed him suffering from emphysema in 1957. "My father had smoked early in his life but had quit 30 years before," she recalled.

Too late. His health continued to decline to the point his character was bedridden in one of his last features, "The Fear Chamber."

He made his final public appearances in a wheelchair. But anyone who thought it was all over when Karloff died in England in February 1969 hadn't counted on one of the things he had left behind: the Daughter of the Frankenstein Monster.

*As surely as her name is Sara Karloff.*

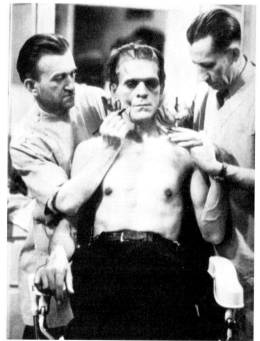

# TIME TO CLOSE THE CRYPT DOOR

## BUT DON'T WORRY . . . I'LL BE BACK IN . . .
## RETURN OF THE
## TV HORROR HOST

# TO SO MANY WHO HELPED OVER THE YEARS, AND LAID THE GROUNDWORK FOR THIS BOOK, WHETHER THEY KNEW/LIKED IT OR NOT . . .

## KTVU, CHANNEL 2

*They worked on CREATURE FEATURES, or watched it happen:* David Ambriz, Bob Austin, Ron Boltz, Sheila Warnado Brown, Caroline Chang, Gwen Clark, Mike Cleary, Ed Cosci, David Eardley, Chris Elliott, Lon Feldman, Lee Gonsalves, Nick Hamil, Flora Harman, Mark Johnsen, Catherine Kendrick, Chris Kievman, Michael Krajac, Ione Larson, Larry Larson, Bill Longen, Ron Louie, George Lum, Pat McCormick, Bob MacKenzie, Rob Neft, Joe Olmedo, Jack Parmeter, Sue Riis, Jeff Rodgers, John Rodrigues, Bob Roth, John Scroggs, Steve Shlisky, Barbara Simpson (now of KSFO Radio), Jim Skinner, Wally Smith, Karen Stoneman, Marilyn Storm, Dick Weise, Mark Welch, Nelson Wong, Ben Woo, Roxanna Zappia.

## THE SAN FRANCISCO CHRONICLE

*To the Late Greats who helped me find my way as a newspaperman:* Scott Newhall, Gordon Pates, Darrell Duncan, Abe Mellinkoff, Dick Demorest, John L. Wasserman, Stanleigh Arnold, Charlie Downie, Helene Rivers, Nancy Griffin, Paine Knickerbocker (he assigned me my first movie reviews), Bill Hogan (he enabled me to write sci-fi novel reviews), Herb Caen (he taught me about the Mystic Energy of the City Room), Terrence O'Flaherty (one of my best friends), Jack Rosenbaum, Al Frankenstein (appropriately), Art Hoppe (still the funniest writer ever), Ralph J. Gleason, Charlie McCabe.
*Among the Still Living:* Sue Adolphson, Calvin Ahlgren, Scott Blakey, Robert Graysmith, Edward Guthmann, Jesse Hamlin, David Kleinberg, Mick LaSalle, Bea Mettasick, David Moore (the annual Santa on "Creature Features"), Gerald Nachman, Joel Pimsleur, Jim Rose (he laid out the fourth "Creature Features Movie Guide"), Joel Selvin, Ruthe Stein, Judy Stone, Marilyn Tucker, Eric Ward, Bernie Weiner, Gail Wrixon, Marian Zailian, Maitland Zane. And a nod to fans Walter Addiego, Joe Brown and Peter Hartlaub.

## THE RANK AND FILE

Bill & Patricia Alex, Gail & Jack Anderson, Bob Anthony, Gene Arceri, Sam Z. Arkoff, Gary Arlington, Dick Arnold, Bill Banning, Jesse Beaton, Vic & Carla Befera, Barbara Bladen, Gene Blodgett, Jim Brachman, Barry Caine, Dan Caldwell, Ingrid Cali, Chris & Larry Campbell, Sandy Clark, Charlie Coane, John Cochran, Tony Cuneo, Cliff Dektar, Bob Ekman, Robert Emmett, Dan Faris, Douglass Fake, Ben Fong-Torres, Gilda & Lee Forrester, Steve Gawley, David & Michael Gibson, Kevin Gilligan, Alex Gordon, Al Guthertz, Don Herron, Roger Hill, Chris Hopkins, Nick Hopkins, Alan Hose, Chuck Jarman, Adrian & Paula Jennings, Charlie Jennings, Paul Jennings, Bob Johnson, Sara Karloff, Pat Kleinberg, Steven Kirk, Bill Lanese, Karen Larsen, Randall Larsen, Elliot Lavine, David Litwin, Richard Lupoff, Leonard Maltin, Mick Martin, John McClintock, Bill McLeod, Gary Meyer, Allen Michaan, Ron Miller, Anita Monga, Eddie Muller, Ben Myron, Gene Nelson, Ray Nelson, Gail & Ray Orwig of "Big Eye," Kit Parker, Viola Parr, Erik Lee Preminger, Augie Ragone, Dick Rojas, John Rothmann, Sue Schneider, Bill Schneider, Michael Snyder, Bill Sparkman, Shelley Spicer, Russ Stanley (fair-haired son), Bob Stephens, Mike & Rita Stevens, Suzy Strauss, Irwin Swan, Steve Talbot, Jim Tedesco, Don Thomson, Suzanne Toner, Will "The Thrill" Viharo & "Tiki Goddess" Monica, Vale Vale, Chris Walis, Tom Walton, Walter Von Hauffe, John Weaver, Malcolm Whyte, Dennis, Sarah & Danny Willis, Sally Wilkins, Jack Wodell, Kurt Wyrsch.

# A Few More Thank Yous . . .

Without cameraman RON WILLIS, who stuck with me through thick and thin during the production days of "Creature Features," I could not have produced all the minimovie material that finally reached the small screen. Not only was Ron an excellent 16 mm cameraman, and later a videotape shooter, but he was great with the still camera. In fact, many of the on-set photos used in this book were snapped by Ron, usually under adverse, hurry-up conditions. Above you see him checking the light level in the Casablanca Restaurant, where we shot "Return to Casablanca" in early 1980. You are a true professional, Ron, and I salute you and your picture-taking prowess.

## Going Loco Over Mr. Lobo

Known to his fans as Mr. Lobo, and to his friends as Eric Lobo, this dynamic, hard-working horror host started out on Sacramento's KXTV-ABC channel, inflicting all kinds of punnish-ment on his fans with his "Cinema Insomnia," which he created, wrote, produced, directed, edited and hosted, with some help from Scott Moon, editor and publisher of "Planet X" magazine. He interspersed his public-domain sci-fi and horror movies with scary skits, comedy cut-ups and physical shtick earmarked by slapstick of a kind endorsed by Moe Howard. For a period of thankless time he stretched his tentacles of terror across 100 cable systems, inflicting his unique form of pain on such unsuspecting territories as Virginia, Louisiana and Arkansas. But then he retrenched in late 2006 for a weekly version of "Cinema Insomnia" carried on KTEH (San Jose, CA), KCAH (Watsonville, CA) and a handful of other small independent stations across the land. He and his girlfriend Sara (known in some quarters as The Queen of Trash) have collaborated on a comic book, and he can be found as one of the floating, talking heads in the horror-host documentary "American Scary." Mr. Lobo is a tireless, driven individual whose ultimate dream is to become acknowledged as a leading horror host of his time. I wish him well and thank him for his continued support to Bob Wilkins and myself.

## Zooming With Zomboo Into Zaniness

Is it true that Zomboo means "the sexiest man alive . . . or dead" in Italian? Indubitably. Ask Frank Leto for the truth and he just bares his fangs. And snarls. A one-time member of the aerospace industry, Frank decided to take a gamble and came to KOLO-TV in Reno, Nevada, in 1997 to become a maker of ordinary, average, every-day commercials. But two years later he accepted a newfound role as a horror host, having been inspired as a youth by Zacherley and Soupy Sales. He patterned his creation, Zomboo, after Lon Chaney's character in "London After Midnight" (1927) and has been going mad weekly ever since. Joining him in the show have been Bianca, the Rack Girl (blonde at left) and Miss Transylvania (brunette at left), just two of the busty and shapely wenches who have appeared consistently on his program. Yes, such female exposure indicates that Zomboo caters to an upper-crust, more intellectual market than most patronizing horror hosts.

I want to thank Zomboo for his willingness to compromise his potential audience and go for the mind instead of the commercialization that he might have otherwise exploited with ruthless abandon.

Don't miss Kurt Wyrsch's scrapbook and treatise on the history of this unusual character, entitled appropriately "The Zomboo Scrapbook." You can find that as well as coffee mugs, DVDs, T-shirts and autographed photos at www.zomboo.com.

And thanks, Mr. Zomboo, for holding Bob Wilkins and myself in your humble reverence.

Can an innocent kid born in tranquil Burlingame, CA, find happiness as a pseudo-sophisticated horror host in liberal-minded Berkeley, CA? Examine the life of Michael Monahan, once fresh-faced kid of the Peninsula, and you will discover that he produced 13 not-soon-to-be-forgotten shows from a dungeony place at Berkeley's Channel 28 under the title "The Hip Crypt of Doktor Goulfinger." (Friends like me call him "Dok.") Though now off the air, he continues to regale audiences with his colorful cigarette-smoking character inspired by Asmodeus, a largely forgotten horror host who emerged on Channel 20 in San Francisco just prior to the coming of Bob Wilkins at KTVU. "I was as equally inspired by Wilkins, John Stanley, Ghoulardi and Zacherley," remarks the bearded sophisticate, who sees the world through special "gross-colored" glasses. The mentally superior Monahan deems himself an historian and archivist. I have discovered that he is endlessly articulate, knows everything about any kind of movie imaginable, works in the book distribution business, and is always asking me for a light. In turn, he has lit up my life on more than one occasion – we freak-quently appear together at horror conventions and special shows.

S O N   O F          G H O U L

Bearing a strange resemblance to a human named Kevin Scarpino, Son of Ghoul is a horror-host hero in Cleveland, Ohio, whom I consider to be in the best Ghoulardi tradition.

# CREATURE FEATURES STORE
## Bob Wilkins & John Stanley

## Creature Features

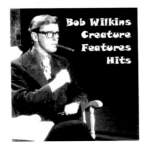

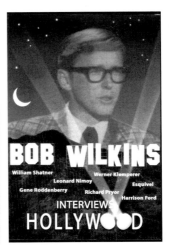

### 1) THE BEST OF BOB WILKINS  DVD

Over 100 Minutes of Creature Features!  Includes: Carmine Infantino, Forrest J. Ackerman, Melvin the Great, Coffin ad, Martian Report, Ernie Fosselius, a Jawa Interview, King Kong Sweater  & much more! Captain Cosmic clips: Anthony Daniels, Halloween shows, and 2T2. Bumper Slide Show: A hilarious group of Bob's handmade commercial bumpers. Bonus material: Behind-the-scenes slide show.  A rare group of photos taken on the Channel 2 set.

### 2) BOB WILKINS INTERVIEWS HOLLYWOOD  DVD

From Bob's personal collection, these vintage interviews were transferred from the original 16mm films. Werner Klemperer, Harrison Ford, Mark Hamill and Richard Pryor. "Star Trek" fans will enjoy Shatner, Nimoy, Takei, Nichols and Roddenberry.  Gahan Wilson draws his idea of a typical "Creature Features" fan, and there is a 1967 interview with the Godfather of Space-Age Bachelor Pad Music, Esquivel. Includes outtakes of Esquivel and his band performing! Also, outtakes with George Takei from the "Captain Cosmic" show and president-to-come Ronald Reagan!

### 3) BOB WILKINS  SUPER HORROR SHOW  DVD

Includes a newly re-mastered transfer of "The Bob Wilkins Super Horror Show" direct to DVD from the studio tapes. You have never seen it with this kind of quality before. Program includes: Bela Lugosi interview, Boris Karloff interview, Universal horror films, King Kong outtakes, The Monster Movie Quiz, Hammer film trailers, Christopher Lee interview, 1970's horror film trailers, and much, much more.

### 4) THE BOB WILKINS CREATURE FEATURES  CD

Track 1:  Gotham City Municipal Swing Band  (Bob's original theme) Track 2:  Creature Features Theme Song  (1975 replacement theme)  Track 3:  A 1976 excerpt from Bob's show. He talks about complaints from fans about his movies. Classic Bob Wilkins. Track 4:   A 22-minute interview with Bob. He explains how he got involved  in hosting horror movies, the show's props, his favorite movies, why he left TV, and a lot more. Track 5:  Captain Cosmic Theme  Track 6: Captain Cosmic Show with 2T2   All re-mastered from original studio tapes. Appx: 45 minutes.

 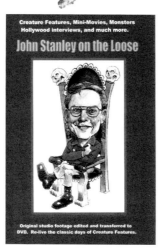  

## 5) JOHN STANLEY'S CREATURE FEATURES   DVD

First up is the "Trailers of Horror" special.  Horror trailers of the 30's & 40's, sci-fi trailers of the 50's, trailers from John's favorite movies, and lots of extras. Next is "Creature Features" interviews with Gary Kurtz of "Dark Crystal," Charlton Heston of "Mother Lode," Ray Bradbury of "Something Wicked This Way Comes."  "Psycho" interview with Richard Franklin, director of "Psycho II." Franklin gives some great insider information on the original "Psycho" and Alfred Hitchcock. Bonus materials include: A behind-the-scenes slide show, a rare group of photos taken on the Channel 2 set, plus many extras.

## 6) JOHN STANLEY ON THE LOOSE    DVD

John's "Creature Features" special a.k.a. "The Best of John Stanley." Guests include the cast of "Star Wars," the "Star Trek II" cast, Robert Bloch, Chuck Norris, Ray Bradbury, Karl Malden and many more. Specials: Private Eye Night, "Creature from the Black Lagoon" show, Bug-Eyed Monsters show, New York Stake skit, The IRS Lady Meets the Werewolf, and John visits the set of "Hee-Haw."  Mini-movies include "The Stanley Cage," "Return of the Channel 2 Dragon," "The Mummy Rises," "Meeting at Morningside (Phantasm)," "Adventure of the Persian Slipper," "Little Shop of Murders," "Attack of the Killer Scarecrow," and "Revenge of the  Channel 2 Dragon." John gives insight on the making of "Creature Features" with lots of show clips and previews.

## 7) JOHN STANLEY'S STAR TREK SPECIAL  DVD

John's 1982 special "Star Trek -- The Roots of Khan" includes rare interviews with William Shatner, Leonard Nimoy, DeForest Kelley and Ricardo Montalban. Special effects artist Ken Ralston, from Industrial Light and Magic, visits the Creature Features set. John reviews the history behind the making of the feature film and Spock's death. Stanley Stardate 7.10.82 Bonus material is a lost 1980 interview with Leonard Nimoy after the making of "Star Trek -- The Motion Picture."

## 8) JOHN STANLEY'S CREATURE FEATURES CD

Track 1:  John's Original "Creature Features" Theme  Track 2:  Alien Show  Track 3: Musharuma, John's Outer Space guest  Track 4: "It Came From Outer Space" show  Track 5: 3-D Movies  Track 6:  "Comin' at Ya!" Special  Track 7: "Wacky World of Creature Features" ads  Track 8:  Bad Movie night  Track 9: 1983 replacement CF theme  Track 10: "Creature Features" background music

DVDs are available for $15.00 each and CD's are $10.00 each, shipping included.  Purchase today at: www.bobwilkins.net - "the best" Bob Wilkins site on the internet.  All DVDs have interactive menus, full color disc and cover art. Packaged in a protective mylar sleeve. If you have any questions or comments write: T. Wyrsch @ tpw1705@aol.com